Foster's Store

Be There Then

Foster's Store

A subculture of the times and of

West Georgia College

Some partied like there was no tomorrow. For some there was no tomorrow.

Semi-sociological déjà vu

By the surviving lab rats

Wayne Eliot Lankford, M. Walter Carmichael, Bob O'Kelley, Terry Farner, Chris Berry, Larry Bowie, Mike Sorrell, Phil Spackman, Richard Duncan, Mark Pitstick, Richard Hurt, Roger Hornsby, Steve Aderhold, and a bunch of other former store mates and friends

Editor
Peter Bryg

Illustrations by Bill Harrell

Books from Oak Valley Press are available at special quantity discounts for Bulk purchases for sales promotions, premiums, fund raising, or educational use. Special books or book excerpts can also be created to fit special needs.

For details write:
Oak Valley Press, Inc.
P. O. Box 36186
Hoover, Al 35244

On the internet: Visit oakvalleypress.com or
Email: webmaster@oakvalleypress.com

Foster's Store
First Oak Valley Press Edition

Copyright March 15, 2006 by Wayne Eliot Lankford

Published by Oak Valley Press, Inc. Hoover, Alabama
Printed in the USA

Edited by Peter Bryg

Cover Design and Layout by Wayne Lankford and Bill Harrell

ISBN 0-9745125-2-4 Hardcover Edition

Numbers that don't mean anything area.

506 4867-3—8999LN677
1 1 1 1 1 1 1 1 1 1 1 1 1 1 1

8-24-06

Beth,
FRog Butts Co. with
LOVE,

Disclaimer

This is a book of essays from a whole bunch of people and the subject matter is from a long time ago. A team of investigative reporters, let alone archaeologists, could not certify the accuracy of events recounted in much of this volume. What you have here is our contributors' best recollections, colored by powerful emotion, of some of the best—and worst—years of their lives. Therefore, Oak Valley Press, Inc. disclaims responsibility for any mishap that might befall any person or institution as a consequence of these faded memories shocked into life by print. While we are unaware that reading this volume will produce dangerous side effects down the road of time, we must warn our readers of a spreading rumor that eating certain pages of this tome will cause its masticators to experience effects not unlike the accounts described herein. Crazy idea! However, we have warned you and therefore deny liability to potential eaters of this book for any debility should you disregard our warning and eat the thing anyway. In fact, *Bon Appetit!*

Oak Valley Press, Inc.

L. R Foster 1955 - Standing in front of Foster's Store

Dedication Page

This book is dedicated to the memory of L. R. Foster and to his daughter Ethel, Mrs. J. T. Marks.

Those of us who lived at Foster's Store got to know L. R. very well. After more than thirty-five years I still remember how much fun Mr. Foster was and how he enjoyed coming by to visit us from time to time. He was 85 when I left West Georgia. He lived to be 97. All of us former store mates cherish our memory of him, and his daughter Ethel, without whom, our partying may have really gotten out of control.

Of course, understand, L.R and Ethel really didn't have any idea as to the things that were happening right under their noses back then. Just like I'm mostly ignorant toady as to what all my own kids are up to right now. Yeah, Right. No, things were different then.

Table of Contents

Introduction

You need to read this before you try to read this book.

This book, you will soon discover, is designed to be a little different than most books you're used to reading. It's mostly a non-fictional account of things and experiences that happened a long time ago all right, but it turns out that, to a lot of us who lived back then, the world hasn't really changed too much. That being the case, maybe, along with these archeological accounts of what life was like for some of us, you'll be able to pick up on what passed for humor for some residents of The Store during part of those times.

What I've tried to do is recreate **that atmosphere,** by including elements from that time - things like Bill Harrell's *Ink Lines,* and other art from those days. Then, in that spirit, we're going to see if we can be successful at continuing that unique thread of creativity that was present back then and connect it up to right now; so no matter whether you are 18 or 90 years old, from Georgia or New Jersey, you'll perhaps get a kick out of what's presented here.

Speaking of connecting things up, since this all happened a long time ago, while setting the book up, I began to notice that some of these chapters might seem to be presented out of order, or the subject matter of one particular chapter seemed to have nothing to do with the chapter preceding or following. I decided a kind of Mini Master of Ceremonies might be helpful. A guy who would travel along with you, keep you on track about where you've been and where you are headed, a tour guide of sorts.

This is what he looks like: Pay attention to his words.

There are a bunch of pictures in this book. Most of them have been hidden away up in attics and garages for the past thirty years. They weren't in that good a condition when I got them. They were taken mostly with cheap cameras. That's all we had. We were college students. My own pictures of those days (only a few survived) were in pretty bad shape and not that great to begin with. Please don't criticize these treasures. They are what they are. I wouldn't have it any other way. The fact that they survived all these years and are now being shared with the rest of the world is a wondrous thing.

As you read, you need to keep in mind too, that just like today, there was a war going on at the same time we were matriculating. You can't have all this without that. It wouldn't be real. But it wouldn't be Foster's if there wasn't an unreal part too. To address and fill that characteristic, for today, we've created a couple of different vehicles. *Advice from a Storemate* is a program where people who miss Mr. Foster's style of advice from years ago get to ask directions from *The Old Spirit of Foster's Store.* Yes, that means that we had to set up two-way communications between the here and now, all the way out to near wherever this lost store mate, this starry sooth resides today, out there somewhere in the ether of the great beyond I guess. I think it worked out pretty good. I had seen a lot of people on talk shows doing the same kind of thing, so I figured, if they could, we could. You decide if we pulled it off or send our celestial styled storemate an email yourself one day and you tell me.

So, the Viet Nam war was real. "Advice from a Storemate" is not real. Or is it *vice versa?*

There are also a lot of book recommendations for you if you decide you'd like some more information and a better feel for the times discussed in this book. We also have a kind of classified section containing items from back then and today. Look for them sprinkled through the pages of this *opus.* Look for all this kind of stuff between the regular book chapters. We've even thrown in some current event reporting from local sources on some matters you may have some interest in today that are ongoing around Foster's Store right now.

The main objective of these writings, though, is to take you back to that place out on the Bowden Highway and introduce or reintroduce a bunch of people who shared a community of fellowship and growth. And remember this: Foster's Store was just one place. The fact is that there were other such places similar to "Foster's Store" scattered all over the country. The problems we faced and the experiences we had were shared by millions, by a whole generation. The two little concrete block buildings we lived in were in every college town in the USA I woke up the other day thinking about all this and realized if somebody didn't start writing all this stuff down, it would all be lost in time. This book came about because it turned out that I wasn't the only person who didn't want to see that happen.

Wayne Lankford

Feed N Seed in Background

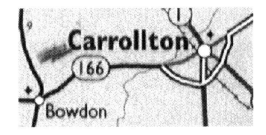

Preface

The following piece appeared in The West Georgia Perspective in January of 2005.

Remembering Foster's Store

By Wayne Lankford

Back in the late 1960's and early 1970's, west on Maple Street toward Bowdon, stood a former country store, converted into a residence of sorts.

I remember it well, but don't worry; I'm not going to mention any names here. (*Maybe worry a little bit.*) There was never any kind of blood oath or anything like that; no ceremony about promising to carry all those episodes to the grave with us when we passed on. What would be the use; I lost all those photographs a long time ago. But you know who you are.

Actually, this article's main purpose is to dispel what I'm sure are a number of misconceptions as to what many people may today believe went on at Foster's Store between the years of 1967 and 1972.

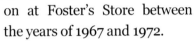

First, there were never any "wild parties" whatsoever on or around the premises that were generally known as "Foster's Store". During the two and half years that I resided there, I swear that I personally never engaged in or witnessed any illegal activity whatsoever. I acknowledge that there were such rumors at the time, and some people still refuse to believe my accounts as to what a typical day of residence at "The Store" was like, while I and others like me were enrolled as students at West Georgia College.

It is true that many hours were spent sitting in circles and discussing, like college kids everywhere, the events of the day and their future ramifications. One topic that was constantly reoccurring among the Business majors at Foster's was the economic law concerning Supply and Demand. It seemed like we were always faced with meager supplies while our demands remained very high for some of the staple items associated with the learning process. Eventually, we'd get enough money together, and somebody would drive to Atlanta and we'd be OK (wink-wink) for another week or two.

But we didn't study all the time. We engaged ourselves in many school-supported activities. You may remember our Intramural Flag Football team, *"The Green Jay Rushers."* For a while there, I really believed we had a chance to win the league championship. Then, unexplainably, for some reason, maybe it was actual competition, my illusions of grandeur melted away. But still, I will always remember the pretty colors.

Green Jay Rushers?

Another area of misconception has to do with reasons for the frequent personal visits from both the City of Carrollton law enforcement units and, to larger degree, calls made to our residence by the Georgia branch of the FBI. I really never understood the motives behind these late night visits. Ultimately, I came to believe that we were a kind of a beta site for them. In the end it was beneficial to both our groups. We got free training in how to wear handcuffs and in standing up against walls for hours while they, in turn, fully acquainted themselves with the folkways of off-campus living and with every nook and cranny of our environment. It was as if they were searching for things that they couldn't ever find. So alike we were. I offered to share my research with them, but I never received what I'd call a favorable response. My best source for this proposed thesis was the American Civil Liberties Union in Atlanta. That was the only reason their phone number was highlighted next to our communal phone. Research had been my only motivation. I swear.

Looking back on those times today, I find myself amazed about how so little has changed. I remember every Thursday evening, the TV news, Walter Cronkite delivering the numbers to us directly as we drank our Pabst Blue Ribbon from returnable brown bottles ($5.17 a case at Skinner's), how many of them we killed or wounded, how many of us they killed or wounded, the MIA's and KIA's, the strange number game that came out of a place we'd never heard of, until a time came, when that was all we heard.

Today, a different Newscaster's voice is heard over new images of new fires and smoke risings tallying the number killed and wounded, while the camera pans the crying and the blanket-covered bodies, the anguish, and what's left of a blown-up automobile, a building or flesh that once held a soul, I'm just as terrified today as I was thirty-something years ago at Foster's. The big difference is that today, it's MY generation who's dropped the ball, who can't find any way better than our fathers' way to try and deflect this current hate that's put on us. I didn't get it then and I don't get it now as I pass this memory on to you.

Have another toke, Brother. Embrace that multi-colored beast again. That picture of that nineteen year old Marine in his Full Dress blues is just as killed in action as all those others a generation ago who died for something I can only just suppose. I don't know, but I'll tell you this: I'm wearing my hair a little longer today and for reasons that you might imagine, I'm remembering a lot today, those years at Foster's Store.

Lankford 1970

Chapter 1

Pioneers of the West

By Walter Carmichael

L. R. Foster welcomed his first tenants to the store and the house in 1966. The first group to occupy the store wasn't rebels looking for a safe refuge in the old store building but friends looking for more room. "We were renting from Dr. Overton, who had a home across from the college," said Jackson native Bob Greer, now a businessman who lives on Lake Lanier north of Atlanta and will make his second attempt to become Georgia's Agriculture Commissioner in the 2006 state elections. "I think he felt, and we did too, that the place was too crowded and we needed more space."

Greer, Jim Crayton, and Larry Mobley went looking for a place with more room and at a price they could afford. "I had transferred to West Georgia from Young Harris to play basketball," said Crayton, who retired as the superintendent of schools in Pike County, where he was raised. "We were on some kind of scholarship for playing basketball but it didn't help us much with expenses."

Riding around looking for space, the students headed out the Bowdon highway. As fate would have it, they spotted L. R.'s daughter, Ethel, outside the store where they noticed some kind of construction going on. They stopped, talked with her and inspected the store, and cut a deal on the spot. It should be noted that at that time there wasn't much rental space around Carrollton for students. The college enrollment started to grow around that time, which caused some entrepreneurs to start building apartments, but they weren't on the scene yet in 1966. The old store may not have been the most fashionable of addresses but the students were looking for low rent and space and they found both.

"The Fosters had built a hall down the middle of the store with bedrooms and a living room on both sides and a bath and kitchen in the rear," Greer remembered. "It was designed like a shotgun shack but it had room, four of us lived there, and it was close to the college. It wasn't much to look at but the girls at the time didn't seem to mind and we had a great time living there." Unlike some of Fosters later residents, the core of the first tenants was built around a Jock mentality. Besides Crayton, Robert "Big Red" Richardson, who was also on the basketball team, along with Bob Holtzclaw lived in the store. Greer also thought Jerry Nacht lived in the basement apartment, and Gene Massey, Jim Haney, and another basketball player, Terry Rutledge, lived in the residence in the rear. The men at the store were also involved with the intramural sports scenes playing for the different tribes like the Sioux, which later became "The Nads", who ruled the flag football scene at the time. People on the sidelines would yell and scream,

"Go Nads, Go".

Bob Greer, one of the first to live at Foster's Store, runs with ball

But like so many others, Crayton and Greer left West Georgia with more than just a degree. They found their life partners, Creighton with Alice from Rockmart and Greer with Betty Jo from East Point. The first pioneer settlers at Foster's Store moved out after that year and some of them ended up at the more fashionable addresses like Jackson Courts or South Park. Several of the early Foster's crew, Greer, Mobley, and Crayton, were charter members of the Cavalier fraternity that later became the Pikes (Pi Kappa Alpha). They found careers and raised families. They ended up as businessmen, educators, and civic leaders in their communities. Speaking from fine homes and offices today, they appreciate the lessons learned at West Georgia and the lessons learned at a broken down shotgun shack of a general store out on the Bowdon Highway.

And Now,

before we all lose completely whatever's left of our collective attention spans, I want to remind you that between each chapter we will have a little break. History is Ok you know, but this book is supposed to be experiential. The Store was all that and more, and you are there now, not where you think you are. So, I know you're all chomping at the bit to read the account of Chris Berry and how the floor was raised in the storehouse, but we already have a question for our spirit guy, a classified ad, and a book recommendation we need to share with you. More things of this nature are out ahead of you as well. Be prepared to encounter the unexpected.

A talk with the Spirit of Foster's Store

Dear Spirit of,

The girls at West Ga. today seem to be more interested in academic pursuits, than good old fashion partying. What can we do to stop this dangerous trend?

Joe Freshman

A reply from the ether

Dear Joe,

You're all a bunch of wimps! You are probably a good boy and maybe just need a little inspiration. So here goes. Just walk right up to every girl you see and invite them over to your dorm room to watch porno movies and smoke some dope. I hear that's what these modern women go for these days. Maybe get real drunk yourself first and just drive your momma's car right thru the front door of the closest female dormitory. That's what I call making an impression! There's nothing like a bad reputation to make a babe magnet out of you. There's a female out there for you somewhere, Joe, whether she's human or not, I'm not too sure.

These little guys and their friends may show up just about anywhere in this book and for no reason at all. Sometimes "no reason" is the best reason of all.

Personal Ad

This is the place to hook up with a new honey or maybe just find that missing piece of jewelry you misplaced at the Johnny Rivers concert.

This is a free service to all of Fosters Children and Friends.

SEARCHING FOR DAD--after years of knowing that I really didn't fit in, my mother confessed to me that my father, who I always thought was Dad, but now I call him Chuck, which is short for his given name, Timothy, is not my father. She is still too ashamed to say she had any kind of relationship with you insincere losers and won't tell me which one of you is Dad. I'm white, female, 34, 5'8" tall, blond, (Chuck is 5'5" and has dark, kinky hair). I want to know you, love you, and find the best possible home for you in your coming years. Some of those places can be so brutal. E-mail attn: 9247Q@fostersstore.com (leave messages for Charlotte in phone box 9247Q

Earth I'm here for a reason. How about you?

Book Reading List Recommendation

How to Make Yourself Attractive to the Opposite Sex

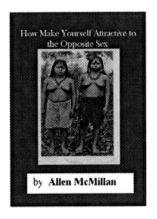

Allen McMillan was not always the dashing blade and ladies man we all remember him to have been. Most of Mac's formative years were spent, as he explains, in quiet desperation. In this partly autobiographical essay, the young McMillan hoboes his way to Texas and then heads south to the wilds of the Amazon Rain Forest in attempt to get a date. It's there, in the most remote and wildest place on earth, that this now wild man encounters a strange tribe of natives who mistake him for a deity and begin to worship him. Besides a lot of sex and barbeque pork, Mac discovers the difference between the two and, eventually, returns to the USA with renewed confidence. This is a crazy book about a crazy storemate. And, if you happen to like books with a lot of explicit descriptions of sexual encounters with multiple partners, this book is for you.

Nothing in a box

Ok, from here on out check out the end of the chapters for more "filler". **Ed**

InkLines

Oh my God! I'm in a book!

Now I'm in the box with nothing.

Nothing is ok.

This next chapter is something Bob O'Kelley thought of. What went on at Foster's Store, the tales of those days, would never fit into one book.

These little snippets are just a few remembrances of one single person. Each could be a book chapter all by itself. Maybe one or two might spark a memory in your own mind about your own set of circumstances during the times of Foster's Store, whether you went to West Georgia or not. I think they just help put the reader in the time and place.

If you find yourself really getting into the spirit of this book and come up with something you remember from your own time and circumstances, feel free to submit them to the Foster's webpage, especially if they are in bad taste.

Piece of a snapshot

Chapter 2

Snapshots - Images from the second year 1967 - 1968

By Bob O'Kelley

Image One – Remember, the Store looked just like a store.

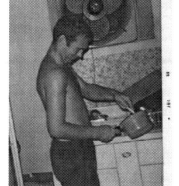

The Ice Cream man delivers.

Bill Craver Cooking in Store

It is early September of 1968; Bill Craver, Jay Heard, Rodney Abernathy, Steve Robinson, and I (Bob O'Kelley) have just finished moving in to the store. We are sitting around the living room shooting the breeze, getting used to each other, and generally enjoying our new digs. For all of us it is our first quarter away from the dorm, and we are well pleased. Without warning the front door opens and a deliveryman walks down the hall with a hand truck full of ice cream. He gets almost to the kitchen before he realizes that something is wrong.

He asks Abernathy, "Where is the freezer?"

Abernathy says, '"What freezer?"

The deliveryman says, "Hey, are you boys living here?"

Abernathy answers affirmatively.

Then the delivery guy says, "Which one of you ordered this ice cream?"

Abernathy says, "No one here ordered it! Our phone isn't even hooked up yet! "

The deliveryman produces a bill-of-lading with the order and our address on it. Abernathy says, "I don't know anything about that. I mean, look around you. You're standing in our living room. This ain't been a real store for a long time".

The deliveryman says, "Well, son of a bitch," and leaves.

We never did figure out who sent him, but Abernathy strongly suspected his buddy Ed R. (Reid Ingram).

It wasn't only the Ice cream man who continued to try and deliver stuff to Foster's long after it was no longer a real retail store. We had guys try to deliver just about everything from vegetables to gasoline. I remember one Saturday morning when a kid comes marching down the hallway with a bicycle inner tube in his hand. I'm in the bathroom taking a leak and he comes right up to me and asks me where the air pump is so he can fix his flat tire. From the outside Foster's Store looked exactly like a real store because that's what it used to be. That fact would produce a lot of funny stories over the years.

Image Two - Steve Robison Preaches

Steve and two friends (possibly Bill Craver and Steve Craft, but I could be very wrong about that) went out carousing one night and ended up at a Pentecostal Tent Revival. I am not sure if it was the Holy Spirit, or a less than Holy Spirit that got into them, but they made the altar call, and that in itself must have been quite a sight.

They arrived back at the store pretty late, but we were still up watching TV. They came in and began telling us about their adventure. Out of the clear blue, the normally reserved Steve says, "I feel the call to preach."

I think it is safe to say that the spirit that was calling Steve to preach had a lot more to do with Jack Daniels than anything Holy. Jay Hurd, who was our resident electronic guru, set his huge stereo to the PA mode and started his reel-to-reel tape recorder. Steve began to preach.

He started slowly by greeting us, "Friends, I wanna thank each and every one of you for being here tonight. Good to see ya, Bob, Rodney, Jay," and continued like that for about half an hour building his up to a crescendo just like the ones on the radio. The normally quiet Steve was hilarious, and he sounded like a real preacher. After a few minutes he had his rhythm down tight and was preaching loudly and rapidly sounding authentic as any of those guys you'd hear in the radio. All of us were "A men-ing" and stuff right along as Steve hit full preach on the throttle.

"I was to traveling-ga.

And on down ta Tuscaloo-sa Alabam-ma.

I stayed at the Holiday Inn-na.

When I heard a knock at my door-ra.

I opened the door-ra

and there she was-sa.

I was staring temptation in the face-sa.

She had ruby lips-sa

and shapely hips-sa.

and I said La-ord what shell I do-ra.

And right at that time there is a knock at the door. It is Ms. Foster from next-door. She says, "Boys, I don't mind preaching in the day time, but at 3:00 in the morning it has got to stop." So it did.

Word got around campus about how funny Steve had been that night. Jay ended up playing the tape for everyone we knew and some we didn't.

I can still see Steve in my mind along with O'Kelley and Abernathy. All of us tried out our own preaching styles on each other. I remember wakening up early on some Sunday mornings to the sound of Reverend Ike on the radio. One store mate's clock radio was set to sound the alarm at 7 every morning. He kept his door locked while he was gone for the weekend so you couldn't get in there to turn off the blaring radio, which at that time was broadcasting a style of preaching very different from the Atlanta GA Presbyterian Church where I was raised.

I'll never forget it. It was almost the same every Sunday.

To quote the Reverend,

"And the rains came-ah

And the winds came-ah,

And the rains came-hah,

And he looked-a out a-pond de-land-da

Children a grace-hah!

Put your hand a-pond the radi-o-hah!

Do you feel the change-ah?

Most certainly he did-ah."

Listening to that with a beer hangover was pretty tough.

Image Three - Mr. Foster Drops By

Mr. Foster and Buffy Wuffy 1968

I was in the store by myself. It may have been a Saturday. There was a knock at the door. Through the window I could see an old man in blue work clothes and a 1950's style fedora hat. It was Mr. Foster. The top button of his shirt was buttoned. Between the button and the hat, he looked very old fashioned, but I suppose when you are ninety years old it is hard not to look old fashioned, and he was about as sweaty as a ninety-year-old man can be. I opened the door and greeted him.

He says, "Phew! It is a hot one! I've been working my worms." Mr. Foster had a worm farm behind his house, which was nextdoor.

He continued. "Say you don't suppose that you have one of those co' beers that I see you boys with, do ya?" I got him a beer and sat with him in the living room while he drank it.

It occurred to me that he must have been born in the 1880's or early 1890's at the latest. Here in Georgia that probably meant that he was very likely the son of a Civil War veteran. I felt like I was talking to a walking history book and wished that I knew him well enough to ask him about his life, but I let the opportunity pass without a question.

Mr. Foster 1940's

He talked of the ins-and-outs of raising "the best red wigglers in the State of Georgia." Then he said, "Say, where are those pretty little gals that I see around here all the time?"

I answered, "You must mean Eileen (Howell), Willy (Linda Wilson), and Kathy (Perkins). Jay dates Eileen, Steve dates Willy, and Rodney just started dating Kathy."

Then he said, "Well what about you. Where's your girl friend".

I told him that I didn't have a girl friend.

He said, "Well there ain't no excuse for that. That college down there has a yard full of pretty gals. Don't be shy. Go down there and get you one, boy." I told him that I would.

When he left, he said what he always said when he dropped by for a cold one. "Now don't tell Ethel." Ethel was his daughter who also lived next door.

Ethel would not have been too pleased to have heard that her father would come by from time to time and accept our offer to share our beer with him. Mr. Foster always made a comment about that fact and we assured him. "We'd never tell Ethel." Truth is that most of the times we would see L. R it would be in the daytime hours when Ethel was at work downtown and during the day, most of the time, there really wasn't that much beer around. Thinking back on it, I doubt if we'd share a beer or two with him more than once a month. I would never characterize him as anything but a fine old man. He and Ethel both were the best kind of people. They were our landlords yes, but they were more like ordinary neighbors not too different really from the ones we'd all left back home somewhere. They were just very good people, but I think we, despite all our shenanigans and hard partying, were the same kind of good people. Mr. Foster had a great personality and was always in a good and cheerful mood. Today, I can't picture him any other way. I make a lot of fun of L.R but that doesn't mean I didn't respect him.

Image Four-The Living Room

This was the year before Chris and Carlos raised, padded and carpeted the floor in the living room, thus making the now infamous "den of inequity" or whatever it became known as in the years that followed. In 1967-1968 it was decorated with posters, including one of King Kong on the Empire State Building. There was a rubber tree plant, which was planted in an old toilet, and an up side down chair nailed to the ceiling, so that it looked like the ceiling was an upside down floor.

Image Five - Abernathy Imitates Elvis

Rodney Abernathy standing in the living room, wearing boxer shorts, a tank top tee shirt, and using Jay's microphone to imitate Elvis. This was a daily occurrence. There were two things about Abernathy. First: when God was handing out personality Abernathy tarried in line and got a double dose. He was the most popular of the store dwellers. My prestige around campus was enhanced just because I was his friend. Second: imitating Elvis was not something that Abernathy did; it was something that Abernathy was. He had done it all his life. When Rodney was being Rodney, which was most of the time, the Elvis program was always playing in the background. Rodney without Elvis just wouldn't be Rodney.

I can still see Rodney demonstrating the Elvis walk, the Elvis look, the Elvis guitar strum, the Elvis "Ah-haugh" and the blurting out singing of "Ya ain't nuttin but a hound dog"!

Image Six – Cooking

All the store mates are in the kitchen preparing our first meal. It was meatloaf. We start by chopping an onion. I don't know if you have ever noticed, but when men cook, we always start by chopping an onion. Each one of us is trying to tell the other how his mother does it. The compromise meat loaf will contain tomato paste and tomato sauce as well as all the seasonings that all our mothers have ever used in a meat loaf. It is glazed with catsup.

"How long do we cook it?" someone asks.

"About four hours", someone answers; so that night we had peas and carrots, which contained stick of butter for seasoning, mashed potatoes, which contained another stick of butter, canned corn, which contained a third stick of butter, canned biscuits with butter, and a **catsup covered carbon ball.**

*With just a little effort, I think it would be possible to produce a **Foster's Store Cookbook**. Besides O'Kelly's meatloaf (aka Catsup Covered Carbon Ball) there's the infamous "Tuna Douche". I remember Dale Teeter used to cook up a tasty rendition of Shrimp Creole. Candee Carmichael could do wonders with a can of Spam. O'Conner and I turned the plain old Bologna and Cheese sandwiches into an art form of sorts. There was the Cole Slaw recipe, which a whole chapter of this book is dedicated to, and my personal favorite, Southern Fried Chicken. But, for our day to day subsistence, I remember standing in line at the T-Burger a whole bunch, mostly at night, whatever buzz I had on fading away and so famished that a T Burger and an order of fries was all I could think of to quench the hunger; it was also the easiest solution.*

Image Seven - Steve Plays the Banjo

Altman's Bay Station was a convenience store. We shopped there a lot, and more or less knew the clerk there who was named Bob. Bob was learning to play the banjo and would practice between customers at the store. He improved rapidly. Steve and I went in the store one day, and Bob was playing with an entire bluegrass band right there in the store.

We were city boys and had never paid any attention to this art form, but we both played folk guitar and had an appreciation for folk music. I think that we both realized that the Greenwich Village folk music the record companies had been feeding us was a bunch of Yankee crap, and that this was the genuine article. Steve was hooked from the get-go on this style of music. He sold all his record albums and bought a banjo. Steve, who was already a damn good folk guitarist, had the banjo mastered within a few weeks, and for a while there, Foster's had bluegrass. A couple of years later I heard that they had some other color grass.

Image Eight - Jay's Microphone

As I stated earlier, Jay was our electronics guru. It would later become his occupation. Jay had the first cordless microphone that any of us had ever seen. For the sake of decorum, I will not mention names, but Jay hid the microphone under someone's bed while he was in the bed room with a girl. The rest of us sat in the living room with dates no less, and listened to every sweet nothing that was whispered. We were a hard lot.

Image Nine - The Foster Bowl

One day we decided that we would host a football game in the pasture next to the store. Word was spread around campus to come for football and beer. On Friday afternoon we got a keg of beer. Jay pulled his huge stereo outside so that we had music and the party began. News of this event had reached Atlanta, and much to my surprise, friends showed up from there. We played ball for about fifteen minutes and partied for about two days. A good time was had by all.

We played a lot of football and basketball at Foster's store.

They even let me play.

I must meet this Sheila.

Classified Ads

Personal Ad

SWS/G-Bi-true female, Sociology major in junior year at U. of Western whatever seeks relationship with any of the legendary lovers from the old days at the Foster's scene. Love guys on the rebound, (gives me the feeling of getting even with my late father), and you guys are famous for hooking up with women with only half a brain; so it only takes them three decades to dump you. So a bunch of you must be available. Send pictures featuring the nipple to knee area. Sheila@fostersstore.com

Book Recommendation (NOT)

Foster's Store 1966 to 1973, *the Bootleg Edition*

Foster's Store
1966 - 1973

by
The People who lived there.

Did you ever see one of those movies where some guy goes out and tries to buy up every newspaper in town because there's a story printed in it that he doesn't want his wife to see? That of course is just one of the not so subliminal marketing plans this unscrupulous publisher has shamelessly come up with to promote, what, to some, may prove anyway to be a very important book about a very turbulent time in the USA, as seen from a place called

"Foster's Store".

We think we already have all the existing copies, so don't waste your time with this cheap and boring knock off written by people who just want to cover their own ass with a bunch of lies.

Historic Photograph

Student Center 1969 From the Collection of Charles Balance aka Capt. Jack

From the Art of Foster's Store Collection

Spanada Bottle - Allen McMillan 1970 Charcoal Pencil

Remember me, your guide?

Chris Berry is about to lay some architectural history on you. This may be the first real creative kernel ever demonstrated at the old storehouse. The raised floor in the womb room was a characteristic not found anywhere else. It was a first. I guess it was a last too. Chris, Dean and Carlos were major developers of the central architectural party grid that became so famous.

Dean Nations 1968.

Dean Nation's old photographs were invaluable in the creation of this book.

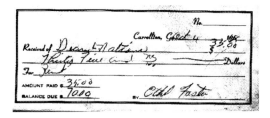

Copy of Dean Nations Rent receipt!

Chapter 3

The Raised Floor at Foster's Store

By Chris Berry

Chris & date

Yes, Dean Nations and I raised the floor. Mostly from materials gathered in midnight raids on construction from WGC. I think we did buy the bamboo curtains from Pier One and the rug from some outlet in Bremen. We sent Carlos to get something tasteful and he came back with the Blue Shag.

We had an old couch which got shot gunned several times one homecoming afternoon, and we needed someplace to recline; so it seemed logical to make a comfortable floor. It always worked well with the babes, as they were immediately reclining upon entry. Well I guess you know all that. It should also be noted that we introduced *Andre's Cold Duck* to West Georgia on that same afternoon, a big step up from Boone's Farm.

Other things attributable to Andre on that very day were: Carlos' convertible stuck in the adjacent cornfield and a passed out Dean Nations dressed up in leather coat and ascot and deposited in the stands at the basketball game, where he eventually woke up and walked home. I think that same evening we had a race down the highway dressed in sheets and the sheriff came in but the German shepherd ran him off. Ah, those were the days.

Bruce Kinney lived at the store one summer with Dean and I don't know who else. Bruce, I believe installed the AC in the TV lounge. There was also a guy named Ran Berry (distant relative) who spent one quarter at the store and curtained all the walls in his room so he wouldn't have to look at the concrete block.

Animals I remember were various dogs, and ducks around Easter who inhabited the spare shower stall.

Dean Nations in front of Store 1968-69

There also was a lady who came in the store plastered every Friday afternoon to use the bathroom. We figured she still thought it was a functioning store.

Beer can baseball was big in front of the back house during spring. I guess we didn't have any baseballs but we always had lots of beer cans. They were hard to catch after several hits had compressed them into sharply pointed mini meteorites.

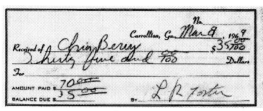

Chris Berry's rent receipt.

Keith and Larry

Classified Ads Work!

Ask the Spirit of Foster's Store

Dear Spirit Guy,

I was wondering. I went to WGC from 1967 to 1972. That floor in the main storehouse wasn't always raised up like it was in the latter years. Do you remember who did that construction and what the idea was behind it? And did the same person collage the walls in there?

Blue-jeaned lady

Spirit Guy Answers

Hey Blue,

What, you some kind of historian of Interior designs? I'm out here beyond the ether trying to give my phony baloney advice to the major partying crowd and you're cluttering up the wave with shit. Let me ask you a question. How much other crap like that have you got floating around in that head of yours? Important stuff is like knowing just how drunk you can get with the little money you have or making some unsuspecting coed to feel sorry enough for you that she'll forget all that stuff her mommy told her and jump in between the sheets with you for a game of hide the salami. Who raised the floor is not as important as why. The why, was so them boys could get closer to you faster and then laugh about how easy you were the next morning. The floor was like a sliding board to sex. Maybe somebody else out there knows the answer to your question. I'd be glad to pass it on if I hear.

Picture taken in "Womb-Room" circa 1974   Females identities unknown From Mark Pistick

Book Recommendation

Big Fun with Tazer Guns

Some might suggest that wiring unruly children to the sharp talons of a tazer gun might be a bit extreme. But not so says West Georgia Graduate Steven Aderhold. "Gentle persuasion, positive role modeling, and systems of reward and punishments are fine for most parents, but some days you're just pooped and maybe would like to *just cut to the chase with these brats*". Ask yourself, do I let it slide if the martini I tell my 10 year old daughter to prepare for me has too much vermouth in it? How many times are you going to have to tell them before they make it right? Tired of your neighbor's dog leaving his offerings in your front yard? Or maybe your sex life has slowed a bit?

Don't laugh, a tazer gun may well be in your future. Book comes with 10% off coupon. While they last.

Paid Advertisement

Clapsaddle Pawn & Jewelry Company since 1951

Remember that Class Ring you pawned just to keep your buzz going a little longer?

Remember? You came into my store with your pupils as black as coal and I gave you the exact change for a case of Pabst Blue Ribbon and 2 hits of Orange Sunshine. Remember that? Here's the deal, **Slomo T. Clapsaddle** still has a bunch of you losers' crap here and I can put it back to you for only about nine times what I gave you for it back in 71. I got your Daddy's golf clubs here too; you know, the ones you told him "got stolen", and all that stuff you sold off to me on the cheap, just to keep your buzz going as long as you could. I'm still in the same place. You know the drill.

And, if you guys ever have a reunion, let me know. I can put you in a name tag maker for cheap. Then all you have to do is remember your own name.

Eclectic Art by Phillip Deloach
1970

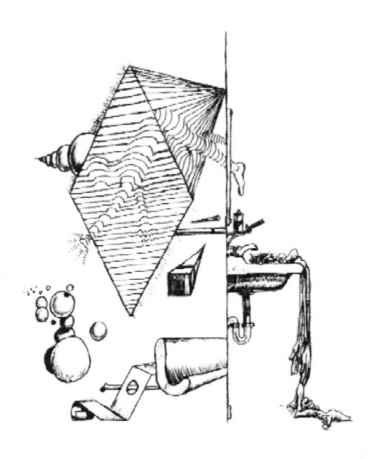

Next

Besides telling us about a crazy party, Terry Farner sets the scene for the late 1960's. We were a pretty paranoid bunch. The draft was eating people like air. All of us needed to form a strategy of some sort or another. We'd either have to surrender to it fully, get into a reserve unit like Terry did, get out on a medical thing, or skip out to Canada or Mexico. There was a war going on that was killing a lot of people. Most of us just really weren't sure why.

Oh yea, there was the other option, you could do nothing and get drafted. It's a funny thing. Historians will tell you that the country was split pretty much down the middle as to their feeling about our involvement in Southeast Asia. Of course the whole county wasn't about to be drafted. Was It?

Chapter 4

Hole in the Wall Party 1968

By Terry Farner

I would like to say that during the recall of all of this, my mind has completely gone on overload with the dates and events. I will try and stick with this one story, as I remember it. I have numerous stories to tell as do Tom Cunningham, Chris Berry and Steve Craft, Carlos Penedo, Dean Nations, Bob O'Kelley, and many others who will surface eventually about all the times we had in school. I suggest we UNLEASH our thoughts to include all of W. GA from 1967 thru 1975 and really hear some true stories that will chill the soul about very good

friends who lived and schooled together during college at a point in time when the Viet Nam war was calling all of us to go

(Not in the Fighting Mood, Chris Berry and Terry Farner in front of Store 1968)

over there and fight. I certainly remember it well...just not the dates!

Unlike Dan Quayle...Terry Farner called a contact in Swainsboro, GA and got his young ass into the National Guard by pulling a string or two, using my Dad's name, credentials and some small town politics to get me in!! Unfortunately I went into boot camp the first Monday after Thanksgiving 1969 at Ft. Polk, LA and found out on December 1st that my draft number was 347. They only took up to 189 that year. Boy, was I pissed, hurt, and stuck with 6 years of obligation. Oh well...better than going SE Asia in my book. I left school then and graduated in the class of 70 the next summer.

As I remember things, it was Fall of 1967 when I came to West Georgia to start my Junior year. I lived in a dorm for one or two quarters but felt I had to get out of there because of the cramped quarters. I moved to the suburbs and found a very beautiful place called Fosters Worm Ranch outside of town on ST. RD 166 West. I believe I might have been one of the first to rent the house (at least that is the way I remember it, unless Tom Cunningham was the first, and I moved in with him...that sounds good for now until we find Tom and he can contribute). Maybe someone did prior to then, but I think not. The rent was $35 per month or $105 per quarter. Mr. Foster rented the old store up front for a year or so before he started renting the house. Previous to Tom and I living there, it was believed that some of Foster's relatives lived there for a while; but when it became vacant the little house with the flat roof was just perfect for college students to rent. (Some believed that Mr. Foster had built the little house for his daughter Ethel in anticipation of her marriage. The tale goes that Ethel was left at the altar, and therefore the house became vacant and rentable. It turned out not to be true at all.)

L to R Terry Farner, Tom Cunningham and Carlos Penedo

The house was like the Ritz Carlton compared to the store at that time. It actually had real designated rooms, some heat and a little AC. It also had a lot of "character". Easy to take care of ... when we had parties ... we came in the next morning and cut off the top of a Ajax can and a bit of soap and threw it on the floor, scrubbed it in with a mop, broom or brush, and hosed the entire front room and kitchen out the back door followed by a squeegee of some type. It was now squeaky clean! Ready for the next event.

The walls in the living room were eventually painted BLACK by me and Steve Craft (or maybe Steve alone that summer of 68. I also lost a few brain cells in the house and cannot remember many things about it, much less the exact time of the events) and we had a couple of black lights there that shone on the various writings on the wall when lighted up for a party. We spray painted several things on the wall with a clear type paint that showed up under the black lights. ANYONE REMEMBER THAT ONE?? Steve also had his Chevy Corvair Engine in the living room for a rebuild. He had seen the *"Thomas Crown Affair"* and was trying to copy the Corvair Steve McQueen used in the movie. Needless to say, it never happened and the motor, as I recall, was trashed from broken bottles (that is another story) and people messing with all the parts during a party.

Dean Nations on Party Patrol talking with Bonnie Bubb - Steve Craft and Cathy Kent cursing on campus

When we were having a great party at the "Worm Farm House" (WFH), people were everywhere. A typical weekend event was led by Terry Farner, Tom Cunningham, Dean Nations, Chris Berry, Carlos Penedo, Skipper Glover, Steve Craft, Bob O'Kelley, Dan* (the karate guy) with his dog named Vigo and many other characters partying at the "WFH". It was a very non luxurious place with a flat roof and bare concrete block walls without insulation as I remember it. If it did, it did not work. We had two bed rooms, one bath, a den, living room (front room with nothing in it) and a kitchen. Steve Craft covered our bedroom walls with bamboo siding during the summer of 68, while I sold Bibles in TN for the Southwestern Company. When I got back in the fall, I lived in it. We also had a few nets tacked to the ceiling with many artifacts on them (use your imagination). It was a cool place to live. I drove a 6-cylinder 3-speed 1964 Mustang half white with a black top.

Here we go again...

Heat was small gas heaters in each room (almost) and the sun. In the warmer weather we did have an AC in the Front room, my BR and the Den ... maybe the other BR, but I think not. My room was on the front of the house and it was the prime suite! Soft beds and plenty of places to rest on the floor.

The partying was intense and the people were packed in the house. I would guess 75 +. Some of the best looking girls at school were there, with and without dates. As you might guess, the single bathroom became a very important and visited spot for everyone at the party, except guys who went outside and used the grass bathroom.

All of a sudden I got the bright idea to punch a very small peep hole

Terry - Storehouse in background

in the kitchen wall that lined up to a full 6-ft. tall, 1-ft. wide mirror in front of the commode in the bath room that backed up to the kitchen. Got the picture and the thought!? By punching a little secret hole in the wall, us Dirty old young men could look into the bathroom and see the girls on the toilet as a direct shot from the mirror on the wall in front of the toilet. Got the picture? All I can say is it was great for a couple of parties until it failed! Carlos screwed it up for all of us! Remember, we had the hole hidden behind an iron skillet that hung on the wall, that was the wall on the W. side of the bathroom. You must remember...there was no insulation so the wall in the bathroom was framed in with 2x4's and wall board.

Carlos and Date

Somewhere along the way, during a party up in the Store house, Carlos Penedo got a little carried away and pushed just a little too hard (maybe because of all the guys standing behind him) on the kitchen wall with his face and hands, and the whole wall between the frames (16") came down and the girl in the bathroom was almost scared to death because she thought the house had finally caved in. I do not remember who she was but she was real cute! Prior to this, my eyes were very tired of looking thru the hole at the ......'so. Do not get me wrong...the girls who knew about it looked at the guys also!

Some of the women at the party tried to figure out what had happened but the truth of the matter is the small PEEP HOLE was destroyed by the big wall board failure that wiped out the entire bathroom behind the toilet. If then were now, we would have countless videos, pictures and documented stories to share. But it was 1969 and we were there dealing with our schooling, grades, Vietnam, the draft and what the hell we were going to do when we graduated.

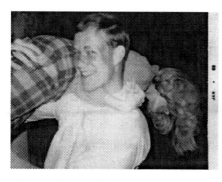

Skipper Glover with date

If anyone can add a little more to this story, I would welcome it! I do believe Steve Craft will be able to add something because he was a great roommate who partied with the best of us for those great years. His dad also packaged the venison for us in packages from Winn Dixie and we cooked more deer meat than the law would allow. Our dates loved the spaghetti and meat balls and the steaks we cooked on the grill.   Never knew they were venison steaks or hamburger patties!

Chapter Notes:

an excited Vee-go. Vee-go was always excited

*From John Horton

Dan "the karate guy's last name was Withrow. His German shepherd WAS named Vego, or maybe Vigo (pronounced vee-go), which was German for something or other.   He trained the dog to respond to only German commands.

Go figure.

Classifieds

Talk To the Spirit guy

Hey Mr. S:

I remember all the fine wines, but was very disappointed not to find the wine of all wines Mother of the Fruit--- BALI HI. This was a regular at the store in the late 60's, accompanied always by a case of tall neck PBR - returnable, of course. I think the Bali was around $1.69 before tax for a gallon. I recall picking one of each up on Friday and next thing you know you're sitting in Class and it's Monday. Now go figure!!!!

Sleepy J

Mr. S answers from the peaceful beyond.

Sleepy,

I was wondering when the space time continuum questioning would start. Let the truth be known: Bali Hi was actually a secret government experiment implemented during the late 1960's and early 1970's. This mind-altering alcoholic beverage, tainted with secret additives that produced psychotic reactions like yelling at the moon and walking around without a shirt on and wishing you could live in a mobile home forever. Very dangerous stuff, but its main purpose was that it made, for its consumers, the solutions to real problems completely unobtainable. It made the Army look good. Some say (not me) that Henry Kissinger thought the deal up during a skull session with his buddyTricky Dick in the oral office. In the end, despite the large price supports given for its production, the brew became popular among only the lowest rung of the populace. You just happened to be standing at ground zero at the time. It's not your fault. Welcome home Flight 19. Retool your mind on the cheap, cheap wine.

Book Recommendation

How to Clean Things Really!

Former store mate Terry Farner shares with the world his cleaning secrets. Gone are the days of simply chopping a large can of *Ajax* in half and sprinkling it all over the place after a long night of partying and then washing it all away with a stream of water from the hose. Farner admits that pure chlorine and army surplus flame throwers can't be found down at your neighborhood Mega Mart, but with a little knowledge of the Import Export business, the tools for those really nasty jobs can be found. "Never give the crime scene guy a break!" Fully instructional and illustrated, learn every cleaning method from A to Z.

Advertisement(s)

Old Store Mate Looking for vintage bottles of "Red Worm".

Party will pay top dollar (pesos) for mescal bottled between the years of 1969 and 1973 prior to US/Mexican Trade agreement forbidding manufacturing of any alcoholic beverage destined for export with untreated river water. The new stuff never rode as well for me. Looks like I'll be crashing with Shelia for a while, email me there.

Ron L

Foster's Store Mug

To order,…..

Go to

www.fostersstore.com

 Here I go,

Are we getting the hang of it yet?

What?

Wake up would you!

What?

Yea, you're getting it.

Historical Photograph

Mr. Foster with Buffy Wuffy and Ponies 1973

L to R – Ponies, Mr. Foster, Bufffy-Wuffy

Chapter 5

The Foster 500

By Bob O'Kelley

It wasn't the fastest race. It wasn't the most exciting. It wasn't 500 miles but it was the most comical race that I have ever seen and, as you might expect, it took place at Foster's Store.

There were two pretty fast cars at the store when I lived there sometime between 1967 and 1969. One was a 1965 light blue Pontiac Lemans that was in every way a GTO, including the size of the engine. It was never clear to me why it wasn't a GTO but the emblem said *Lemans*. The other was a white 1966 GTO. The Lemans was owned by **Rodney Abernathy** and the GTO by **Marvin Ramos**. For those of you who have never had the pleasure, Abernathy was an easy going guy, who was very popular, handsome and funny. He kept everyone entertained with his shenanigans, including imitating Elvis. He could charm the chrome off a trailer hitch, and, oh yes, the girls thought that he was the cat's pajamas. Marvin was more of a regular guy, except more intense than most. He was well liked by everyone, but it seemed that if Marvin did something wrong he always paid the price. Escaping the reaping of what he had sown was not his forte. It seemed to be Abernathy's.

Bearded Rodney Abernathy and Terry Farner

Somewhere there is a law of physics that, simply stated, says that if two young men with fast cars live in the same dwelling, there will be a race. One day, Marvin issued the challenge, "My car can out run yours, Abernathy." As you might expect, Abernathy could not let this challenge pass. After all he had recently faced Ed R. (Reid Ingram) in a race which had taken place on the Newnan Road at the Chattahoochee river bridge. Half the campus in a procession longer than Kennedy's funeral had followed the racers to the bridge. Abernathy had a reputation to protect. So, the two would-be Richard Pettys, decided to race. This was to be a private affair, unlike Abernathy's last event. They headed out of town from Fosters Store towards Bowden, to a

Dan Withrow with Beer beside race course 166

straight flat place on Hwy 166. As we awaited the results of the big race, the rest of the store dwellers were sitting around under the portico that covers the now nonexistent gas pumps. We were playing guitars and generally screwing around, expecting one or the other to return with the big head and the other with his tail between his legs. But that wasn't going to be the case for this pair of racers this racing afternoon. Back up the highway, the racers pulled into a driveway to get turned around and discuss the particulars of the race. They then lined up on the highway paying no attention to the man sitting on his front porch. As luck would have it, he was the County Sheriff and he heard every word they said. He put on his hat then got into his squad car, which was not visible from the highway. When they started racing, the sheriff started after them with the lights flashing and his siren blaring!

Much to our surprise, back at the store, Abernathy came roaring by the store about 80 or 90 and made no attempt to turn in to the parking lot.

A few seconds later, Marvin came flying into the parking lot and did a 180 degree fish tail so that his car stopped under the portico, facing the direction from which it had come and sending fellow store mates flying for cover. I was never sure whether I had seen an exhibition of driving skill or good luck. Marvin jumped from his car and ran into the store. The sheriff turned in the lot with his lights still flashing. He got out. Walked slowly up to me and said in no uncertain terms, "Get me the boy what was driving **that** car." I whimpered, "Yes Sir." Marvin, having heard the sheriff and knowing that he had no escape route, came out before I could go into the store to get him. At that exact moment, for reasons known only to him, Abernathy returns. He gets out of his car, walks up to the sheriff and says, "Officer, what seems to be the problem, here"?

The sheriff's face turned red. Then it turned redder. The veins in his neck expanded so that his collar looked too tight and his eyes bulged. He stared at Abernathy and in a good slow Georgia accent said, "**What seems to be the problem**? What seems to be the problem? Boy, you know God damn good and well what the problem is." Abernathy said, "Yes, Sir." Then Marvin said, "Yes Sir." Then Abernathy again, then Marvin.

He must have chewed on them for twenty minutes. They must have said "Yes, Sir." fifty times each. But in the end they didn't even get a ticket. Probably in the entire history of racing, no one else has staged a race in the County Sheriff's driveway while he watched.

O'Kelley lived beneath the store back then

Wavy Guy Coffee Mug

This might be an example of subliminal advertising.

Now that you have seen this mug you will want one tomorrow when you wake up and start to drink coffee out of an ordinary coffee mug. You will say to yourself, "What in the hell am I doing here! Where's my *Wavy Guy Foster's Store* coffee mug?" Then you will remember that you don't have one and you will go back to this book and read through it until you find an advertisement for the cup and order it. Then you will feel much better.

Talk To Mr. Sprit of Foster's Store guy

Dear Mr. Foster,

...harkening an era when time moved slowly, fast cars and fast women developed legendary proportions, hair plentiful - money short.

Thank you so much for the valuable consumer information. I only wish we had access to such information in the late 60's and early 70's: Zig-Zags, condoms, wine...these subjects pretty much cover the necessary staples for life.

As I mature should I be placing my attention toward other things?

Sincerely,

Heywood Jablome

Spirit Speaks,

Heywood,

Yea, you idiot. rolling papers, condoms, and wine are just part of the support system to a life of debauchery; they are NOT THE LIFE! Stop concentrating on the tangibles and go right for the tits. You college boys and your crazy misconceptions would just kill me if I weren't already something else. Getting drunk and stoned are number two and number three. Number one is getting laid! Do the math, then invert the equation by getting your dates inebriated in a way of their own choosing, then, when they reach that plateau where they "Just don't care," *you* be there to help them out of their underwear. And, as for your maturity question, other things you might want to focus your attention on might be making videos of your sexual conquests and sharing them with the rest of us.

Book Recommend

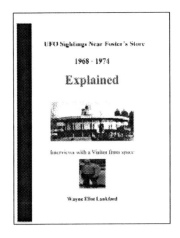

UFO Sightings near Foster's Store Explained

Thru the Author, **Wayne Lankford**, Mr. Foster relates numerous personal contacts with visitors from other planets. One visitor, by the name of Lars, made several inappropriate advances toward not only Mr. Foster himself, but his French poodle dog "Buffy-Wuffy" as well. We are talking crop circles, cow mutilations, and big lights in the sky. Some theorize that Mr. Foster may have unknowingly ingested some sort of mind altering chemical as a result of his small farming activities. Others, like myself, believe every account, no matter how strange or bizarre. You decide yourself in this 400+ page dialog.

Paid Advertisement

The West Georgian newspapers dated 6/30/67, 9/22/67 and 11/17/67. Ed Tant Editorial

In VOLUME XXXIV--NUMBER 11. Also have "very rare" First Edition "the east village BUBBLEDRUPP" January 23, 1968, a publication of AYCOCK HALL. All 3 pages.

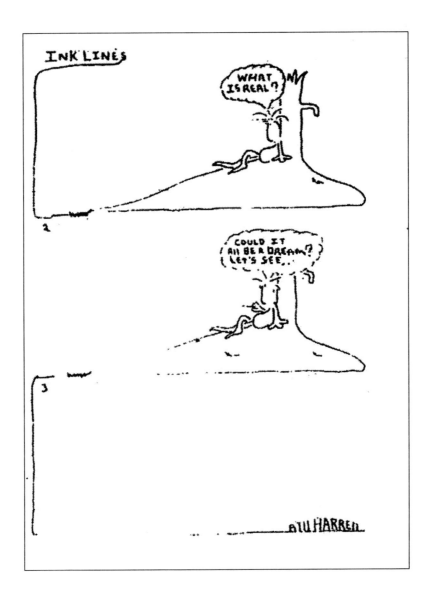

Eclectic Art 1970

Sylvia Hanson

Maybe...

a little more pre chapter explaining to do here.   The late sixties were real strange, just like this book I guess. This next chapter is about an emerging subculture that was everywhere else at the time, but still in its infancy at WGC. Mike Sorrell, then an aspiring song writer, was the first person I had ever met who had actually smoked marijuana. We became fast friends. It turned out that I already knew a lot of people who smoked pot back then, I just didn't know that I knew people like that .That's the way it was in the beginning. In the end, four years later, I'd look around and realize that I didn't know anybody who didn't smoke the stuff. That's just the way it was.

and,

A train full of crazy was headed to town. Nobody was going to stop it. Only fools would try. **Mike Sorrell** was my personal conductor for a while. Here's a chapter from him about part of all that.

Chapter 6

Meanwhile, over in the parallel universe about 3 miles from Foster's Store...

By Mike Sorrell aka: Kangarooman

 Mike Sorrell

"Well, I've had my fun, if I never get well no more."

Goin' Down Slow
-    Howlin' Wolf

At this point in our lives, we have all faced the fire and stood either first in line or in close proximity to death, divorce and self-destruction, but nothing quite slaps you upside the head like the realization that we have less time in front of us than we had behind us.

They say if you have a clear recollection of the '60s, then you weren't an active participant. While I'm not an official alumnus of Foster's Store, I have known a few and was most certainly an active participant.

I was 20 years old when I transferred to WGC January of 1968. Coming from a small textile town in Alabama, I was naïve and innocent in many ways, but worldly in others. I'd always had a fascination with the blues, a passing interest in Zen Buddhism, the ability to quote long passages of Dylan and, thanks to my friend Dave Roberts (who played upright bass at a late-night jazz club in Columbus), a working knowledge of marijuana. I saw myself more of a hipster than a hippie, some sort of holdover from the Beat Generation.

Aycock Dorm Winter 1968. Sorrell and Lankford's room. (**Point of interest on the Dope Tour, see end of chapter for tour details**)

Karma and fate aside, I've always believed life was a cosmic crapshoot – you just ante up and roll 'em again. Having said that, I kinda think that Wayne Lankford and I would have to have crossed paths at some point. It's rare that I find someone who shares my exact same streak of whimsical anarchy. I think we both subconsciously sensed a kindred spirit, someone who used his eccentricities to protect his creativity and that we were destined to stay up late and travel down some strange roads together. The fact that we ended up roommates and lifelong friends was in no way coincidental.

I know time fades everything, and we remember pretty much what we want to. Let me think. What can I clear up? I do remember turning the police car around, but I don't know if I took the keys. I know we met with the ACLU lawyer, but I don't recall his name. (Al Horne?) I will admit that it was my cherry bomb that blew the fire alarm button off the wall at 2 a.m. on the top floor of Aycock Dorm, but there were co-conspirators.

All this was going down in the midst of figuring out who we were and trying out who we wanted to be. There were always these weird conflicts, equal parts *Animal House* behavior and hippie commune idealism, the juxtaposition of the cultural battles of the '60s small-town life in Georgia.

Sid Short behind the wheel

One particularly fine April afternoon, I was sitting top down in a white MGB (with red leather interior) while Sid was negotiating a marijuana purchase with a floor counselor at a Georgia Tech dorm. Whatever I was listening to on the radio got interrupted by the news of the King assassination. I remember having two thoughts: One – something was fundamentally wrong with America; and two – Atlanta, Ga., right then was no place for two white boys in a convertible.

Chipping in to buy weed was common. Most everybody had a friend that knew a guy who could fix you up. Trouble was, you had no idea what you were really getting-talk about "Pot Luck." One time somebody returned from Atlanta with an ounce of marijuana that was covered in white dust. We were told it was cured in something called "peace." Not knowing diddley about large animal tranquilizers, we proceeded to pile it all up on a piece of newspaper while the usual suspects formed a circle. Rollin!

After the third one, Doug remembered he had a date that night. I was amazed how well he was able to function. He showered, changed clothes and left. A few minutes later, he nudged me and passed me the joint. "Decided you couldn't make it?" "Make what?" "The date." "I just got back". "From where? " "The date. We went to the movie."

Somewhere I had lost three hours, and I'm sure a few brain cells. I guess that is small change compared to what PCP cost James Brown.

In the summer of '67, a long-haul trucker gave one of my friends a half-pint fruit jar full of pills, various sizes and colors and as near as we could tell, all amphetamines. This neatly dovetailed with a three-day run down to Panama City. A couple of days later, after too much beer, not enough food and no sleep, things at the motel got a little weird and a lot wired. About 4 a.m., I took a bedspread out on the sand dunes in an effort to escape. Somewhere off in the distance, I heard these mumblings, then a dragging sound.

These drunks had torn down an old neon restaurant sign that was in the shape of a fish. They were stepping on and stumbling over the dangling wires, grunting and groaning, pushing this thing through the sand, apparently attempting to return it to the sea. In the background, I could hear "Like a Rolling Stone." Somehow it all seemed to make sense. I guess visions are where you find them. Before WGC, this was as close as I had come to a hallucinatory experience.

Hallucinogens, oh hell yes, LSD became a kind of rite of passage for us. Those were experimental times. What is this stuff? Should I take two of them? OK, I'll take two, and if it's any good, give me the other one later, and here, hold my pocketknife so I don't kill anybody.

I can't speak for anyone else. For me it was always about sailing uncharted waters, dipping a toe in the great unknown, never knowing when you would go right past enlightenment and over the edge into grinding paranoia.

I have a very vivid memory of crawling into Sid's kitchen, reaching up, opening the refrigerator and shivering in the blast of cold air. Hmmm, must be something in here worth trying. My eyes fell on a small yellow plastic lemon. I unscrewed the little green top, tilted my head back and squeezed. My taste buds exploded. They came out of my mouth in a multicolor arc of fireworks. Sort of a rainbow effect – thrilling, terrifying and mystifying, all at the same time.

Another time, a friend at Auburn gave me two tabs of really good New Mexico mescaline. I made a present of one to Sid. In return, he gave me something. He put his in his pocket. I swallowed mine. He told me it was 500 units of LSD with a 250-psilocybin kicker, whatever that was. (He told me this after the fact.) Somehow, later that night, we ended up at the old A&W Root Beer joint (not a real good place to go on an LSD trip). On the way back after going over a dip in the road, for a little while there, I lost all the feeling in the lower half of my body.

Later that night, I thought Larry Bowie, a friend who I thought resembled Glen Campbell, actually was Glen Campbell. I mean I knew that he wasn't really Glen Campbell, but then again, how many chances do you get to hang out with Glen Campbell? In a mobile home? In rural Carroll County? Crazy little thoughts like that happen when you'd take LSD and such. Hell, if they didn't, you'd want your money back wouldn't you!

I really don't want to get that deep into the spring of '68 drug bust. Life is too short. I have tried to think who told me while I was coming out of class that it was going down – I guess I have blocked it out. I just remember they said that they already had Sid in custody. I headed across campus to where I knew Doug had a history class. I was going to warn him, but there he was being escorted by a campus cop.

I took a left turn, loaded up, told Wayne to clean up and left town. It was all a set up, of course, but good people got hurt and lives were changed. At times like that, you learn who friends are and what they are made of. Some people were forced to say things they did not want to say. I understand that; others, however, told not only all they knew but also what they suspected.

I received a call that fall from someone in the D.A.'s office. I told him that I would not voluntarily testify and that they would need to get a warrant and come and get me, and if they did, I would take the 5th. He told me not to ever come back to Carroll County. I ignored him. I was back in Auburn for the fall quarter. Disciplinary expulsion, my ass.

I last saw Sid briefly some years ago in Helen. We just stood there and grinned at each other like maniacs – everything else was understood. I hope to reach a place in my life where I can go back and hang out and maybe we can spend a little more time.

Someway, somehow and to some degree, we all survived. God, we were fearless fools. In the occasional surreal moment, I think I knew more then than now. But I'm still the same optimistic cynic I've always been. I'm pretty sure I wouldn't want to go back and relive those days, but then again, I have no real regrets.

Some people may have better stories about me than I do, and some may remember things differently. I have no quarrel with that; their memory is probably holding up better than mine. If there is any case where the statute of limitations has not expired, I not only deny the allegations, but would be willing to wrestle with the alligators, as well.

Let me wind this up. May you all find whatever redemption you are seeking and may the God of your choice bless you real good.

Foster's Store Tours

Request for Historic Dope and Alcohol Tour Information Form

Fuck the new Library! Show me where all the real History Happened!

Send tour highlights, dates and times to me!

Contact Information

Name_____

Address 1_____

Address 2_____

City_____State_____zip_____

Email_____

Mail to: Foster's Store Tours – History Department

P. O. Box 36186

Hoover, AL 35244

Or email: editor@fostersstore.com Attention: History Tour Information

Announcement!

Franchises still available!

$250,000 minimum Investment

Mr. Foster's Favorite Red Wigglers

Contact Butch Gungii

Gungii, Clappsaddle & Obberwolfer

Atlanta, GA

Now that last piece was a real segway, but we needed to let everybody know that, like Dylan had said, "The Times, they were a changing."

Life was crazy! It is not an accident that I put an advertisement for Mr. Foster's Red Wrigglers in between these two stories.

Anybody want a sandwich? Here's the top piece of bread from Terry Farner, *Liquor 101*.

Something needs to go here but I don't know what.

How about the other half of that picture of Chris?

Half of Chris Berry and all of Terri Scruggs.

Terri said it was OK to use her picture in the book. Thanks Terry!

Eclectic Art Fall 1970

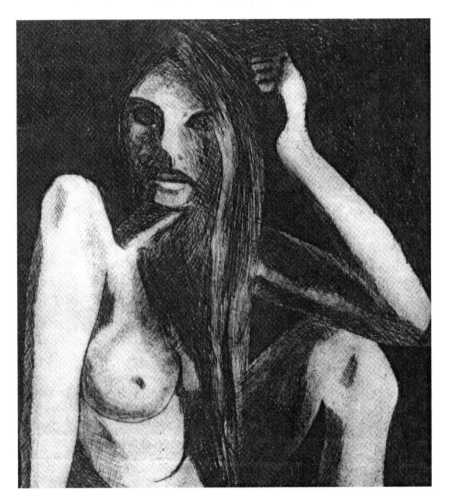

Oliver W. Boyd

Chapter 7
Liquor 101

By Terry Farner

During spring of 1967, a bunch of future Foster's Store residents were living at Jackson Court Apartments. I tell you, a little warm weather will start a whole rekindling of the parting thought process. Spring is about breaking out and new beginnings. From time to time we'd feel a need to wrinkle our standard Jackson Courts party planning, which actually was no planning at all; just a short drive down to Skinner's Grocery and pick up a case or two of the PBR's and try to find some willing coeds to engage with us in our usual debauchery. Yea, but spring requires a leap of thought and sometimes you just get sick of the beer thing. Yeah, some hard liquor would up the volume on our sophistication meter a click or two and would put a proper mark to the end of the cold weather of winter.

Waiting on Terry and the Booze run

Future Storemates - Party Scene at Jackson Courts

As you might recall, in those days Carrollton was a "Dry" county for liquor; so when the urge hit us, we had to travel over to Fulton County in order to buy the stuff. As in many cases, we'd prepare a shopping list which would more than likely include not only the liquor for our little party, but maybe for several other parties that might be planned; or, as it would often happen on weekends, breakout spontaneously throughout the whole complex.   Bourbon, vodka, rum were the favorite choices of libation, but there would always be somebody who'd want some Sangria or something to add a bit of sophistication to their particular *soiree*, Jackson Courts style. The news of "the liquor run to Atlanta" would travel through the Courts pretty fast and it

Farner, Terry Peotrowski, John Grant, Bill Harrell, Linda Mason

& Bill Bateman

wouldn't be too long before a pretty good sized order had been compiled and money collected.

We took turns making such trips and this weekend it was my time to drive over to Atlanta and get the booze and deliver it to the masses back at the courts. Even though I myself was underage to purchase liquor legally (I still had about six months to go before I was 21 and legal), I could still drive the car, something I was more than happy to do.

A fellow partier and Courts resident, Bill, (I can't remember his last name), was 21 and, as I remember it, we left Carrollton about 3:00 pm and hauled it toward the Fulton Industrial Blvd. Exit on I-20 just inside the Fulton County line (about 45 minutes). We had made this trip many times without a glitch: Hwy 166, out to Hwy 5 to Douglasville, where we would pick up I-20 and, the skyline of Atlanta would appear as we topped the big hill just before the Six Flags Exit, where we knew were just minutes away from our destination.

Once we arrived, I backed my car right up the front of the store to make it easier to load the liquor into the trunk of my 65 Mustang. On this day, the salesman filled our order for the 20-30 bottles of booze, wine & beer and noticed the decal on the back windshield of my 1965 Mustang that read, "West Georgia College", and made a comment about what a great school it was. As a matter of fact, he asked us if we went there and if we were having a party that night. We said "hell yes" and we thanked him for the booze. I believe we got a 10% discount because we bought so much.

Even though Bill was of legal age to buy this booze now all tucked safely into the trunk for transport back to school, I admit I was feeling a bit of pride and accomplishment in my voluntary contribution to such an admirable mission: bringing so much joy juice back to Carrollton and the smiling faces of my partying friends. There's just a lot of self confidence and good feeling you get from these above and beyond the call of duty missions.

Farner, White, Hardigree, and Berry with liquor

As we got back on I-20 W. toward school Bill and I discussed the finer points of mixed drinking and were dreaming out loud about just how many drinks it might take our dates to be talked out of their outer garments and into our bedrooms. We were discussing the merits of drinking Johnnie Walker Red on the rocks against the alcohol standard of college age drinking, Rum and coke, when all of a sudden we saw a police car (lights flashing) on the East direction/opposite side of the road going full bore after someone toward Atlanta. We commented how he was sure in hot pursuit of somebody for something. The next thing I know is I'm seeing a blue flashing light closing the distance behind us and I hear a siren and he's right on my tail, his headlights on bright and flashing, blinking me to the emergency lane on the side of the highway. Quite dutifully I pulled over and stopped as fast as I could manage it and get out of the car, as you did in those days, and immediately handed the policeman my license. Thinking back on the episode today, it kind of reminded me of a "Dukes of Hazard" episode or "Smokey and the Bandit" with Buford T. after you. Know what I mean? The accent and the body language were unbelievable. This guy got out of his cruiser with his "John Wayne" pistol belt hanging on his side and spoke very unhurried and so "SOUTHERN" English.

"So, what are you boys doing out here swerving like you were back there all along the way?" As I handed him my driver's license, I informed him that we were just driving back to college not realizing why we had been stopped. I was puzzled as to his description of my driving and I guess I looked it as well. To my knowledge, we had not broken any laws—yet. It was still before 5 PM.

While attaching my license to his clipboard, he gave my car a good once over with his eyes. He said it looked to him like we were "swerving all over the road", maybe because the rear end of the car was so low to the ground."

All I could think was: "What?" I was really surprised and alarmed at the same time now. "No, I don't know how that could happen," I told him. "My car is in very good shape and has no problems that I know of. Maybe the wind was blowing pretty hard today, maybe that's what you noticed."

I believe whatever I could have said wouldn't have mattered at that point. He was all business when he asked me quite plainly, "Open the trunk so I can see why the back end is sitting so low?"

The Mustang wasn't sitting low to the ground at all. I knew that and so did he. None of that mattered. Bill was now standing in front of the car. I remember we made eye contact with each other and held our collective breath as I unlocked and raised the lid of the trunk, revealing the 20 to 30 bottles of booze all stowed away neatly in 3 different cardboard boxes.

"Well, looks like you boys were going to have a party somewhere." My heart sank right through the concrete and just sank deeper as he emotionlessly, without any discussion beforehand, read us our rights, saying we were "transporting illegal amounts of alcohol across a dry county" and were "now under arrest." He continued, "Please follow me to the "Villa Rica" Sheriff's office for a hearing immediately." Then he just turned around and walked off to his patrol car, his back to us.

I thought about it. My Mustang was pretty fast, but if we tried to outrun him, he would eventually get us. I couldn't outrun a radio. Hell! He had my driver's license still stuck to his clipboard. I was not going to be more stupid. It pissed me off that I knew he knew it too.

It was only a few miles back up the road to downtown Villa Rica. Our contraband liquor was still in the trunk. I felt like a caught fish being tugged in at the end of a line as we followed the still flashing blue light of our captor to the small Police office. Eventually we were to be greeted by this heavyset and overweight Boss Hog-like character. My god!!! What a joke someone

1968 Yearbook Picture

had played on this man, or was it on us? He was the Sheriff? Magistrate? I didn't know what I was in for here, what kind of person he was, just sitting behind a wooden desk with an open beer on the side counter next to him. It was our beer he had already helped himself to.

All I remember is he said something like we were "in BIG trouble" and could "both go to jail for this kind of crime," that they "took bootlegging seriously, this is a dry county, you know?"

"Bootlegging?" I gasped! "We're not bootleggers; we're just throwing a party back at school!"

Quite unimpressed with my defense, the Magistrate guy told me to watch what I had to say, reading both of us the law again from the statute book. I felt like I was going to burst, but at the same time sensed that the worst was over. The Deputy had already unloaded the liquor from my car and given me back my keys. They seemed in fact, as anxious to get rid of the two of us as we were to get away from them. The big guy told us he was going to let us go because we looked like good college students but he would keep the booze. He made it clear, even without coming right out and saying so directly, that if we made any waves or called anyone, and it got back to him, they would come get my car and sell it at public auction, as it had been used to haul illegal amounts of booze across a dry county line. I later found out he was correct. He could have done it.

It was always my guess that the salesman at the Fulton Industrial Boulevard liquor store was in cahoots with this guy and they had a scam going to collect large amounts of booze and maybe sell it back to the store. Who knows?

We could only imagine the look on our fellow partiers' faces as we would begin to tell them that their pre-purchased bottles of alcohol had been intercepted like some miss-thrown pass and were now resting comfortably within the confines of the Villa Rica Police Department. The sudden and unplanned absence of that much hard liquor, so anticipated by so many, could cause such an immediate void in the ether that the entire Jackson Courts Apartment Complex might be sucked completely out of existence, so great was this sorrow. Then we imagined our fellow brothers and now all but deflated partiers changing their mood, becoming distraught at first, moved to tears just before the real backlash of anger and lust for retribution would set in, focused on Bill and me directly. The initial state of mourning would not last long, I reckoned. I imagined a mob forming quickly, torches, tires burning in the parking lot with a lot of black smoke rising. And as we pulled in and up to my apartment, they were all there waiting on us, just smiling with anticipation.

Only after a few minutes of their hearing us out did it start to sink in that what I was saying about the cops and the booze was the truth. I had not hid the stuff somewhere else. "I'm telling the truth, really!" Bill was backing me up, we backed each other up. Hell! I was as disappointed as they were. More so. I too would have to go through the trouble of plying my date with Pabst Blue Ribbon instead of Bacardi rum as I had planned. So much time and money had been wasted already today.

Jackson Court Party 1968

At the end of the day I guessed that only a couple of people continued to believe that we actually had ripped them off for the money. My God!! Isn't there any slack given for those people who volunteer their lives to drive up and down the roads of life to get whisky for others? I hope so, and I believe we were rewarded in the end. After all, nobody shot us.

In the end I think they came to accept our story about how we lost all the booze. Thank God for reality and the true friendship we had with all the investors. Even though it was a BEER night for all.

Farner's Trunk Stuffed with Beer

Classifieds

Ask The Spirit

Dear Spirit of:

I was trying to create an old Foster's Store favorite recipe and need a bit of assistance.

I pretty much have the stuff I need to create the infamous "TUNA DOUCHE"
I can tell you it costs a lot more than 50 cents a pop to serve nowadays with inflation and all...
What I was wondering is will it taste as good if the tuna is not stolen???

Tuna breath wannabe

Dear Wanna,

If you get tired of fried cat in a shoebox, another Foster's favorite, then "Tuna Douche" is a great choice for all them wayward boys what has spent all their momma's money on Bali Hi and grease weed. Hell, once you've killed off as many brain cells as you guys did, the idea of a civilized cuisine is kind of out of the reach of those shaky hands of yours. The recipe for that concoction, besides an "I don't give a shit anymore" attitude, was a can of tuna, a can of cream of mushroom soup, an onion and a couple of chopped up stalks of celery, can of water. Mix all that crap together in a frying pan and pour it all over a bunch of cooked egg noodles. Take a nap, and then go reload the hookah.

Hey, It's ME! I think it's me.

The Art of Foster's

Phillip Deloach 1969

News Item

<u>Confiscated Counterfeit T shirt found in Hong Kong</u>

Warning!

Because of the popularity of all things having to do with Foster's Store these days, I find it necessary to warn everybody about all the counterfeit stuff that is already hitting the marketplace. What's weird is that the knock- off artists making this stuff, are charging more for this crap than Walter and I. The photograph above was sent to us from one of our agents in Hong Kong. It seems that the unscrupulous manufacturer who is ripping us off on the T-shirt biz is not only selling inferior shirts, but is maintaining a workplace where the temperature is so hot that the workers, mostly young Asian women, in order to stay cool, have to work all day in the nude.

I'll try to get some pictures and post them on the website as they become available.

People were changing

Jim Kent 1969 Yearbook Picture

1973 Foster's Store

Chapter 8

Rodney needs his Cooking Utensil

By Wayne Lankford

There was this chapter I wanted to do about recipes. I felt like from a historical perspective people living in the future might want to know what kind of food we ate during the days of Foster's Store. Personally, I could only remember a few of the staples like bologna sandwiches and Tuna Fish Surprise; mostly I remember going to the T Burger a lot.

I did remember one night when Bob O'Kelley, Rodney Abernathy and I decided we would try to fix ourselves a down home southern favorite, Chitterlings. (Pronounced "chit-lins") They were supposed to be real cheap. I had seen them in the grocery store many times and wondered what something that sold for almost nothing tasted like. I knew what they were, hog intestines, and that fact was a turn off for sure, but the price was right. You could get five gallons of the things for about three dollars. We weren't poor, but if we could find ways to save money on food, then it follows that we could spend what money we had on things that were more enjoyable.

In researching this chapter I called O'Kelley and we talked about that night. His recollection of what happened that night and a few days later was very different from mine so I called Rodney Abernathy and yes, Rodney remembered that episode back then too, but his recollection was altogether different from mine and Bob's. Not only that, but Abernathy really didn't seem to think that the deal with the chit-lens was all that big and not really worth me doing much with it. But he goes on to describe just how you are supposed to prepare the things, how to wash them, clean them and, then, and how you are supposed to par boil them for a few hours because if you didn't, they would be so tough that you wouldn't even be able to chew, much less eat them. Basically, the recipe calls for the preparer to literally, "cook the shit out of them".

Yea, Rodney's not really too excited about all this at all, I can tell, and right there, in the middle of his cooking instructions, he asks me, "Do you remember that Big Panty Raid we had back in the Fall of 68?"

eorgian

EORGIA, 30117   FRIDAY, DECEMBER 1,

Six Raiders Receive Penalty Not Panty

One West Georgia student has been suspended and five placed on social probation for the remainder of the academ. for their part in a recent attempted panty raid.

According to an onlooker in Old Mandeville, where the raid was staged on November 2, a small group of boys were stopped by a counselor at the bottom steps leading to the old dormitory. She told them to leave and they did.

Kruay Golightly, judiciary chairman of the S.G.A, said, "Six boys from Row Hall were tried this past Monday and it was recommended that one of the boys be suspended and the remaining five be placed on social probation for the duration of the academic year."

The names of the students were not released by the Office of Student Affairs, but Dean Pershing said that the recommendation made by the judiciary com-

Golightly registered no interest on the boys' behavior

"Well Gee Whiz, Rodney, that was a long time ago, I remember some Panty Raids, but I'm not sure about any dates. That was a long time ago", I responded.

Rodney just continues talking and I'm picking up a little sadness in his voice, like a lament, maybe like he isn't even talking to me directly; he's remembering something that's maybe important to him, but I can't figure that out and just ask him if he was living at Foster's then.

"Yeah! Me and Hoke (Hoke is what a lot of us called Bob O'Kelley, his middle name) were living there then with Steve Robison or somebody." He continues, "Well, we were all up at the college for this panty raid thing one night and there was a bunch of people outside the girls dorms, and the campus cops came and Dean Pershing drives up and parks his car right near where I'm standing. He gets out leaving the door open and the keys still in the ignition."

Listening to this, I can tell that whatever this is about, Rodney has thought about it for a long time. It was one of those things where I'm pretty sure my chitlin story is never going to happen anyway, so out of politeness I just listen to Rodney continue on about whatever it is that he wants to talk about.

"Well I'm the person who stole Dean Pershing's keys that night."

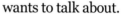

The Keyless Dr. John J. Pershing

I guess my interest level increased a notch or two just then, but it was a 'who cares' thing to me. That was so long ago.

I didn't personally remember anything about any missing keys. But Rodney went on.

"I guess the devil got me. They were just there. It was so easy. I did it before I even thought about it. Then I just went back to the Store and would have forgotten about it, but then all those notices about 'the missing keys' started appearing all over campus."

Listening, I respond, "Gee, Rodney, I really don't remember any of that. Let's talk about chitlins some more."

Totally ignoring me, and with that thousand miles away sound in his voice, he continues, "Yeah, not only posters saying that the person who had the keys would not get into any trouble if they returned them, but it was all over the school newspaper too. I was really getting all shook up about it."

"Well Rodney, why didn't you just go and turn them in?" I ask him.

"I don't know, it was like I thought I might be getting set up or something."

Now I'm interested really; so I ask as genuinely as I know how, and with a real caring tone in my voice, "What did you do Rodney?"

"Two or three days went by when I guess I figured a way to get the keys back and not get caught. I was afraid that they might fingerprint the keys and catch me that way; so, I decided what I would do is put the keys in a jar of peanut butter and mail them back to the school."

I'm imagining him doing all this, the peanut butter, the box, the label, the post office, the relief as he puts the package down the shoot. "So they never knew who stole the keys?"

"No, I never got caught."

"Rodney, I had no idea you were such a bad boy!"

After a pause Rodney came back still totally serious, "It was just one of those stupid things you do when you're young; I had no intention of doing anything wrong, it just happened."

Then, in attempt to get back to the chitlin mission, I got Rodney to tell me really how you are supposed to cook chitlins. For a few more minutes we discussed our ill fated hog intestines from so long ago.

After talking to Rodney I decided that I couldn't use his account of our chitlin experience. Nor could I use the tale told to me by O'Kelley. There were just too many inconsistencies between them.

This is supposed to be a truthful retelling of things, and the only way I can stay true to that objective is to just tell you my own version, like you really care now, of the night we burned them hog guts.

As I remember it, Hoke and I had discussed a couple of times back and forth an interest in trying out a traditional southern favorite that was supposed to be flavorful and cheap. If grits were OK, and they were by our standards, then we just needed to try chitlins. After all, we were living right in the heart of Dixie weren't we?

Finally the day came. We thawed them out and rinsed them off as best we could and put them in this biggest pot we could find. We could barely fit them all in the pot. It was a Saturday afternoon. I seem to recall that the raw innards did not smell all that great even before we got the heat up on the stove and the things began to boil slowly as per Chef Rodney's instructions. We observed right away that these things already smelled pretty bad, and we'd just started them. Just after a few minutes the smell was driving us from the kitchen. The simmer time on these babies would be about three hours. Maybe they would smell better the longer they cooked. It would be a while before supper. After we cooked them here, we were supposed to clean them again and cut them up into small strips and pan fry the things. It was beginning to look like it would probably be after dark before we'd be ready to eat the things.

I don't exactly remember where we all went, but with a cover on the pot and the heat on low, we figured everything would be all right for a couple of hours while we were visiting friends somewhere else. I don't remember. I do believe that while we were gone we all consumed a number of beers and maybe lost track of exactly how long the chitlins had been on the stove. I do remember coming back eventually and seeing smoke coming out of the kitchen window in the back of the house where the kitchen was located.

Drunk, but undaunted, we ran down the hall thru the smoke and got to the kitchen to see white smoke coming up from underneath the heavy metal pot lid.

Somehow, O'Kelley and I got the smoking pot and its even worse now, stinking contents outside and set it all out next to the store where they would be out of the way. Stinking, that is the word. I got a small cook pot and filled it with tap water and while Bob lifted the lid, I poured the water over the smoking chitlins. It, they, everything, smelled awful, stunk to high heaven!

Bob and I were just looking at each other thru our collective beer buzz, really kind of proud of the fact that we'd just saved the store house from being burned down by a pot of runaway hog guts when Abernathy pulls up with his girl friend and takes a whiff of the air and says something like, "Good God Almighty! What the Hell have you two been doing", and "What's my cook pot doing out here on the driveway?"

We explain that we were just cooking these chitlins and guessed we didn't put enough water in the pot and just about then the girlfriend interrupts and says, "Rodney, you need to take me back to the dorm, this is awful! Look there's still smoke coming from inside the house!" (Note: I wish I could remember her name. She was a cute little thing. She would always wear these very short shorts. She followed Rodney around like a little puppy dog, sat on his lap out in front of the store even when he did his Elvis Presley impression.)

It would be a few days until the next garbage pickup. God knows we weren't going to ever eat any of this smelly mess that was now just contained and smell-secured by the heavy metal pot lid. There really wasn't much we could do except maybe go out into the cow pasture beside the store and dig a hole and bury the things. I remember thinking that that would be a lot of trouble and I wondered about burying part of a hog all by itself out there and we joked about the hog guts, or the spirit of the disembodied hog guts coming back to haunt us and future residents. That didn't seem like a good idea as we just kept drinking our beers out there in front of the store until we decided to leave it there where it was until the next garbage day.

The cook pot would have been beside the tree pictured here

The next day Abernathy is bugging Hoke about the damn things just sitting out there in his best cook pot. So after about three days of complaining Bob does get around to it and rediscovers that, when he lifts the pot lid, that not only do these things smell even worse, but they are stuck to the sides of the pot because of the scorching last weekend. He doesn't know what to do now. If it were me, I would throw the whole thing out, pot and all. That was my universal answer to cook pots I'd ruined in the learning to cook process while I was living away from home for the first time. But, Bob, two years older than me, decided to let the hose run some water into the thing and let the water supposedly soften up the hog guts while he was off to his morning classes. That's what he did.

Around noon Bob gets back to the store just in time to find a pack of stray dogs out front. He sees a couple of them with their heads in the chitlin pot just a licking away like crazy. When he gets out of the car he yells at the dogs and runs towards them shoeing them away. To his surprise, it appears that the hungry dogs have completely eaten every trace of what was left of a five pound bucket of burned up stinking chitlins. Not only that, but upon further inspection, it appears that these stray dogs have literally licked the pot clean, so clean that now there's not a trace that anything was ever in this pot. I imagine his relief. The pot is so clean that he takes it into the store house and sets it in the sink thinking that he'll finish washing it later after his afternoon class and goes into his bedroom to sleep for a couple of hours.

Of course, he forgets all about the pot he left back there in the kitchen earlier, awakes form his nap and goes on to his afternoon class, then doesn't return until after five o'clock when he finds Rodney, and his girlfriend at the time, in the kitchen making a big pot of spaghetti in you know what.

"Hey Hoke, great job on the pot cleaning deal! I knew you could do it. But how did you ever get it so clean?"

Bob is a bit surprised and is curious at the same time of course, wondering if Abernathy thought to wash the pot out with dishwashing soap and hot water thinking about the dogs and what all might have been growing in the thing that he couldn't see for the last two or three days. Bob starts his answer saying, "Yea, it really wasn't too hard a job after all those da-ah" but stops himself mid word and continues as he now stares into the boiling pot of spaghetti noodles, "after I let it soak for a couple of hours."

Abernathy is really pleased saying, "You going to help us eat all this spaghetti aren't you? We made plenty!"

"Well you know I'd like too, but Lankford and I have to get back to Atlanta to work tonight; we'll have to get something on the way I guess. Bob knew that Abernathy would be really pissed at him, probably even more pissed at him than he was about the thing in the first place if he knew his washing job was subcontracted to a pack of wild dogs. Bob figured that, hey the water is boiling there, that's how you sterilize everything anyway. What good would it do to tell Abernathy all the details? Right then and there he decided to maybe wait until some time in the future when maybe he would be more forgiving.

I wonder today, if Dean Pershing was still alive, if he would have forgiven Abernathy about stealing his keys and then returning them to him packed in all that peanut butter?

Probably not. I wonder today, if Abernathy had known about those wild dogs,...

Campus dogs at Jackson Courts

Historic Photograph

Remember living in the dorm, fixing your hair up in all those big rollers, and drinking bourbon?

This is another one of those, meanwhile, back at the ranch chapters.

Larry Bowie got a little closer to the law than he had intended and the next chapter is about all that. Chitterlings and car races were colliding with changing attitudes about some other laws that a lot of college students in the country were getting all too familiar with in a hurry.

But please, feel free to admire the picture of the duck below first.

Gratuitous Picture of one of Dean Nations Ducks

Chapter 9

The First Annual West Georgia Pot Bust

By Larry Bowie

I was never a resident of Foster's Store, not in body anyway. I guess the thing with everybody during these times was a kind of a kinship we all felt for each other. Maybe it's best described as a kind of togetherness, not unlike a tractor trailer truck loaded with chickens and headed full speed down the interstate towards the processing plant. We were the chickens. I did, however, pass by that old store daily on my way to and from school when I lived in Mama Kate's fishing shack out on the pond.

Mama Kate's old Fishing shack was a great place to live. It was a little cabin on a little lake out beyond Foster's Store, maybe just a couple of miles down Tyus road as I recall. Mama Kate ran the snack food concession at the student center. If it wasn't for her and her home cooking, many of us would have starved. I remember visiting a few times over at Foster's. They had some fast cars over there in those days and I remember being stopped one afternoon by their caution flag man just as a drag race was being started out in front of the place. They had these two trash barrels, metal garbage cans full of garbage set on fire, smoke everywhere, their race starter was up all wrapped in white sheets like an Arab holding a big checkered flag with "Budweiser Beer" printed on it, ready just then to start the race between a couple of guys, one in a GTO and the other contestant in a big Plymouth or something. It was all cool to me. All of us chickens were crazy or close to it in those days. For sure, we all shared a similar state of mind.

During my years at West Georgia, 1964 to 1968, I stayed pretty busy playing in one band or another; and if I wasn't in the band playing the parties, I was throwing up the cafeteria spaghetti along with everyone else who had a meal ticket and a wish to get crazy on the weekends. I do believe that included just about anybody I ever knew who went to West Georgia in those days. . You have to appreciate the sick humor of a kitchen staff that always served spaghetti on the day of the big dance. God, I can still see that picture of that plate of spaghetti on that plate, on that brown serving tray, sliding across those three stainless steel tubes in the serving line. I won't describe what else I can also imagine.

My tenure at W.G. was a bit of the old Dr. Jekyll and Mr. Hyde. There were primarily two reasons I was in college. The first was that it was expected. Having survived the Depression, my family wanted me to have a better life, a better opportunity. College was very high on their list. They had high hopes for me. The second reason and, truthfully, the main reason for me was the old college deferment that would keep me out of the jungles of war by the skin of a grade for four wonderful years.

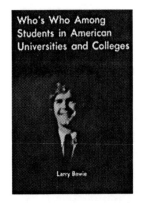

Who's Who Among Students in American Universities and Colleges

Larry Bowie

I, on the other hand, only wanted to make music.

My college life followed two very different directions. On the "expected" side; I was involved in class politics, wrote for the school paper, participated in plays and was a member of the Debate Club. You name it, I did it. I must have done a fairly good job. I won awards, plaques, contests, class offices; and as a result for $45.00 and a book order I managed to get in *Who's Who among College Students*. On the dark side, the Registrar informed me at graduation that, had it not been for Political Science, Speech, Drama, and Debate, I would not have had an average at all. I couldn't help but notice that she listed all the bullshit arts.

Yes, I only wanted to make music. My other life was an adventure. Our group, *The Rock Garden*, performed all over the Chitlin' Circuit during the summer, and all around Alabama, Georgia, and Florida on weekends. What a life, but that's another story.

Like everybody else my age, the war was beginning to occupy a lot of my thoughts. After graduation, what? I couldn't get any kind of deferment until I had a job, but I couldn't get a job without a deferment. *Catch 22*, and I only wanted to make music. I became involved in Anti-war efforts. My senior year the war loomed large.

After graduation I had a job offer from Tommy Roe. Mike Huey, his drummer, had worked with me in the *Rock Garden*. However, on the Friday before I was scheduled to leave with Roe on Monday, I was offered a gig with *The Candy Men*, former back up band for Roy Orbison, and my favorite band in the world at the time. I took it!

Rock Garden, Bowie is front right.

My adventures in music as well as my experiences with the draft board, the military, my conscience, and the rest of the world are stories for another day. Like a lot of people during those times I went to some pretty extreme measures to keep from being drafted, things that could fill another full book, but all were in the end, just my futile attempts to keep from being drafted. I eventually received a

Conscientious Objector Status and avoided having to go to the Vietnam War all together. Yea, that's for another day, maybe.

For now, and for this history's sake, because I was actually involved, I would like to recall for the purposes of this book, the *First Annual West Georgia Pot Bust*. My recollections may be a bit hazy, but what follows is the best I can do at this time. Recovered memories are still a new area.

At the time, I lived in a house trailer with one of my band mates on the outside of Carrollton. In Carrollton they would say we lived in the middle of nowhere. It was great. My room mate and I kept very different hours because of our class schedules. I was participating in a school play at the time, and we were in nightly rehearsals. Most of the time, my roommate and I would see each other as we passed on the way in or out and on weekends when we performed. This particular night I came straight home and went to bed without even seeing my roommate.

The next morning over coffee he told me that an old acquaintance from his high school had dropped in to visit the night before. They had listened to music, talked about old times and smoked some great pot his friend had brought with him to share. Share is a big word here. That's what people did back then, and for a lot of years. I never really knew anybody who sold pot to make money. People shared it, and other people would gladly share the cost of sharing it. Pretty simple really, nothing diabolical, or to do with big deal drug dealing at all. Just sharing some stuff like you might share a six pack of beer with somebody, nothing more than that. Nobody went out and robbed liquor stores to get money to buy pot.

I remember my roommate expressing a little surprise because the friend who had given him the pot the night before had been such a straight arrow in high school, a guy who in his words was the "last person I'd ever expect to smoke pot." Funny, that phrase really describes us all back then. This is a perfect example of how rare pot was at this time. A guy shows up you haven't seen in three or four years, a straight arrow, who somehow finds you in the middle of nowhere to get you high and sell you pot and no alarm bells of any kind go off? But that's natural; we were all straight arrows in the beginning days that marijuana was around. We didn't know anything about alarm bells, pot wise. They'd not even been invented yet. Even though we were beginning to experiment with pot, we didn't consider ourselves, or anybody else sinister or character flawed because they smoked pot or drank beer, which too was illegal, as most of us at the time were under twenty-one. "Duh?" is all I can say, we just really wanted bad to get high on something. That's what the party crowd had always done, always felt.

Anyway, as I was leaving for class, he showed me a dime ($10.00) box of pot, a penny matchbox that his "friend", had sold him. Really, all we had here was just about enough marijuana to roll two marijuana cigarettes, packaged, as it were, in a *Blue Diamond* penny match box, the kind that they sold you for a penny when you purchased a pack of cigarettes. (You Know, cigarettes, the things that are legal and give you lung cancer and cause you to die because you smoke them.) I headed for class. Not much later that day all hell broke loose. Students were being pulled out of class and escorted, some in handcuffs, by campus police to the Dean's office for questioning about what we knew about this marijuana thing. A lot of us learned that day how it feels to wait, wondering when they will come to take you away. Talk about tight butt cheeks.

It didn't take long to realize that my roommate's "friend" from the night before had visited four or five old friends around Carrollton. All of whom were raided and busted. Here's to old friends. I dodged the bullet of their inquisition by simply not saying much at all. Somewhere along the line there, they presented me with a confession and wanted me to sign it. All it said was that I had smoked some pot with my roommate and that was about it, along with the fact as to where exactly the match box full of pot had come from. For some reason, something inside me told me not to sign that piece of paper. I had taken a law course of some kind a year or so earlier and remembered about it being a bad idea for anybody to incriminate themselves about things where they didn't have a good idea about what was going on. I took some heat about it but after a while they told me I could go. That's why I never got busted it turned out. I didn't confess anything on paper and sign it like everybody else did. They were going to charge me just because marijuana was found in the trailer I lived in even though it wasn't even mine, nor did I even know the person it came from.

For the next few days everyone knew someone or had been someone called to the Dean's office for questioning. Since truth is a matter of perspective, the stories varied in color and scale. There were, however, some constants. Everyone was asked to tell everything they knew about pot and the West Georgia student body. What, when, where, how and who. Most people said as little as possible if for no other reason than we were all scared shitless. So far everything was flying under the radar. Parents hadn't been notified. The City of Carrollton law enforcement was not involved. The school was attempting to handle this problem "in-house." So, everyone told their story, or some part of it, to the Dean. You were then asked to write and sign a statement including all your pot knowledge. This statement was to be placed in your permanent folder and appropriate school punishment would be handed out, some kind of disciplinary probation we presumed. It was better than jail.

Hunter Thompson stated that "when the going gets tough, the weird turn pro," and this was no exception. There were some individuals, one in particular, who took this as an opportunity to thumb their noses at the establishment by expanding while expounding upon the pot culture of the beloved institution. There was one person who told of everyone he knew who smoked pot and, for good measure, threw in a few he just suspected to be users. Of course everyone was called in and questioned. Needless to say, there was no love lost on this "singer of sad songs."

You need to remember that both schools of thought regarding the casual and recreational use of marijuana were new. Nobody knew anything about it. It was against the law, sure, but after smoking it a time or two and comparing it to alcohol that was legal, I naturally began to ask why one was illegal and the other wasn't? It made no sense at all as to the degree of differing severity punishment wise between the two offenses. It still doesn't.

Suddenly a tight little college bust had been turned into a parade of "pot heads." At the same time, marijuana use had been tied to a definition about telling easily which side of a political fence you stood on. It was easy to patch together the anti-war movement with the pot heads and characterize them as communists or worse. The whole Peace movement was characterized by some as simply "Un-American." Un-American meant you were for the enemy, whoever they were. So when you find pot smokers, you also find enemies of the United States of America. They were believed to be the same thing, in California, and Carrollton, everywhere. To add to that, it began to be a time when people who had disagreements with the government and their policies, especially where a war might be concerned, felt an obligation to voice those differences in many different ways, many of which became defiant in nature. That type of defiance became commonplace and pretty loud sometimes.

Peace Signs were New

So, something like this was a little hard to keep quiet in the community of Carrollton and the larger community of the Good Old USA and the news media. The times were changing before, but now they had changed completely and some were refusing to recognize it. They would do anything they could to put that Genie back in the bottle, especially those genies that reared up in their face and shoveled the obvious truth right at them. Carrollton was everywhere.

It would be hard for today's West Georgia College student to hate the Carrollton we knew for a while back then. I remember even a particular dry cleaner downtown refusing to take in a load of my dirty shirts just because I was a college student. This was a perfect opportunity for the town to put a stop to shenanigans going on at the college. Of course they never would have known about all this if there hadn't been students who were refusing to go quietly into the night for the first time about more than just smoking a match box of marijuana. In their defense, they did get a lot of us in a lot of trouble, jail time even for some, but they felt that they had a higher mission to be true to. It wasn't about pot, it was about believing that a government in a country that they loved was lying to them and sacrificing good people for the wrong reasons. A pot bust was more an opportunity to join the cause of freedom. It was a whole lot more than a pot bust.

But once challenged by this boisterous and albeit immature challenge, the local D.A. staff had no choice but to become involved. They collected the information gathered by the college investigations, prosecuted and eventually convicted several students. A few students were expelled and some placed on probation, but by and large most students were innocent.

Since then, the laws about marijuana became less and less stringent. There are new fears today, marijuana seems pretty harmless to most of us. One day we can only hope a saner tone about such things will prevail.

Bowie with longer hair in 1970's

On a personal note here I have to say that Dean John J. Pershing was a decent man. He treated me with more respect than my smart ass deserved. He helped an expelled student I knew to enroll in an out of state college. He did all he could to protect us from ruining our lives, and we owe him a thanks every now and then among the cussing. Righteousness and politics along with a dose of stupidity brought us down. After the smoke settled, I realized that I only wanted to make music. And that's the truth.

Classified Section

Book Recommendation

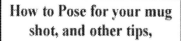

How to Pose for your mug shot, and other tips, while you wait for your lawyer to get there.

By
Butch Gungii, Attorney at Law

"Whether it's your first offense or you're a long-time career criminal, there are things in this book you need to know!" So says its author Butch Gungii, Attorney at Law. Gungii literally lays down the law in this tell-all-tale of the inner workings of our American system of Incarceration.

Ever wonder the proper etiquette you need to follow for Judge Bribing? How do you get an extra blanket when you're in the slammer? Is it within my rights to ask for a new bar of soap? Will you still be able use your credit cards for phone sex while in the slammer?

These questions and more are candidly handled by Gungii who it turns out, received his own Law Degree thru a correspondence course while serving a six to ten year stretch in Folsom Prison for impersonating a Playwright. This guy knows the deal. If you are there already, or planning a visit to a correctional facility of any type, this 682 page book is mandatory reading!

You can figure that if there is a Part 1 that there is a part 2 somewhere. Be patient!

The kids will love you for it. Or hate you. I don't know.

Foster's Store – Milo 3 Button Black short sleeve.

Chapter 10

THE DRAFT Part 1

By Bob O'Kelley

"How did you get out of going to war, Daddy"?

During my time at West Georgia, the draft hung over every male student like the plague hung over Europe in the Middle Ages. The Viet Nam war was unpopular. Staying in school could literally be a life or death matter. To flunk out could easily mean a free ticket to Viet Nam. We all knew the draft regulations as well as we knew the traffic laws, but over the years people have forgotten how it was, or, because they are too young, never knew; so let me recount the conditions that we lived under here:

Any male between eighteen and twenty-six could be drafted into military service for two years. We all had to carry draft cards.

If you were a college student and got drafted, you could apply for a draft deferment, which would allow you to finish school. Many a degree was earned by those whose main reason for being in college was to avoid the draft. The colleges were filled to capacity.

The National Guard and the Army Reserves were rarely used in the Viet Nam war. There was a long waiting list to get in either. If you could get in one or the other, you would have to complete either six months or two years' active duty, depending on your program, and either a four or six-year enlistment, again depending on your program.

There was a waiting list for slots in the Guard and Reserves. Political power or social prominence could put you at the top of the list. Some bribed their way into units. The unconnected never seemed to make to the top of the list.

Anti War Poster

It was possible to declare yourself a conscientious objector, but it was difficult to convince the draft board that you were sincere. One way was to become a Quaker; Quakers were given conscientious objector status. There were anti-war groups who, on religious grounds, would help you with this process.

If drafted, your last hope was to be declared unfit for service by flunking the physical. [Many bogus letters from doctors were presented to the draft board doctors, describing bogus physical problems in hopes of getting declared unfit for service.] Some took drugs to raise their blood pressure to an unacceptable level. Some, even college students, tried to flunk the I Q test. Any and every means were used to flunk the physical.

If all this failed, you had the choice of going in the Army or running to Canada, which a lot did. When I took my draft physical, a high school friend was also there for his. We were goofing around together, when his demeanor suddenly changed. He looked at me, said, "Fuck this," and walked out the door. I never saw him again, and I was unable to find out what happened to him. I always assumed that he went to Canada.

Some time in 1969, Congress decided that it would be fairer to conduct a lottery to decide who would be drafted, rather than having the local draft boards make the decision. This was to be done by birthday. Those born on the first date pulled would be the first to go, and the process continued until all dates were drawn. The lucky could get on with their lives uninterrupted.

By the time of the lottery, I had moved out of Foster's Store and was living with Charley Walker in a trailer on Burson Street. The night of the lottery, Charley had a date with Kathy Larson and I had a date with Kathy Holland. We sat, drinking beer, and watching TV as the drawing took place. It was sort of an impromptu "let's see who is going to get drafted party." I had a student deferment, and was not sure whether I was included in the lottery or not. Charley drew a high number, and was safe. I drew number fifteen and with a number that low, it didn't matter whether I was included. Either way I lost. I had been unable to get in the Guard and Reserves. I was unwilling to be a conscientious objector, go to Canada, or lie about my physical condition. I might as well have bent over to kiss my butt good-by that night. I was out of options.

Book Recommendation

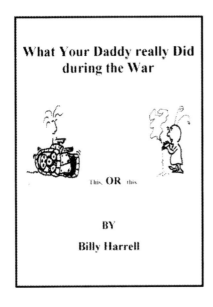

What Your Daddy Really Did During the War

By Billy Harrell

To this reviewer, this book falls into that category of an ever growing number of books that try to revise history in a way favorable to the authors' current political view and has little or nothing to do with what the title of the book may lead you to believe you are about to read. In fact, there's really not very much verbiage at all in this thing. The author, Harrell, remember, was, at the time of the Viet Nam war, a famous cartoonist. Then at the war's end he mysteriously disappears for almost thirty years. There is no clue here to his whereabouts thru those missing years, but now, all of a sudden; he spins out this cartoon book. I got to tell you, it's really quite entertaining. Try it out for yourself. Then screw up your courage and volunteer for Iraq. Wars are great fodder for cartoonists if nothing else.

The Art of Foster's Store

One of Harrell's Ink Line Characters as graffiti on US Aircraft Carrier.

I miss the communists some days. They had neat uniforms.

Bad guys today don't wear uniforms too much.

The Russians could really march.

Chapter 11

Proud Mary

Chris Berry and Haliburton on Mary's front end

By Bob O'Kelley and Wayne Lankford

Sometime in 1969, Lankford and I were at my parents' home in College Park, and, for whatever reason, one Sunday afternoon we decided to see if we could get back to Carrollton by driving only on dirt roads. We were in his old 1953 Plymouth, which was known to all as the "Proud Mary". It was named after the song, of course. The only vehicle that has ever been built that is more indestructible than a 1953 Plymouth is a Sherman Tank, and if Wayne hadn't destroyed it, I think that it would still be running today. We found a dirt road in College Park that looked like it headed west and got on it. Any time that we found another dirt road that looked like it headed in a more westerly direction, we would take it. We repeated this process until we got to the outskirts of Carrollton. There were a lot more dirt roads in 1969 than there are today. This is just one of the memories that I have of the "Proud Mary". She was a good old car and served us well.

I finished West Georgia in the winter of 1969 and was immediately drafted. I went to Viet Nam, served in the infantry, and in less than two years I was back. It was October of 1971 when I was discharged. The war was scaling down and they released me a little early. I had been home for only a couple of days, when I decided to visit Wayne, who was living at Foster's and in his senior year at West Georgia. After all, it was Homecoming. I get the feeling that everyone expects me to write some dark piece about how screwed up I was after being in a war, but nothing could be further from the truth. That was behind me, and I was optimistic. I was ready to get on with my life.

When I arrived at Foster's Store, the "Proud Mary" was being decorated for the Homecoming parade. In typical college craziness, the store dwellers had chopped off her top, tied a beer keg to the front and painted her colorfully. "Proud Mary" was not an officially registered float in the home coming parade. Just like in the movie *Animal House* we were crashing the parade, only we did it before John Belushie ever thought about it. I remember Carmichael and McMillan being there, as well as others. I knew the guys, but

Tom Cunningham, Dale Teeter, Richard Haliburton, Lankford & O'Conner

not all that well. They had moved into the store after I had graduated. Everyone was dressed as Arabs, pirates, prisoners, and such.

As a former Fosterian I was invited to ride on the float, which I did. But when the accompanying photo was taken, I was having one of those life-changing epiphanies. I didn't want to do this. I knew that there was a time when I would have thought that this was totally cool, but now it just seemed stupid. I had been around the world, faced death and destruction, and was well beyond this silliness. I wonder if I would have had the same reaction, if I been in Atlanta working instead of in Viet Nam? I guess I will never know, but the accompanying picture was taken at almost the exact moment that I was realizing that I had changed.

Then Wayne remembers:

Yea, I remember that day and how it started off a little earlier in the week. I was sitting in the student center when Bruce Hildebrand or somebody comes up to me and says that he's learned that the Foster's Store people wanted to drive "Proud Mary" in the homecoming parade. It was news to me but, I remember replying almost at once that, "yeah, we'd do that for sure!"

Bruce said "Ok" and told me what time we should show up and where Saturday morning. I remember store mates Dale Teeter and Richard Haliburton, along with Steve Zoromsky and David Ethridge, all of us doing our impression of car decorating with some old house paint that had been sitting in the barn for a long time. I remember Dale Teeter suggesting we shoot it a few times, that bullet holes would add some charm or something. That was fun for a few shots, until we noticed that the bullets were ricocheting off the engine block. Teeter also had the idea to write "fuck you' across the rear bumper. Dale painted it in German, so actually nobody knew what it said anyway.

I remember waking up early and waking everybody else up. We were going to be late anyway, but I wanted to get there just before the thing started. If we timed our entry right the organizers wouldn't have time to react and maybe change their mind about inviting us in the first place. Teeter was nowhere to be found, but out of the blue, Mike Mobley and Chris Berry shows up all dressed for the thing wearing a pith helmet and a gas mask. We load up and head over to the other side of town with Z behind the wheel and I'm thinking, "They're never going to let us join the parade; we look like a bunch of refugees from a Turkish prison." That feeling only solidifies as we begin to pass the rest of the already positioned floats and convertibles; all with these dressed up babes showing all this cleavage while we are passing around cans of warm Old Milwaukee just out of sight of the other float riders and the throngs who are already lined up along the parade route.

Cunningham, Teeter, Mr. Foster, Haliburton

So if you can picture this, there we were, told to wait until the rest of the parade proceeded out ahead of us. We were to be the last "float" in the whole parade. We didn't care. It was just too early to care, or maybe it was too late to care. It was a you pick it I guess. But when we got rolling, we were really in the Homecoming Parade (!) and that was something; riding on the top of an old car that a few weeks earlier I had chopped the metal hard top off of with an ax. I had no idea at all what would come of that action, that we'd all be here riding down the center of town with what seemed like every citizen of Carroll county and their kids all lined up along the Maple Street.

I remember Z working that all but worn out clutch. I could hear it, it was almost gone, and the friction point was way out there. I worried that the thing might just give up right in the middle of the street. I remember the smell of oil and how slow we were going. I can see Haliburton jumping off the front of the thing every so often and picking up candy from the street. I was just amazed that we were actually there and that we were there and it was so early at the same time. I could see candy on the street, freshly thrown, but it had not been picked up yet by the many kids that lined the corridor. This candy had been thrown by legitimate paraders who had proceeded us. I see him passing it around and all of us tossing it back to the crowd. I think I see Chris offering someone a can of beer. I can hear the clutch grinding and the sounds of sticks being beat on the sides of the car as we moved along, I hear the school band playing somewhere far ahead of us. We have a band? I see Haliburton waving a Beer flag. It's so early, I think to myself. Where did all these people come from? They must live here I guess. I wonder what happened to Dale Teeter? He was just about the most enthusiastic of all of us. Where the heck is he? But we just keep on rolling, just like song *Proud Mary*.

After about 30 or 40 minutes, the parade ends with a right turn on to the campus. All the other floats are unloading all around the place. We just keep on going. Proud Mary is on her end, almost no clutch at all now. If we stop now; we might never get started again.

Richard Haliburton 1970

I think it was Haliburton who suggested it. We had to pass the College President's house on the way back to Foster's Store. I remember driving down this long driveway and when we got right in front of the house, Z stopped the car and we all got out and mooned the house. I don't know if anybody saw us, but afterwards, we parked the car behind the store house so it wouldn't be visible from the main highway. After that day, Proud Mary was never the same. Her clutch was just worn out. We moved her eventually up closer to the road and parked her under the shade of a big tree there in front of the barn. About a year later,

O'Connor and David Jack, tied a chain to her and dragged her behind Mr. Foster's pick up truck to the county land fill. They took along a couple of gallons of gasoline and set her on fire right there in the dump. It was sort of like a Viking funeral, we reckoned. What a great car.

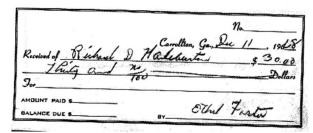

Evidence of residency

Store mates preparing for party Fall 1970

Richard Haliburton, Dale Teeter and Tom Cunningham

Chapter 12

The Cusp of Change

By Wayne Lankford

Between the years of 1968 and 1974, that's where we were, at Foster's Store, living on the cusp of change in society, psychology and politics. It was like living on a seismic fault line. The beliefs we were grounded in became ground that was certainly shaking. At least for our generation it was the time in our lives when we together and individually began to ponder the universe and all that was around us. So it goes with every generation, I suppose. But for so long, since 1959, when the first Americans were killed in Vietnam, until the war's end in 1974, that sword of Damocles hung over our draft-able heads. Today I have a theory: how long that sword hung over you affected your attitude towards the war and other things.

As I started my tenure at WGC in 1967, I was as sure as I could be that the Vietnam War would be over by the time I graduated. I mean World War II only lasted four years after America joined the fight in 1941. We had already been in Vietnam in one way or another since 1961, when Kennedy sent in "advisors" to help the South Vietnamese learn better how to kill the North Vietnamese, who, we understood, were communists—and all communists needed killing, of course. I mean they were *communist*; they didn't have an atom bomb so they were fair game. We go over there, kill them all, and everyone will be happy for ever and ever. Better dead than red. Or *they* would see the light and forget about all that communism shit and everyone would learn to live in peace. Maybe we could make Baptists out of them. Who cares; the war would end before I reached the end of my college deferment.

So it was like a game in a way. I was rooting for the home team all the way. But by the time my older brother graduated from military college in 1968 and a few months later volunteered as a First Lieutenant to go to Viet Nam, I found myself rooting for my brother, whose very life was now on the line, and I found myself sitting on the fence between still thinking my country knew what it was doing, and just trying not to think about the fact that a lot of people were now lining up in full opposition to this adventure called Vietnam.

I remember watching the news one day and this guy saying that marijuana was some sort of communist plot used by our enemies to undermine our efforts in defending the free people of South Vietnam. "Oh my God, this shit I'm smoking is a communist plot!" was not the first thought I had at all. I want to tell you something: the longer that sword hung up there in the air the better that marijuana seemed to be. The more crap we saw on the evening news, that made no sense anymore, the less sense we saw in the government and individual citizens calling other citizens un-American. Do you remember? It was like the government had reinstituted the Committee on Un-American Activities, but just wasn't using any kind of formal name like that. Jane Fonda seemed to be Number One on their hit list. My God! She was using her right to free speech. "Kill the bitch! . . . Carpet bombing is a good thing!" Carpet Bombing—I think Vietnam was the first time I heard that expression. Sounds so benign, doesn't it? "Yes, we'll just carpet bomb here and carpet bomb there and after a while everything in Vietnam will look like a nice smooth carpet down there." (Like today we have these things called daisy cutter bombs. "Oh, nothing; we are just cutting back some daisies today.") Do you remember that point in time when the news reported that we had now dropped more bombs in Vietnam than we did in all of World War II? Meanwhile, I was just on the fence taking it all in; being brain dead was, to me, a better thing. I mean compared to all these smart people who were running things with such smart brains and a thing for bombs.

But, back to the sword, and to this theory of mine. It was about time. The longer your head was underneath the sword and the longer the war dragged on with no end in sight, the more time you had to question what was going on as you got older. And speaking of older, you began to notice that the people who were getting killed in this war were getting younger and younger, and darker and darker. The questions we asked had no real answers any more, or the answer was always something real broad, like "we need to be afraid of this threat of communism," but it just didn't make any sense at all anymore. Nobody was asking questions like "Why don't these people, the communists who live in grass huts give up?" Or, it wasn't asked enough, and the answer supplied, when there was even an attempt to answer it, no longer made sense to me any more.

It was all about time; it seems to me, looking back on it today. The longer the time under the sword, the more time you had to develop an opinion and the more information you had to develop that opinion.

The difference between my brother and me was the amount of information and the flavors of information we individually were exposed to. I was exposed to more between the time I was eighteen and the time I was twenty one than he was. And the flavors of information that were around when I was twenty-one weren't around when he was. Things like the Mi Lai Massacre, the killing of eight war protesters at Kent State in May of 1970 or the assassinations of Martin Luther King, Jr. and Bobby Kennedy. That kind of information wasn't available to a lot of guys who went to Nam early on, simply because it just hadn't happened yet. And it just didn't seem to matter who was driving the boat, Kennedy, Johnson or Nixon. All of them seemed to be without a compass. Yet, at the same time, my generation was being called on to fight for something that just wasn't clear any more. The reason we were there just kept getting foggier and foggier all the time. It wasn't the LSD or the marijuana smoke that was making it hard to see; it was just more of the same bad news about the lost compass and how much it was costing in our ever failing attempts to find it.

Something else wasn't available in 1968 that was everywhere two years later. West Georgia College was awash in more than marijuana smoke. By 1970 and 71 the same guys we went to high school with were returning home from military service and Vietnam. The GI bill was there to put them through West Georgia College and colleges and universities all over the country. It was a time in the history of that war when we, as a generation, had the opportunity to learn a little more, first hand, about what was going on over there. It was a specific point in history, where we had a war that lasted so long that there would be more people back from it than there would be going towards it. We didn't know that then, of course, but what that meant was that the very people, who knew most about it, were now living under the same roofs as the people who were most likely to have to go there themselves in the near future. When in our history books had that ever happened? We would be exposed to more than what information we could get from newspapers and television, or, especially, Presidents of the United

States of America. There was real first hand knowledge everywhere, fresh on the minds of people all around you. It didn't even matter that most of the returning Vets almost never talked about what they had experienced. Not talking about it was information enough. The bad was so bad that most these guys couldn't even talk about it. Some still haven't. Twenty five years would have to go by before my own brother could go to sleep at night without a loaded 45 caliber automatic pistol under his pillow. He made a career in the army. Twenty five years later he was a Lieutenant Colonel, and it was only then, when he began having the same nightmare over and over, that he got some help, and was able to put the gun somewhere else and sleep through the whole night.

Our Buddy Ho

Going to a war where you think you believe what you're there for is completely different from going to a war and not knowing that. Being against the war never meant to me for a second that I was against the guys who were there fighting in it like my own brother. It was just that by 1970 and 71 the people then being drafted seemed to have a whole different mindset than those who got drafted in 65-69, based on more years of information, more images of what was going on, and feeling pretty certain where their country would ask them to go. They had the draft, and the lottery system because, not everyone was rushing down to his favorite recruiter for a chance to kill commies as fast as was required by those in power, who had hung their political careers on winning this thing. So, next time you hear somebody say, like Nixon used to repeat all the time, "Peace with Honor", remember, that could be politics-speak for, "We don't know what the fuck we are doing anymore".

They say that sometimes the leading edge is also the ragged edge. Every generation has its own crosses to bear. And every generation handles things a little differently than the last one. We were no different from the guys who were a few years in front of us; we were just exposed to different things that they never had opportunity to be exposed to themselves. We partied pretty hard sometimes, as we moved from kegs to kilos, from whiskey to hallucinogens, and back and forth. That's where a lot of us were around 1970, living on a fault line at Foster's Store, with piles of bad news, with body counts. No way out of it. No exit. The cusp of change.

The Look of Revolution on Campus 1970

A Response from Store mate Bob O'Kelly

Hey Longhair;

You know that I love you like a brother. We attended the same elementary school, high school and college. We lived like brothers in my parents' house for a while. I first met your older brother in 1952 and you a little later, but sometime before we left Cascade School. I can barely remember when I did not know someone named Lankford. You entered WGC in 1967 and I entered in 1965, and we both lived at the store.

It seems impossible that two people with such similar backgrounds could think so differently. I got drafted and you didn't. Maybe that's what makes the difference. If what I am going to say alienates me from the Foster's Store crowd, then so be it. I am going to speak my mind.

In your piece the "Cusp of Change," you speak of not having information about the war and you are right, we didn't have good information about the war. The press, then and now, made it seem as though we were the bad guys over there. America is naïve. You have never seen tyranny. I have. Have you ever actually been to Mi Lai? I have. We were not the bad guys over there. The communists committed atrocities like the butchery at Mi Lai regularly.

Did you ever wonder why vets generally support war efforts? It is not because vets love to kill; it is because we know that there is something worse than war. In Viet Nam I learned first hand to hate war, but I also, more importantly, learned this: as long as there is someone in the world, who will raise his hand to you in violence, there must be someone to stop him, or he will rule you. We live in a world governed by the aggressive use of force.

In my view Viet Nam was a battle in the larger cold war. We lost the battle but we did win the war against worldwide communism. I sat at home, by myself, and cried as I saw desperate Vietnamese clinging to the helicopter runners, as the last of us pulled out of our embassy over there. They knew what it meant, and I knew what it meant. The evil bastards killed three million people in the chaos that followed in Viet Nam, Laos and Cambodia.

Yes, I said evil. It exists. I've seen it.

It is easy to say that you don't believe in war, to set yourself above the fray, and criticize those who are engaged in it, but that doesn't solve the problem. It does keep you out of the fight, however, as long as there is someone who will protect you. You could not smoke dope at Fosters, unless there is some twenty-year-old Marine somewhere in the world watching the gate, and who isn't smoking dope. Sorry guys, the "Age of Aquarius" never arrived, and it is folly to think that it did.

See how all this is working out yet?

We put something serious in here but we frame it with a bunch of crazy silly shit. Ask any media expert and they'd be quick to tell you that the way we are doing this book is just plain wrong.

"Just plain Wrong"

"Crazy silly shit"

But, life is just that way sometimes, especially at Foster's Store. .

Classified Ad

Worms

Mr. Foster's Favorite

Big Red Wigglers

In Season Now

Talk to the big light in sky for a while.

Dear Spirit guy,

I understand that, besides marijuana, worms were also sold during the days of the store from out in back of the house. Tell me; just what did people buy so many worms for?

Sincerely, Tee Ball Boy

Spirit guy Speaks!

Tee Boy? Does your Momma call you that? To answer your question, I suppose most people used them worms to try and catch fish with. Your question makes me wonder though. Up here in all this cosmic connectedness I find myself today wondering a lot, mostly about how all you idiots can manage to come up with such stupid questions. Yeah! Here you go, Tee Boy, they taste great! People eat them. Get you a bunch and put em in your mouth yourself. You'll see. You'll see colors. Now get out of here.

Foster's Store living Today

by

Steve Craft

Book Recommend Foster's **Store Living Today -** Long to get back to the carefree days of your youth, cheap wine and a house full of roaches, ants, and mice? Remember waking up each morning with a headache and a desire to puke your guts up from the all the cheap wine you drank the night before? Those were the good ole days. And look, if you didn't exactly set the world on fire financially, trying to find a place to retire to without a big pile of money could be a problem.

But, "No Problemo" says former store mate and now author Steve Craft. Just ease into this guide to find the cheapest places in the USA to live. Well, you might ot call it living, but it's surviving on the edge. Just like back at Foster's. No Dry counties represented.

-The T Shirt Deal -

Enter the information requested below, then tear this page out of the book and mail it along with 20 bucks, plus 3 dollars a shirt for return postage, to me, Wayne Lankford, Foster's Store T Shirt Deal, P. O. Box 36186, Hoover, AL 35244.

All T Shirts 100% Cotton

S M L XL 2XL

Name_____Size_____

Mailing
Address_____

City_____State_____Zip_____

Number of Shirts ordered_____ Sises_____Amount
Enclosed_____

Chapter 13

A SOLDIER'S STORY

By Bob O'Kelley

The young man raised his rifle and put the man squarely in his sight. All he had to do now was pull the trigger . . . pull the trigger . . . pull the trigger—damn it, pull the trigger!

The young man was in Viet Nam, an infantryman on patrol, his platoon in the jungle several months. By now, he'd seen combat. He's seen his friend, Frenchy, hoisted up to a helicopter in a harness, dead, killed in an ambush. He was sickened by the sight. He'd seen the enemy blown apart. He'd seen Americans shot, American feet blown off by Viet Cong booby traps. He'd fired his weapon into the jungle concealing the Viet Cong who killed Frenchy. Yet he was not hardened to war. He had not killed. He could not let war harden him. He must not. He knew if he became a warrior he would always be a warrior. Even if he killed, he must not allow himself to fall into the dark place of the true warrior. But could he escape?

Only months before, the young man had been a senior at West Georgia College. Life was good—calm and peaceful. All that he knew of the life in which he now found himself was what he had seen on TV. Viet Nam was far away. The draft was the greatest fear of college men. The war had become unpopular. The young man had graduated. He no longer had a draft deferment. His life of college life ease was over. He knew he would be drafted, but never believed that he would end up an infantryman in Viet Nam. After all, he was a college graduate. Surely, the Army would put his education to use. The Army did not.

On this day his platoon was on routine patrol somewhere in the jungle near Cambodia, dropped in by helicopter. It was calm . . . seemed safe. Lee, Martin and the young man had walked some yards ahead of the rest of the platoon. Unwise. They were irritated the rest of the platoon did not seem able to keep up. They found themselves at the top of a ravine, a rapidly flowing white water creek at the bottom.

Martin was from North Carolina.

Lee was from Ohio. Lee was a trained sniper. He carried a specialized sniper rifle with a scope. Before his tour was over Lee, by far the most "productive" in the platoon, would have eight personal kills,. To meet him you would never suspect this. He was a tall blond good looking guy with a gentle nature. I am sure that wherever he is today, his friends and family have no idea of his stellar sniper record. Nor would they suspect it. Nor would he tell it. Lee would never dwell in the dark place. It just wasn't in his nature.

The three started down into the ravine. To their surprise, all three fell. What appeared to be solid ground covered in leaves was in fact a pile of loose leaves. Sliding down into the ravine, the young man was emotionally transported to his childhood in Georgia where there was an abundance of such leaves in the fall of the year. This was not typical of the jungle. Rolling down the hill, laughing and playing like children, the three came to a stop some fifty feet from the roaring whitewater creek. Dreams of childhood and home ended abruptly - the young man saw three Viet Cong at the water's edge.

The Cong had not heard the soldiers above the roaring water. They could not see them behind the jungle screen.

The rest of the platoon came. The Viet Cong still had not heard or seen any of them. The young man alerted all to the presence of the Viet Cong. Captain Yeager had the platoon spread out along the bank for an ambush. One Viet Cong was standing to the front of Lee and Martin and the young man. The other two were out of their sight but in the sight of others in the platoon.

Now, all he had to do was pull the trigger. The young man's brain was on fire, thinking, "Dear God, he's playing in the water. Like a little kid. He's playing in the water just like I would. His rifle's on the bank." The Viet Cong is in the young man's sights. "You have to pull the damn trigger. He would kill you. Maybe he killed Frenchy. You have to pull the trigger. . . If only I hated him. If only he would shoot at me. If only I hated him. . . I hate him. I hate him!"

He pulled the trigger. It was not a steady shot. The young man, Lee and Martin fired simultaneously. The Viet Cong fell dead. He was hit twice. He was hit only twice.

The young man knew that Lee had not missed such an easy shot, but what he did not know and never will know is whether the second hit was Martin's or his. He will never know if he had killed. Had he killed? Could he kill? Had he unconsciously forced himself to miss?

To this day, no longer young, he does not know. He does know for sure that he is no warrior. He never went to the dark place. He is just a soldier.

Just a soldier.

Bobby shares with us an earlier view of the world from WGC.

Wayne Lankford and I grew up in the same Southwest Atlanta neighborhood. We have known each other since grade school. And I love him like a brother. In fact when his family moved from Atlanta to Birmingham, Wayne lived with my family one summer and we both worked at my father's business. There is three years difference in our age, with me being the older. I was originally a friend of Wayne's older brother, the late Neil, but over time Wayne and I became close, especially after he came to West Georgia. I practically willed my job at Dun & Bradstreet to Wayne. He graduated from West Georgia in 72 and needed a job while at the same time, I was leaving D&B; so I let him know that my job would be available and he was hired. He worked for Dun & Bradstreet for 17 years, which is far longer than I ever worked anywhere.

I lost contact with Wayne for a long time when D&B started transferring him around the country. When my name appeared in the *West Georgia Perspective*, he called me and it seemed as though it had only been a few days since we had last talked, even though we both had, children, wives, and/or ex-wives who were nonexistent the last time we had been together. It seems so strange to talk to his son. Wayne sent me a copy of his book, *The Bike Path*, and I was impressed.

The three years difference in our ages makes a huge difference in what we recall from Foster's Store. There were few if any drugs at Foster's Store when I was there. There was plenty of beer, parties and girls. The only time I remember the police being there was when the Sheriff came about the drag race recounted in the story "*Foster 500.*"

Change is constant, but during the years when I first came to West Georgia in 1965 to the time Foster's Store ceased to exist around 1975, the campus and the world were going through some major changes. I remember when girls could not be seen on campus in shorts; so when girls went to the gym, they wore long London Fog coats to hide their gym clothes. On Sundays, if you actually stayed on campus, men were required to wear a coat and tie to the cafeteria, which at that time was under the old gym. The accepted dress was preppy. I am told that just a few years before I arrived at West Georgia, chapel was mandatory for those who stayed on campus during the weekend. Services were actually held in the chapel on campus. Today, this would send the American Civil Liberties Union into cardiac arrest. Partying consisted of drinking beer if you could find a place to do it. We listened to top 40 and soul music. Girls had curfews which varied, depending on their class. The girls were ladies and the men treated them that way. West Georgia was Mayberry in 1965.

In contrast, just four years latter, in 1970 when I graduated and left Carrollton, the campus was wide open. The sexual revolution had taken place. We had co-ed dorms and pot was on campus. Dress had changed from preppy to hippy and hair from short to long. The preferred music was hard rock. The rules of interaction between men and women were under change. I was never sure whether to adopt the new rules or stay with the old when I met a new girl. What had been assumed to be true by everyone was under question. The Viet Nam war was in full force and, until they put in the lottery system for drafting, all men knew that they would be drafted if they flunked out. Talk about an incentive to stay in school! It was a time of great tribulation, change and turmoil and to me it was uncomfortable. I was happier in Mayberry.

Ask Mr. Spirit of Foster's Store

Dear Mr. Spirit of,

I was wondering. Today, some physicists hypothesize that the universe may be held together by some sort of a structure consisting of some kind of collection of tiny threads of sub particle molecular matter, kinda like what they call "string theory" or something like that. I'm just a liberal arts major so all that confuses me. I just was curious if you ever got involved with such goings on where you are now and maybe you'd like to share with us your own personal understanding of what you might see as relevant and what on the other hand you might characterize as non relevant as your thinking pertains to the quest for truth and knowledge in general, whether that quest be into the physical or metaphysical worlds?

Confused and Confounded

Mr. Spirit of Answers from the Great Beyond!

Dear C & C

Didn't you read the disclaimer in the front of this book? You need to get down to the OD tent ASAP!

Disclaimer or not, Please don't eat any more of these things.

Truth is though that I'm not too much worried about people like you. It's the people who believe they are actually someplace right now and are actually engaged in the activity of reading this book and not where they really are, which is where I am, where we all are. They don't realize that all the pages in this imaginary book are blank and so is much of the universe. There is no such thing as time. How could there be? I tell you C, it's a long way out here between one intelligent molecule to another. But when you finally get a handle on one of them, tie a string to it. They make great yo-yo's. That's all there is to my string theory which is just a thread to somebody else's consciousness.

Chapter 14

Backyard Ball at Foster's and the Night the Coach fired the team.

By Anonymous and Wayne Lankford

This is a picture of Store mate and the usually glassy eyed and braless Candee Carmichael. But that's not what this story is about. No, it's about basketball. In this picture, just behind Candee, you'll notice a makeshift barn and nailed to the front of the barn you'll also notice a homemade basketball backboard and net-less iron hoop. We played a lot of basketball at Foster's Store. We played it "Make It-Take It" style. We mostly played at half speed in my days there. Others before may have been more aggressive, but in 1970 we had slowed it down a bit.

We killed a lot of time playing our backyard down-in-the-dirt style of round ball. Yours truly, O'Connor, Steve Zoromsky, and anybody who'd venture by got the invite and the ball passed easily between friends as we waited for our afternoon buzz of the day to kick in. Lots of stuff got passed around in those days. Candee played too. She was pretty good and always such fun to guard. She'd dribble the ball around our dusty court as her black cocker spaniel Jason barked and snapped at the bouncing ball before she'd lose control, and we'd all laugh as the ball rolled down the gentle hill with that little black dog chasing it all along its way. Pretty ideal, I'd say. We'd play one on one, or two on two, or whatever on whomever, or, we'd play HORSE, or PIG, or OX, depending on how much daylight was available to play. Some days we'd play AUSTRAILOPITHICUS AFRICANUS, if we had the time. I remember how long it took just to get to the first farewells. We never tired of it.

I have no idea today where store mates Dan O'Conner or Steve Zoromsky disappeared to. But I imagine, wherever they are, pretty close by them, even today, you can still find a basketball ready for play. (Mine's right here . . . ah . . . somewhere.)

Dan O'Conner

Steve Zoromsky

Yeah, the guys at Foster's store had a tradition of supporting the basketball team. Some of our residents were players. In my time there they were O'Conner and Zoromsky. Members of the basketball team had lived at Foster's Store off and on since the first days of 1966 when Bob Greer and Jim Crayton and the rest of that bunch lived there. Personally, I can't really recall even going to a WGC basketball game past my junior year, but my roommate O'Connor was on the team, and even when he threw in the towel, we remained friends with many of the team's active players. We weren't anti Varsity Basketball, or anything like that; we'd just rather do it than watch it. That friendship meant that we'd sometimes party together as a group, not regularly or

anything, I mean these guys played *real basketball*! To us, most of my store mates, by this time that was just crazy.

But today, in the interest of our in-house History, we will look a little deeper into the WGC Basketball program and its connection to Foster's store. The true story cries out to be told.

Coach Jim Bennett

This is a picture of Coach Bennett. He looks happy here, but some have come forward today to paint a less than happy picture of the head coach. In fact, today, in an exclusive interview, after all these years, a ball player has come forward to tell us what really happened one infamous night and repercussions that followed. In exchange for this interview, we have agreed to keep our source's identity secret.

We will simply refer to him as player number 42. We promised to keep his real identity confidential if he'd agree to be interviewed for this special expose of the incident that became know as *"The Foul Outs at Foster's Store."*

"Yeah, I had a great Career going for myself until that night at Foster's Store. I could've been a contender."

--Quote from Unidentified player # 42

Lankford: Now Jimmy, you're jumping a little ahead of us. What about just giving our readers a little of the background leading up to that mass suspension?

Number 42: *OK, yea, the week before the party we had had our ass kicked by a team we were favored to beat by twenty points. Bennett went nuts. You know, he ain't the Mr. Smiley guy all the time, like he'd like you to believe. When he was pissed off about anything he'd sort of freeze up and his face would get all red and you could see his jaw muscles contracting so hard, that I thought sometimes, he might have a stroke right then and there. No one ever dared to even make eye contact with him when he was in a fit like that. It was real freaky.*

Lankford: So what did he say to you losers?

Number 42: *The usual thing, you know, crap like: "You guys were dragging like a bunch of old ladies out there." Or: "I don't remember* it being in the playbook to pass the ball to the other team." Crap like that, nothing out of the ordinary really. Hell, we were all just white guys. What did he expect?

Lankford: Really! Sounds pretty typical to me based on my own experiences from playing any kind of organized ball?

Tingle: *Yeah, everybody knows the drill. But this time, I saw it in his eyes. Looking back on it today, I realize he must have been under a pile of pressure. The sport was changing fast. And another thing: coaches were becoming "personalities," and that meant getting exposure for themselves in order to move up to the next level.*

Lankford: So what happened next?

Number 42: *I'm not sure who suggested it, but my teammates and I thought a party was in order. You know. We'd get together some place and knock down a few cold ones and talk together about what a shit Coach Bennett was.*

Lankford: And that's how Foster's Store came up?

Tingle: *Yea, Dan O'Connor was living out at Foster's at the time. Bennett had already kicked Dan off the team the year before. He didn't like his attitude, you know what I mean. I don't know, we just ended up out there at the store with our dates one night and pretty much just drank a few beers and just blew off a little steam for a couple of hours. Not a big deal at all, a few beers, nobody was pukin' or anything.*

Lankford: Sounds pretty harmless to me. But what happened next?

Number 42: *The next practice, with all the assistants, Bennett walks in the gym with this real stern look on his face, tells us to forget about warming up for the day and to take a seat in the stands. I remember it like it was yesterday. He pauses for the longest time. You could hear a pin drop. Then he starts it. Saying he already knows about what had happened at Foster's store and who was there, and what was going on, the beer drinking. He wanted to know who was "going to be a man and own up" to the fact that they were "out breaking training," doing whatever with "those potheads at Foster's Store."*

Lankford: Sounds pretty scary.

Number 42: *Yeah, no kidding, definitely fucked up. Get kicked off the team, lose your scholarship, have to leave school, and in those days, ninety days later you could find yourself cruising the lanes in Southeast Asia with a M-16, all because of a few beers and some old friends with a bad reputation. Talk about the fuckin' sword of Damocles.*

Lankford: So what happened next?

Number 42: *Well, we are all pretty much stunned by the whole thing, especially after he asks that the "transgressors" raise their hands and identify themselves. But after a bit of hesitation and looking around at each other, we begin one by one, and end up with eight out of the eleven of us with our hands raised. Then real quiet, while his assistant is writing down all our names, he tells us that were all suspended until further notice.*

Lankford: What a fuck head.

Number 42: *It turned out to be only a week's suspension, but we did have to forfeit one game. The next day all of us were pretty surprised to see a story about us and the party in the **Atlanta Constitution**, with Bennett's interview about how he felt compelled to take action and was not going to put up with players who weren't fully dedicated* *to the program. All that same lazy sports dogma that coaches always spout off when they find themselves in that kind of media glow. That he just wanted some more publicity was my end-of-the-day take on the thing. Foster's Store was a good excuse for that.*

Lankford: So, ya'll really cleaned up your act after that as a team?

Number 42: *Yea. Right! Bennett got it on the sports record that he was a strict disciplinarian and we went about our business as usual. I look back on it as some kind of a coaching management exercise. I was who I was and it didn't motivate or de-motivate me one way or another.*

Lankford: Thanks for you time, Number 42.

Number 42: *Most welcome. When's the next party?*

Yeah, those were the days, and this is just one of the many glimpses of what made up part of the reputation that was Foster's Store. We made the *Atlanta Constitution* Sports Section and got a little more famous. Mr. Foster, had he known about all this at the time, could have maybe justified a little rent increase. So, who's up for a little game of AUSTRAILOPITHICUS AFRICANUS?

Foster's Store Basketball Barn

Basketball Fans

The Art of Foster's Store

Pencil Drawing 1970 – Allen McMillan

The Art of Foster's Store

Lankford   McMillan   O'Conner

Chapter 15

Editorial Page

Walter showing Peace Sign with feet.

Authenticity of T-Shirt Idea Disputed

All persons interested in t-shirts should from this date forward email inquires to Walter Carmichael, the T shirt Genius at: editor@fosterstore.com

By Walter Carmichael

This is a notice to other friends of Foster's Store to be aware of certain activities being carried out without conscience by the site's founder and head guru, Wayne Lankford or White Longhair, or whatever name Tex is using this week. Those of us who have lived with Wayne, or lived around him over the years have always suspected that he was a cyclepath, but now, this condition is manifesting itself in mostly benign ways, but my T-shirt Idea must have incited some sort of negative brain chemistry to occur and resulted in his convenient lapses in memory regarding the ownership of said T-Shirt Creation.

So, you can understand, I was still a little taken aback, to see the design that I created for the Left Georgia T-shirt for sale.

My original intention for the T-shirt was that it would be a shirt manufactured by the people, sold by the people and worn proudly by the people. Instead Longhair stole my original design and is taking full advantage of the current fan craze for anything to do with Foster's Store to line his own pockets with the sale of this shirt. At $20 each, this shirt is not for the people, but is strictly marketed towards his bourgeois friends, who use it to make people believe that at one time in their lives they were hip.

Then to add insult to injury, Longhair uses the word "Hippie" extensively in his sick marketing campaign. The fact is there were no Hippies at Foster's Store.

I won't deny that the brothers of the store didn't take full advantage of the "Hippie" craze of the 60s to attract and psychologically imprison innocent co-eds and young girls from the Carrollton community. But the brothers of the store kept a deep secret locked away from family

and friends who were not privy to workings of the inner circle. That closely guarded secret, which could have brought an end to whole scene, was that these guys worked for a living.

In fact working was a fact for

most of my friends during my years at WGC. That's why we partied so hard Monday through Friday, because about half of the time, most of us weren't even there on the weekends. We were working.

I went home one weekend a month to put on an army uniform and serve with the National Guard, as did a bunch of other WGC draft dodgers who didn't have the grades to keep up a deferment. The other three weekends a month I was home working in a variety of different jobs from insurance to the mobile home business. My parents supported my college education but they were working people who had two other children to put through college. To live in the style I wanted to live, which was to live with the appearance of no style at all, required cash.

Other friends worked loading for trucking companies, retail jobs, restaurant jobs, whatever jobs students could find. The wild looking deadbeats in Candee's photos, like Richard and Phil, worked pipeline construction. This was true for a lot of the girls also. I always felt this gave the Left Georgia crowd a big advantage over our friends whose families had the money to send them more prestigious schools where they joined Frats, stayed drunk for four years and then had the unfortunate experience of having a degree but no knowledge of having a boss.

But we did long to live the lifestyle of the hippies from the West Coast that we heard so much about. To sleep late, stay stoned all day, and have free love all night, sounded great, but we never could figure out how our West Coast brothers pulled that off without money. Southern women may have spoken of free love, but they expected, demanded and got something out of the deal or it was no deal.

I don't remember when the "Hippie" thing got to be, but I think it really took off around 68. Until that time most of us were still in the 'straight head' frame of mind. Meaning you just drank beer and let the government do their thing.

Then all of a sudden it all turned around. When our returning brothers from Vietnam started telling us the truth about what was going on over there, the baby boomer generation turned on, dropped out, and tried to put a stop to the killing of our friends and the Vietnamese over a cause that has never been explained.

A lot of people still don't know the thing that expanded drug use overnight across the country was the war. The returning veterans who turned on while overseas to turn off what was going on around them spread drug use across the country, even to the south. Don't you think so Bob?

So it went from one day when the girls were wearing these fiberglass water buffalo hairdos, virgin pins, nice sweaters and skirts, and wouldn't go out with anybody suspected of using any kind of drug or of speaking against the government—to the next day where they were burning bras, putting on the patched up bell bottoms and shot-gunning everyone (even their cats) into Blissville.

And once the girls flipped, that was it for the square-head young Republican crowd. You also have to remember that within a decade the denim turned to polyester, the no hair cut turned into $40 beauty parlor cuts, and we were doing the John Travolta thing on the dance floor. The late seventies scene pointed out and proved a timeless truth for us guys.

It's sad to admit but it is true (and since I'm an old married man now, I'll share it with you girls who haven't already figured it out). No matter what the guys may say, they go where the girls go and they get looking like the girls want them to look. Anyway that's the only way I can explain us going from singing "The Times They are a Changing" to bumping and grinding on strobe-light-lit dance floors to "Staying Alive".

Now back to the Lankford's miscue on the T-shirt deal. Even in the days of the sixties, several of us suspected that White was hiding his real identity behind that mask of an idealistic airhead. But by borrowing my design and test marketing the item in question to the masses for $20 a piece—the truth is out. WAYNE LANKFORD IS A CLOSET CAPITALIST and may he be trampled by bargain basement "going out of business sale" shoppers in his next life.

Special Notice!!!

From now on all persons interested in t-shirts should from this date forward email inquires to Walter Carmichael, The T-Shirt Genius at

editor@fostersstore.com

As a result of this editorial, Lankford has apologized and promises no more t-shirt ventures.

Except maybe

For this one.

-The T Shirt Deal # 2 –

Fill out the missing information below, tear this page out of the book and mail it along with 20 bucks, to me, Wayne Lankford, c/o Foster's Store T Shirt Deal, P. O. Box 36186., Hoover, AL 35244.   Send four more dollars for postage, and your address.

All T Shirts 100% Cotton

One Size XL

Name_____

Mailing Address_____

City_____State_____Zip_____

Number of Shirts ordered_____ Amount Enclosed_____

About this next Chapter: Chapter 16. The Puke Chapter

My editorial review committee headed up by Peter Bryg has begged me not to include the next chapter. Peter says that these little pieces, these small wet little chunks of our history may have the potential to undo much of the goodwill so far extended towards the creation of this remembrance. Peter says, "It is not witty. It is not funny. It is highly something else that starts with a "dispe---------" that I just can't quite make out because his hand writing gets so bad there. It's like he is getting sick or something.

I spoke with Walter about all this and even told him that I was about to ditch the whole chapter, that I really agreed with Peter and everybody else about this.

But Walter said, "Fuck em! Just put a note in front of the chapter and tell people who have queasy stomachs or think they are too sensitive, or might be grossed out so much as to become ill and puke while they are reading this chapter to just skip it!"

Walter said that is what he always used to do when he worked for the newspaper, when he wrote an article that he knew would offend a lot of people.

I am so easily influenced. Ladies and Gentlemen, I present to you without further delay, Chapter 15, Tales from the Okeefeenokee Swamp.

Note: This chapter could not have been included without the technical support of Real Admiral Richard Duncan of the Okeefeenokee Swamp Club. His extensive knowledge of the subject matter here was indispensable. (if not flushable) We who are about to puke salute you!

Chapter 16

Tales from the Okeefeenokee Swamp

Or, *The Vomit Chronicles!*

Warning! This chapter may make you puke!

By various and sundry store mates

Since the WGC Alumni News first reported news about the existence of a website about Foster's Store, I have heard from many people who, like me, still feel a very real and dear connection to the place. I've head from people all over with nothing but raves about our efforts here. Former store mates have promised to write their tales of remembrance about their time spent there and some can't wait, they blurt it out in the first email. It's with some amazement that a number of former store mates and friends feel compelled to relate episodes about the subject of vomiting at Foster's Store at one time or another. This seemed curious to me. So I, in the name of research, broadcast an email to about thirty people requesting stories regarding Foster's Store and vomiting. What follows then is a recap of some of those more memorable accounts with my being careful not to reveal any contributor's identity.

Just a note before we begin! I pretty much lived in the middle of the time stream that was Foster's Store. I've found that attitudes about things were very different over the years, but this vomit thing, there's a thread here that connects all us store mates no matter how long our hair was, our political leanings, what particular ways we partied, or what we consumed in that effort.

Passed out partier

Yucky!!!!!!!!

Contribution 1

This Foster's store deal is so strange. In the last week three different people have told me stories about puking at Foster's store or other places. I think now I'm going to do a whole chapter just on throwing up, Foster's style. I know you think this is crazy, but It looks like puking your guts up is a common thread among store mates, no matter what year they resided there. These older guys seem to frown about smoking pot, think that was a bad thing, but

go on and on about force, volume, and velocity, describing their upchucking experiences.

The obvious contrast is that the 60's guys had only alcohol to use for recreational purposes. Our people, us, were able to moderate our alcohol intake due to the fact that we were too zonked to get up and get another beer. I mean, personally, I remember my drinking limit to be about 12 beers maximum, but as a sophomore, When I wasn't smoking so much weed, I would often drink a whole case.

God, I loved college.

Contribution 2

I was talking to Steve Craft the other night. We were talking about pukin off the balconies of Jackson Courts. You know, really hurling the stuff. I remember one night, a big party weekend, this guy I knew had a hot date with a girl he knew from Atlanta. Personally, I thought she was really too sophisticated for the Jackson Court party crowd. Anyway, the party is really roaring and at one point her date got to feeling kind a queasy and stepped outside on the front porch and threw up a stomach full of beer, I mean real hard flying parallel to the ground for about 6 to 8 feet before gravity got it and took it down to the asphalt parking lot. Well, about that time his date, the ballerina, walks out on the balcony looking for him. He walks right up to her and plants a big wet kiss right in and on her open and outstretched mouth.

What a great party!

Here's another!

Oh, God, do I have puke stories. My family has puked all over the world. A friend of mine bought a boat (60' Ocean Sixty) in England; so I flew over to take the maiden voyage from the southern coast of England to the Canary Islands off Africa. I lost ten pounds the first week, orally over the side. I was praying that we would sink and die just so I could stop heaving. To make matters worse, I took these patches that you stuck on your skin behind you ear to keep you from getting sick (didn't work). Turns out they were like taking LSD. I had the weirdest dreams and had a hard time keeping up with which parts were dreams and which parts were real. The storms were so bad one night we literally had to batten down the hatches and pray that we would be there the next morning. We were in forty foot waves off the Bay of Biscayne. But, after we got closer to the islands and into smooth sailing, it was beautiful and I could see how my friend got hooked on sailing when you have control of the wind and water.

My sister's X-husband had a small plane and every time he took my sister up she puked. He took my brother up once and had him take off his shirt to puke in so it wouldn't mess up the plane. So, when he offered to take me up, I loaded up with vomit bags knowing if my sister and brother got sick, I would too. He took us over the Master's Golf Course when it was in full bloom, I kept trying to focus on the beautiful golf course and not on my stomach, but sure enough felt it coming, whipped out the vomit bag, started puking my guts out and heard my brother-in-law cussing and screaming and looked over the vomit bag to see that the bottom of it was out and puke was flowing all over the plane. He never took any of us up again.

When we were growing up my mother always had the glove box in the car crammed with small brown bags and lots of Kleenex. My sister was always the first to get sick. Back then in cars with no air conditioners, in the heat of the summer, in the back seat, if one of us started, it only triggered the other two. Mom could take a quick look at my sister, whip out one of those bags, stuff it with Kleenex and manage to get it under her drooling mouth before the vomit made it out and whip up two more bags to give my brother and me. If it had been me with those children, I would never have taken them anywhere!

The first time my husband and I went to El Paso to visit his son and see him get married, we had lunch with his X-mom in law. Right after the lunch we flew out and had a stop over in Houston. After about an hour in Houston we were loading on to our next plane and before we could get to our seats, I jumped into the first seat I could get to and rambled through the magazine pocket just in time to whip out the vomit bag and started puking then, and puked all the way back to Georgia with all the other passengers trying not to get too close to me.

Why are you doing an article on puking?

Contribution 4

My 1966 High School classmates created a club called the OYC (Okeefeenokee Yacht Club). We have gone on a 4 day camping trip for the last 25 years. We may go to Cumberland Island, Okeefenokee Swamp, or paddle down the Suwannee River). We have paddled all the way across the swamp and all the way down the Suwannee River to the Gulf of Mexico. Well the purpose of this information is that we have created a game known as "Name That Puke". You try to give as short a hint as possible and the others have to name the person and event! We have one person who leads the way by miles (actually 2, Richard D and Robert K). The club is open to any classmate ....male or female..... but in reality there are about 25 who go and of that number there are about 12 who go every year. We do enforce the 50 mile rule and I have gotten dangerously close to violation here.

Uno Mass

You can't use my name on this one, but my best puke story is that my good friend and her boyfriend and I had to take a friend of theirs from Atlanta to the hospital in Carrollton (Tanner ?) because he had fallen on his arm while we were doing some CRAZY stuff and was in a lot of pain even though he was still under the influence of #$%^^. We were sure it was broken. Well, he passed me a 714, a Quaalude, in the emergency room and even though I had already had one on an empty stomach earlier, I took this one down too. I was so messed up that right after I ate it, I puked the thing up, picked it out of the puke (in the emergency room no less) and ate it again!!!

> Gross???

Contribution 6

I do remember drinking almost a whole bottle of Boone's Farm one afternoon (from the bottle, no less) and puking my guts out, but I think I made it safely to my little bathroom in the basement. And didn't knock myself out on the sewer pipe you had to duck going in or out of the bathroom because I was crawling.

My college career began the Fall of 1972 and it didn't take me long to seek out Foster's store for a multitude of reasons!!! One memory that immediately came to mind after reading the article in *The Perspective* was.........eating a can of baked beans bought from a small store down the road from Foster's. I mixed it with some mustard and ketchup for lunch. Back then I was living off Tyus Road, or was it Resurrection City? Anyway, after selling one of my text books and making a short drive out towards Atlanta for some Johnny Walker Black, I proceeded to drink the whole bottle, probably a pint, on my way back to the store. (God, I hope not a quart!) Straight from the bottle and puked those baked beans in my friend's yellow Dodge Colt. I puked those beans so hard and with such velocity that a lot of them ended up in her 8 track tape player. At least I had the decency not to make a mess in Foster's parking lot ! I lived in Carrollton until March 1977

Contribution Last

Finally, there is the story of another Store Mate who had a date with this girl one night who got real sick and threw up on the front end of his Pontiac, which at the time, was parked out in front of the store. Her puke was left to sink in where it fell on the driver's side front end. After about a week, another store mate and I were sitting outside in front of the Store when we notice a patch on the end of our friend's car where the paint is pealing off. It looks like a splash spot that spreads down and around the headlight and down the left side all the way. On the hood there are spots where it must have splashed up almost all the way to the windshield wipers.

It didn't seem like a big deal at all back then.

 Here we see unidentified WGC Co-ed feeding beer to a goat. I wonder. What does a girl do with a drunken goat?

The Art of Foster's

Big thing in sky

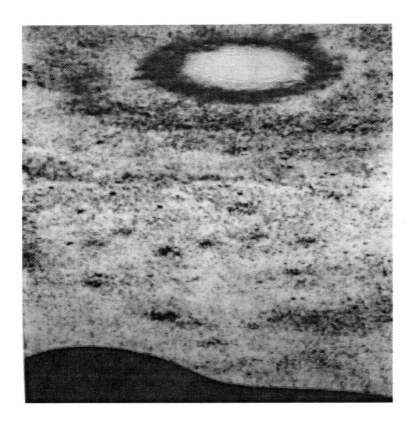

Bill Harrell 1970

Need a Band?!!!! Doesn't Everybody!

Foster's Store's Official Band

Swami Gone Bananas

Contact Information

Booking Information: Gary Dreyfusss or **Jerry Sorn**

swamigonebananas@hotmail.com

Swami Gone Bananas is an Atlanta based band whose roots and material are
in the legendary music of the 60's and 70's. Heavily influenced by the Grateful
Dead and the Allman Brothers, these rockers cast off the rust and chains of the
years, and bring an exciting rendition of timeless classics to the stage. They've
become something of a local legend due to the tight, high energy treatment of
tunes that lure the "jam lovers" to their regular gig at Mike 'n' Angelo's as
well as other venues around the area. Whether you are 16 or 60, if you love
psychedelia, you'll love,...*Swami Gone Bananas.*

November 22, 1968

Chapter 17

By The Editors

Current Events

We interrupt this book to bring you an update regarding the controversy about Foster's Store today.

Investor Group Announces Plans to Rebuild Foster's Store

Carrollton, GA

Butch Gungi, General Partner, Gungi, Clapsaddle & Obberwolfer, announced today the issuance of a $475,000,000 Investment Fund for the purpose of Rebuilding Foster's Store.

"This is a great Day for Education, The Arts, and all of us who believe that there are still ways left today for this type of creative investment vehicle." Gungi went on to say, "This one is a honey!" Then Butch laid out some basic information concerning the need for such a facility here, and the future benefits, not only for The University of West Georgia, but for the "The Whole World".

The General Prospectus (available soon) details the proposed Mega-Structure-Facility. ***Here are a few of the Highlights*** that the plan calls for at inception reviewed by Gungi.

Archeological Site Survey - Part of the main theme of "The New Foster's Store" will be to highlight the historic significance, of not only the site itself, but the cultural and sociological revolutions which were taking place here during the years of 1965-1975. Gungi cited important artifacts, like a dozen or so brown glass bottles, Possibly Pabst Blue Ribbon, and a fragment of what looked like the mouth piece that might attached to a water pipe of some kind, all recently unearthed by the survey team. "We Must conserve first" Gungi insisted, "The very fabric of History is in play here today, we must not forget!"

About Artist's Conception - "We think we've come up with a pretty good conception of what we want as far as the main Building and the adjoining acreage is concerned," The Main building will house not only the Art Galley but will also offer exhibition facility and meeting rooms.

The adjoining Hotel and Convention center, The *Buf-Wuf,* will act as a gathering place for all group activities and tours. A Casino is also part of the designed hotel facility.

The Netherlands (The Country) has been asked and granted special compensation and will operate an Embassy here. "Actually," Gungi explained, "the entire site has been given to the country of The Netherlands; we will actually lease from the Embassy itself, which means," Gungi pointed out, "that we will not actually be part of or governed legally by US law, a circumstance which we plan to exploit freely when in full operation."

Lake Keith- Larry Island

Additionally! Two 30 feet tall Iron Statues of Keith and Larry will Grace the shoreline of the 175 acre meditation lake. "This is very little payback to a couple of guys who inspired so much", Gungi lamented sadly.

In closing, Gungi seemed a bit tearful as he ended with wishes that the whole world might embrace the proposed project with love and respect for the man who made all this possible. "I know if L. R. was here right now, all that he'd need to be happy would be that you let him have a can of beer or two, maybe buy a carton of fresh red wigglers from him: it's that kind of selfless spirituality we want to evoke with all those wishing to connect financially to this worthy philanthropic project."

More details to follow.

the editors

New Big Name Rehab Center Headed for Bowden Road?

Carrollton GA.

"This proposed development will transform Carrollton's west side" so stated General Partner Felix Oberwolfer, of Gungi, Clapsaddle and Obberwolfer. Oberwolfer went on to describe how, with the development of **The New Foster's Store Mega-site**, other avenues of investment would naturally open up. Oberwolfer said that he had already contacted the **Big Name** people in Arizona (who for now wish to remain anonymous) and reported that they had warmed to the idea of expanding their operations into Carrollton. Oberwolfer further explained, "neither that little on campus crisis center or the wider medical facilities of the municipality would come close to covering the future needs that will bloom as this development matures, not to mention Carroll County's outdated criminal justice system."

Oberwolfer then pointed to a number of photographs that had recently surfaced which he suggested, "demonstrate most empirically the types of dementia and disturbed conditions that raised their heads around here 30+ years ago, when so little treatment was available. "We must not be so unprepared this time!"

(from Oberwolfer Exhibit) **Oberwolfer points to painting example described as "hallucinogenic" and a self portrait, Former Store resident Candy Carmichael before 2nd lobotomy.**

"They call this art, we say it's psychosis", Oberwolfer then describes nuances of the investment vehicle.

New Bond Issue on its way

Working from prepared notes, Oberwolfer continued his talk by announcing a proposed **150 million dollar Bond Issue for Carroll County**. "This will be a great investment for our whole community". The proceeds from the bond issue will be used to fund the construction of two new projects directly across the street from TNFS and adjacent to the **(Name to be announced later) Center & Spa.** "All this new traffic will require processing. Our existing Criminal Justice, Jail and Rehabilitation services will be completely overwhelmed within months without these needed and necessary expansions." "Look" Obberwolfer turned serious, "we will be drawing nut cases from all over the globe with this little concession, and we need to be ready". At that point, a rough diagram was distributed to the crowd of reporters who had gathered at the Bowden road clearing. "This is all about convenience, they'll cook em', we'll clean em. We'll all make money!"

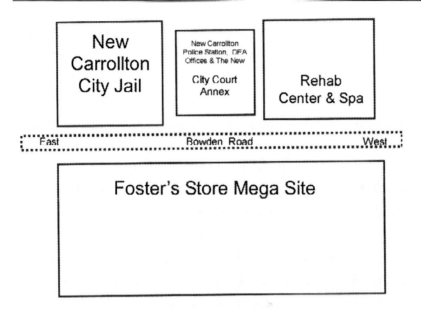

University to Profit ?

Oberwolfer then closed with an outline as to how, in his vision, the **University of West Georgia** might profit in this investment scenario. "In five years TNFS will most probably employ over 1000 people, *but the good paying jobs will be across the street.* The qualifications that will be required then are just the ones West Georgia trains students for right now. Psychologists, Sociologists, Psycho-Therapists, educators and Criminal Justice majors will all be in high demand at both the Big Name Rehab center, and the publicly funded rehab and incarceration structure this bond issue will enable." "If you look at that map, and then in your imagination, draw little arrows circling through the buildings described on that page, see the beauty of the overall plan. They enter the TNFS facility, stay a week or two, exit either headed East or West, and we intervene legally, jail, try, and fine. The new defendants would all be served right there just west of our principal business districts. We can't lose. And the extra benefit to our county: our newly degreed Graduates will never have to travel far for employment in these sectors. The revenue won't either. "

staff

Paid Advertisement

Talk To Spirit

Dear Spirit dude:

"...on several occasions, I went long with The Green Jay Rushers. I just walked back and saw everybody had moved. Who won? What was the final score?
Still Kind' a Out' a Breath, but still in the game,"
Heywood Jablome

 The dude speaks from somewhere not here,

Heywood! Hooty Who to you too!

Smokin so much wacky tabaki will do it every time. Was a time when they had some real ball players at the old store, but them rushers weren't nothing but dope fiends and sex perverts, which I guess, is why we got along so well. No matter how much dope you smoked you seemed to all be pretty one-headed as the babes were concerned. I'll give you that. My guess was that you'd a had better luck with more scoring, both on and off the field, ifin you wouldn't ah drunk so much PBR's and held your head so long in that towel full of Pertussin you use to pass around like it some kind of a I don't know what. Some of that still confuses this spirit.

Haywood, if you might bother to take a quick glance at the scoreboard down there over the end zone, you might notice it's saying your well in ta the second half of whatever game of life you must be in right now. Isn't that your score now today too, the big fat 0?

Classified Ad

Just like Mr. Foster himself!

Chapter 18

The Halloween Party 1970

The Pirates of the Caribbean drop anchor at Carrollton before returning to the Twilight Zone.

Part 1:

An account by someone who wasn't there and wishes to remain unidentified.

I guess it's up to me to get this thing started. What I want to do here is try to piece together from each of our memories just what happened that night, that Halloween night so long ago at Foster's store. I wasn't even there, but, maybe, what I do remember about the days prior to the party may jog somebody else's memory, who then might contribute also to this account of the Halloween night they raided Foster's.

Let me lay some groundwork here. I mean, thinking back on it, one of the biggest reasons our parties were so successful (or so unsuccessful, depending how you looked at it) was that we were in no way affiliated with any school or fraternity, nor did we adhere, in any way, to any formal organizational ground rules. In fact, we were about as outlaw a party group as could be. We had heard of these things called boundaries. They were in fact, for many of my store mates, things that needed to be passed through, exceeded every time, like the sound barrier, for a party to even be considered successful.

Then one fine fall quarter day somebody suggested we needed to throw a Halloween Party at the store. I remember that taking place about ten days prior to the thirty-first of October and then almost immediately, everyday afterwards, I recall people coming up to me on campus or wherever asking me about the party, asking what were we planning and such, like costumes, orgy, kegs, all that kind of stuff, and our replying yeah, orgy, kegs, giant joints, LSD and all the usual party favors of the day. Everything seemed pretty normal right up until the Monday before the infamous Halloween Friday night.

Store mates and Mr. Foster . L to R David Jack, Dan O'Conner, Allen McMillan & White Longhair

I remember this part pretty clearly. I meet this guy in front of the student center. When I walk up between classes, he's talking to a small crowd including fellow store mates and some would-be party goers. He's telling everybody that he heard about our planned Halloween party at a party when he was up in Athens, at the University, where he was in attendance, that past weekend. (Wow, I thought, at first, they'd heard about our party even at the University!) But really, almost immediately, to me, this guy seemed a bit out of place, and it seemed awfully strange for a guy to come all the way from Athens, almost a week early, to get ready to go to a party that won't even happen for five days. Anyway, too, I'm struck by how awake this guy is, you know what I mean, really awake like he's taken a hit or two of speed or something. Then he starts saying that he had heard up in Athens that one of the things we were planning at the party was to "bob for apples in Electric Kool Aid". Now this was the first I'd heard of this, and I lived there. I just sort of blew it off and dismissed this guy as some kind of a nut and went on with my school week. It was a good idea though, bobbing for apples in a wash tub full of LSD. I would not personally do such a thing, but others, if they wanted to, why not? Friday was four days away.

The next day this same guy is out at the store with a bag of pot and giving it all away, still talking up the Halloween party and of course all my store mates are beginning to become more excited with the anticipation of what might well be the biggest social event of the fall season. We were all being swept up in an enthusiastic fugue of major proportion. It was looking like the whole school was going to show up that weekend at Foster's store!

Then, later that night, somebody drops by, I forget who, but they say, they say that they are sure too, that this guy from Athens is a narcotics agent. More definitely, he is working undercover to save his own skin, telling the GBI (Georgia Bureau of Investigation) in order to save his own neck, that he can deliver every pot smoking acid dropping hippie left wing radical at West Georgia College (We figured he meant us). This, you may remember, was right after an *Atlanta Journal* article decrying us, WGC, as the most drug using campus in the state. (What a joke that was, but that's another story)

By Thursday afternoon, the 30th, it's clear to me that whoever goes to this party is going to be busted. What's weird to me is, that my store mates, so crazed now with this thing, they're totally deaf and dumb to all these warnings. I implored them, "Guys, the cops are coming, you are all going to go to jail, remember Ed Tant, this is Carrollton, they're going to make a statement about all this, using this party, our party, busting everybody will be the message, the exact message to everybody who might think about so flagrantly breaking the drug laws. What is wrong with you guys? Do you want to go to jail?" I try every argument I can think of, but it's like they just can't imagine the police really coming, or they just didn't care. I remember the look in their eyes. They all were just wild with anticipation. Crazed describes it better, repeating over and over again, "Electric Kool Aid, orgy, chicks, pot, chicks, acid, orgy, chicks, keg party, bobbing for apples in electric Kool-Aid, Halloween Party, chicks."

I'm being careful not to mention any names here (I'm Not even mentioning my own). You guys know who you are, but I really would like to hear what you have to say, what you guys, or any of your dates remember about that night. As I said earlier, I left town. I went to Atlanta for the weekend and it was after dark that Sunday night when I got back to the store.

I remember it was real quiet that night, the Sunday after the Friday night party, when I got back to the Feed n' Seed. I was met with a pretty strange sight. In my bedroom, all of my clothes were in the middle of the room in a big pile, all the drawers were pulled out and had been emptied, the whole place had been ransacked, everything up-side-down. There were cars up by the store, so I headed up that way and went inside to find you all up there, sitting in the Womb Room, real quiet, real straight looking. And that's when I learned that my prediction had come true, that every cop in Carroll County, along with the GBI, had shown up at the party Friday night and handcuffed, and "up against the walled" everybody. I then learned that they even came back Saturday night to try and catch you guys again. Try to catch you when there weren't so many people from Carrollton there. Their idea had been to get the guys from out of town, the law defying radicals, students from out of town, the bad influences, the leaders. They hadn't bargained that some of you were dating their daughters who were from Carrollton. They couldn't arrest their own kids.

I know it was a good 24 hours before anyone lit a joint in the storehouse. That's how paranoid everybody was. Yea, you guys wouldn't know paranoia if it hit you over the head.

Jim Kent called me yesterday promising to add his own account here. I asked him what his costume consisted of that night and he remembered vividly, "I went as a Priest and my date was dressed as a Nun, we were making out when the cops walked in on us."

Part 2

Now, from $#*&, or Anonymous II:

Barry Edwards with beard

I remember at the time Barry Edwards had a great beard, he went as a pirate. Head scarf, fake earring, sash around the waist with a dagger or small sword—looked like he had stepped from a 20th Century Fox soundstage filming Sinbad. We were raided by the Carrolton Police, Carroll County Sheriff's office and the GBI. Barry was in your front bedroom with his date when the raid started and I heard one of the officers scream, "Watch out! He's got a sword!" Barry got tickled and couldn't stop laughing and giggling. That made them even madder.

I had an old full dress tuxedo, the one with the long tails I had talked you into giving me when you used to work at the formal shop in Atlanta. It was well-worn, but had tails, none-the-less. I went as Groucho Marx, complete with cigar, painted on mustache and eyebrows. Denise Jackson, Bobo's girlfriend, introduced me to my date. She was dressed as a princess and was a looker. I'm almost positive her father was the Sheriff at the time . . . he could have been a deputy or something. When we were raided, one of the officers singled her out and gave us a lecture about the severity of the circumstances— neither of us could see the big deal. Her father called me personally and asked that we not see each other again—we did anyway.

David Jack

By design, most or all of the dope had been hidden within easy reach in the pasture behind the Feed & Seed. Sleepy had a friend with a necklace made out of hashish chunks from Monroe, I believe. He was one of the few to be arrested . . . I think on a parole violation and he stayed high for several days with his necklace in the Carrollton jail.

We were all lined up against the wall in the front room of the Feed & Seed where we were frisked. While they frisked one person, the rest were busy passing various and sundry forms of dope, mostly marijuana, back and forth, so as not to be in possession. The police were just not prepared . . . people would be frisked and just walk off, go get something to eat, maybe return, maybe not, and it was just chaotic in a benign and funny way.

I don't believe the police ever asked us to quit drinking, so some of us just continued to drink while they frisked us and tore the place apart. They would frisk a few, and those people would just wander off. I was frisked several times during the evening. I don't think anybody present was too committed to the situation. I think the police were expecting a heavy duty drug raid with junkies and mass quantities of drugs—I think they were surprised. They wound up at a Halloween Party with some of the funniest liquored-up misfits in America. Everybody present had one purpose—to have a good time. Nobody got mad or too upset.

Not to mention names . . .when drugs were found on our person we would pass them along to one of our members, who would just nod and swallow—no telling what all he took; but if memory serves correct he was up for a few days. Thankfully, no one was arrested for possession.

I remember one of our Store mates, who at the time wanted to be a lawyer, was acting as attorney and general legal counsel for all present. Most of his legal maneuvering he got from a Perry Mason episode . . . he told several cops what they could or couldn't do. He told them he was in pre-law and the way I figure it he had about as much legal experience as they did. They did tell him to shut up a few times . . . I don't think he minded. We had a cowboy with a set of pistols that caused a disturbance—can't remember much about it. A couple of girls complained about being groped, i.e., searched by the cops. We had a flapper with a flask in her garter.

We had some pretty good eats and I'm pretty sure two kegs of beer. I really believe several of the GBI agents ended up drinking a few beers with us before they left. The Carrollton cops did try to scare us by saying we were being watched and they'd be back. But you know, cops have to say that kind of stuff. It's in a code somewhere.

The next day after the raid I got religion and went to talk with a local minister. Believe it or not and to my surprise, he was on the Carrollton City Council (or something like that) and had something to do with the police. I'll leave that story for another time.

Part 3

A third partier reports:

As reported above, it seemed the whole property was under siege that fateful night. Of course, the majority of the action was down at the Feed & Seed and not the main store, where, as I recall, some of the partiers had coupled off earlier and were, by the time the local constabularies arrived, deep into the process of that coupling and perhaps even re-coupling—there was a lot of screwing going on up there.

I too was attired as a pirate. I remember I wore a purple tank top and white bell bottoms that started at the waist and just kept right on going. This is as close to a costume as I would tolerate at that stage of my life. Maybe I was something between a Pirate and a Piss-ant, probably just a First Mate to a more decorated sailor that night.

There were a couple of people there for sure that were not well known to us or trusted. We suspected that what was to come down would, that the earlier predictions of "the man" arriving would come true. We did nothing to counter those predictions, but neither did we proclaim the possibilities, leaving certain of our guests believing that all in our forecast was clear. I can't remember their names . . . that guy from Athens with the wild eyes, but that's not important to our story.

We didn't know any of the cops, but it is true that after the dust of the initial invasion took place, some of them were not so bad and overall we were not too roughed up, but considering the state of my mind, I'm not sure it would have mattered much either way.

For some reason, there seemed to be a lot of store mates dressed as pirates that night, we had a Blue Beard, a Black Beard and maybe an "I lost my beard." I was one of those Beards.

At one point during the evening, while the cops were searching everybody—pirates expect to be searched when their ship is boarded, they're pirates after all—I looked down on the floor and noticed what had to be some lost trick-or-treat candy. I remember they were blue, pink and white candies, the real yummy kind, you know the ones, where the flavor lasts for hours and hours, sometimes till the next day. I was so afraid the cops would see them too, so I was just about to jump on them and eat them myself when another one of my pirate-attired store mates beat me to the floor, mouth first. Like a bullet, he slid past the cops and a couple of GBI agents who immediately tried to keep him from reaching the candy. No doubt, they probably wanted it all for themselves, but they were just too late; this pirate wasn't going to share anything with anybody.

The other pirate just had position on me like in some hallway basketball game. All I could do then was to assist with a body check against the GBI team, while the other pirate went in for the score. I mean, we were on the same side. It was close. To get to his goal, he added, instead of a head fake, what appeared to all of us as a real seizure, something you might see at a football game as the running back tries to submarine the defensive line, a big pile up kind of scene with a lot of foaming at the mouth thrown in for effect, which I believe, he may really have experienced later that night when all the good candy kicked in, a real Jimi Hendrix experience.

Later, we were all lined up against the wall down in the Feed n' Seed with hands high for a while, then down, with handcuffs and without. It was little like playing Simon Says for about an hour or so. Eventually all the partiers they could find had been rounded up and directed into place for that infamous "line up at Foster's Store."

At the end of all this, no shots were fired, although, with all the hair in the room, I think a couple of good old boys might have had some itchy trigger fingers. Not sure who informed us about informers, but again, all that meant little, and the Party went on.

It was definitely worth it by the way!!!

No doubt, a lass named Kathy was in the picture for this pirate for a while. As you may recall, she was a bit on the amorous side and I so loved her nymphomaniac ways. "Up against the wall—Foster's Style", became a favorite of ours.

I think she still has my fake beard.

Not much has changed but the dates on the calendar. Fair weather to you, mate.

Pirate Number 3.

The Art of Foster's Store

Exactly What It Looks Like

by Dan O'Conner

The Art of Foster's Store

Allen McMillan 1970

Chapter 18

Talking with the Beatles

By Wayne Lankford

In spring of 1970, Z and David Etheridge were living down in the Feed and Seed. Future store mates, Dan O'Conner and I shared an apartment in Jackson Courts and future store mate, Sleepy Jack, was renting there too. One Sunday night I halved a hit of mescaline with Sleepy, and we tripped all night. I must confess, it was, to this day, probably the most enjoyable drug experience of my life. There was a point that night where, as Sleepy and I looked at the cover of the Beatles Sgt Pepper's album, the Beatles themselves were actually talking to us. I mean really talking to us. Do you understand what I mean? I decided that night, based on my experience with the mescaline, I would soon have to try some LSD.

Vietnam

David Etheridge had been my roommate at Aycock Dorm for a while my freshman year. By spring of 1970 he had dropped out of school and was making quite a good living as a professional poker player. Etheridge had lucked out on the lottery—he'd never see Nam. All I thought at the time was, "Hey, he's good at it, why shouldn't he?" He ended up renting out the "Feed N Seed" with Z, who had just fucked up, or run-out-of, a Basketball Scholarship, somehow, and was basically just waiting to be drafted by the Army.

I remember Z yelling all the time there, "Well fuck it! There goes my god damn meal ticket! Can you believe this shit?" Within 30 days, Z was a big time basketball jock, and ex-jock, got married, divorced, was out of school, then just surviving at Foster's, mainly just waiting for the

next shoe to drop. He had Vietnam written all over him. He was also fuckin nuts. But who wouldn't be?

Double Vision Quest

For several weeks previous, Z had been on a personal mission of sorts, maybe a "quest" might better characterize it. Without basketball and school and his marriage of less than 30 days to dominate his life, he was out to see just exactly how fucked up he could get, just short of killing himself. But then, not wanting to do all this alone, he enlisted me to accompany him on his own personal kind of a last hurrah before a boot camp of some kind to somewhere.

I never in my life saw anybody take to the drug culture like Z. It was fuckin scary. My roommate O'Conner, also an ex Basketballer now, was the first to get him to try marijuana, and really, just three days later, he did his first hit of acid and never missed a lick, while never slowing at all his already massive Pabst Blue Ribbon beer consumption pace. That long necked brown bottle was a part of his right hand now. Thing was, without school, a girlfriend (wife) relationship, an athletic scholarship, and no money, getting fucked up all day while waiting just be drafted, seemed plainly to be, to me and everyone else, a "most viable option for him indeed!"

I guess he could have done all this "vision tripping " by himself, but it didn't work out that way. I remember being in a Sociology class one morning and Z showing up at the door, while the class was still in session, his eyes black as saucers. Barging in and saying to the Instructor, Dr. Somebody, that I had a family emergency, real serious, and he was there to "collect me".

We get outside and I ask, "What the fuck's going on, Z?" and he says, "Come on man I got us a couple of cases back at the store, we need you to help us party!" "We", of course, was just him, of course, and now me. I mean, for a couple of months there, Z had the wildest look in his eyes, all over. The once pride of Haines City Florida, once healthy and tanned, seemed overnight to be transformed to chalk white faced derelict of self design. He was already caught in the headlights of life with nothing to look forward to but an inevitable step into its crosshairs.

But, being the friend that I was, I really felt for him. I would just shrug and go along with whatever insanity he chose. I guess I was a kind of security blanket for him, somebody to dump all his problems on, a sounding board, and maybe be there for him when he might eventually try really to blow his brains out using something besides beer, pot, and LSD. In a crazy kind of way, I guess I was honored to have the responsibility. I knew if our circumstances were reversed that he'd do the same for me. He'd hear from the Army soon; this wouldn't last forever. This same bad movie was in infinite repeat mode, constantly playing across every college campus in the country, all at once, everywhere for everybody.

At that exact time I was still clinging on to my hallucinogenic virgin status, but mind expanding drugs were catching on fast. The whole culture was taking on body paint and bellbottoms. Sid Shortt's *Headquarters* Head shop was doing land office sales on Maple street downtown, and everybody already had a head with hair. Hard rock music filled the air.

Dan O'Conner Artwork.

- LSD Man - Notice chin

Misinformation and the Hari Krishna

Added to all the lies the government could make up about the evils of marijuana, we were now being told the same about LSD. I remembered earlier Ed Tant's articles in *The West Georgian* Newspaper quoting a scientist refuting the government accusations that LSD caused chromosome damage(in mice no less) and caused babies conceived by parents who had used LSD to be ill-formed at birth. Thru Tant's, and others' articles, we heard that chromosome damage like that was just as likely to occur from drinking Coca-Cola. We all had enough real shit to be really afraid of, so being concerned about having a "Bad Trip" really seemed inconsequential. *The Age of Aquarius* was already feeling the light of the noon day sun, even in our minute little outpost, sleepy little Carrollton, Georgia.

So there's the scene for you. One of my best friends is all but psychotic. What the fuck good to you is an education if you're just going to end up on the raw end of a bungii stick or worse in just a few months anyway? All that shit about truth was just a lie. The fucking solid knowledge ground is moving all around you. The *Hari Krishna* guys and girls are all dressed in white and orange sheets with their heads shaved, chanting and dancing in circles in front of the student center, banging tambourines and bells.

One day, the *Hari Krishnas* are out there in front of the Student Center dancing around as I'm going by. All of a sudden one of them, a guy, breaks from the circle and grabs my arm saying, "Hey Wayne, It's me Jerry! Remember our freshman year up in Aycock?"

It was like I was being chased by a mad dog all of a sudden. There's this guy with every hair on his head completely shaved off, no eyebrows even, dressed in a sheet and barefooted, clinking some kind of bell things at me while I'm just trying to get past as fast as I can.

"Hey man, it ain't me, you, I,.. I've never seen you before in my life." I can still see his face in my mind. Then, above all that kind of nonsense, about every four-point-five days, there's a bomb scare somewhere on campus and everybody misses their scheduled classes for an hour or two.

If I decided one day I just want to have a really good conversation with a plant, I'm just going to. I've just learned how to read and find myself just amazed! I see this guy, Wayne somebody, selling bags of grass between class changes outside the front door of the library; you know the building with the most recent bomb scare. He just smiled when I suggested that calling in a bomb scare might be a good way to create a crowd and more dope buying traffic all at once.

Z had an easier time talking me into taking acid with him than he did convincing me to ditch a Philosophy final that I had studied for. One that I knew I'd would make an A in. "Fuck it, you can do a make it up! Let's party!"

Hallucinogenic Mission Statement

Then a few days later, it was a Saturday afternoon down at The Feed N' Seed; the usual contingent of store mates were moving into comfortable weekend lines to work or to play. David Etheridge would be away all weekend in a poker game David Jack, Z, and I along with a couple of others had been smoking the Mary Jane and listening to the *Abbey Road* album all afternoon, pretty much killing time till the acid finally showed up from somewhere thru somebody.

It was free; seems like LSD was always free.   There were a lot of people who dealt in acid who did it for nothing.   They were like missionaries with a higher calling trying to spread the word about something revolutionary. The prospect of a new devotee and they were beside themselves with joy at finding another convert to bring into the folds of the faithful.

 **Public Service Announcement!**

This Chapter is temporarily interrupted to bring the reader the following information and warning!

Go to next page to observe the warning.

Then you may continue.

Warning!!!
Please!!! Do not eat any part of this book!

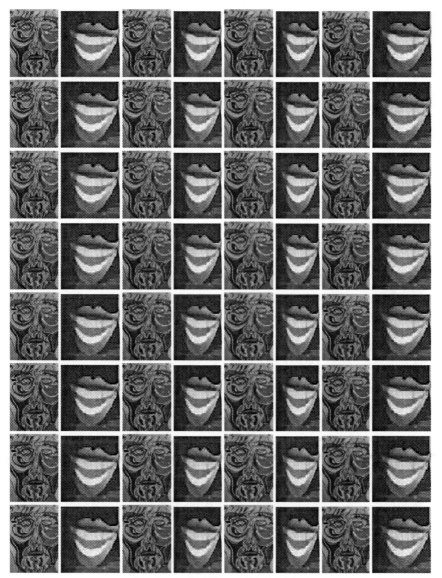

Especially This Page!

You may now continue with your reading.

Acid was the big answer for a lot of people to the question: "Where do I worship?' Maybe that's another reason so many joined the Flower Power Revolution. They naturally had trouble philosophically about how bad communism could be for people who didn't have anything anyway. "We're going to carpet bomb them over this?"

Up was up. At least it used to be? Where's that universal dose of Ammonium A D when we really need it? Why right then, right after completing all the credit hours I needed for my degree in Sociology, do I decide to change my major to Philosophy, a subject West Georgia doesn't even offer a degree in at the time? Steve and I are as one single mind, sitting out on that piece of shit couch, right out there on the front porch of Feed n Seed. Single minded, just in different time zones. Who could I get to sit on the porch with me in a few months when it was my turn?

Forgive my sombrero dancing here, but even as long ago as this event was, it still scares me to think of it. I came close to clocking out that night.

Of oil on the water and Fu Dogs

O. K., I'm about to describe to you what a certain LSD trip was like for me. But, so you will be better able to comprehend what I'm about to tell you, I need to put a couple of pictures in your head.

The first picture is of oil on the water, maybe motor oil, like the kind that you might see at a boat marina, either very early in the morning or at the end of the day, very slowly moving on the surface of dark and very still water. It's a common sight: a very thin lawyer of oil or gas spreads out and over the surface of the water. Just a drop or two can produce a swirling mix of every color in the rainbow, right there on the surface of the water, totally invisible until your angle of view changes to a place where the last rays of the day's light reflect off the water to your eyes—and there it is, all this swirling around of brilliant colors. Anywhere water and gasoline-like chemicals might meet, this effect may occur.   That easy.   Something invisible becomes visible, sparked into your awareness merely by the angle of the sun on the horizon and the absence of any wind to disturb the still water.

The next picture I need to describe is a Fu dog. To my knowledge I had never seen or had even heard of a thing called a "Fu dog" in 1970. Back then there weren't so many Chinese restaurants everywhere and I hadn't encountered this staple of their décor. At that point in time, the Fu dog did not exist, at least not in my very limited knowledge of such things. Maybe I'd seen one in a History book? Who knows?   But that night, when I saw one walk across the floor down in the Feed N Seed, to say I was a bit puzzled would be an understatement of huge proportion.

I was twenty-five before I was actually able to put the name with the thing. Reading James Clavel novels sparked an interest in me to find out more about Chinese culture. I ran across its picture in a book I'd found about Hong Kong. My monster was real. Turns out they're supposed to produce good luck. They are protectors. I wish I had known that then.

Are you with me now? It was much like swirling colors on the water, every color in the rainbow down there.

About thirty minutes after Z and I ate our hit of "blessed" LSD, I remember standing in the front room of the Feed N Seed, back behind the large bar that was there at the time. It was painted black, pretty much the whole room was. I was wearing a pair of jeans and my high school football practice jersey. I got somebody to take a picture of me.

I wanted a record of just how large my pupils were at the time.

Actual Picture taken that Day at the Feed N Seed

I thought that was really cool. Deeper in to the house I could hear the Abbey Road album going which had been on infinite repeat just about all day by now. I had found this orange scarf or something and made it into a headband. I was wearing it when I first noticed the movement.

Nothing in the physical world, but something between my eyes and the walls was beginning to form. It had the effect of the rainbow colors swirling on the water, but there wasn't any color yet. I could see thru its grey-like and still-undefined patterns some kind of microscopic matter trying to form.

"Now this is cool," I thought, "I'm obviously beginning to see things in other dimensions." Notice, I did not think at first that I was beginning to hallucinate. Rather, I personally was able now to see into other dimensions. Not only that, I was really feeling great! I was feeling more intensely alive than I ever had in my life. Everything was amplified! All I needed to do was to put my attention to it and it was, suddenly, turned up, fuller, brighter, and it all vibrated and breathed, everything was alive at once and I had control over it all.

After a while, that grayscale wall of swirls began to take shape. There was something alive beginning to form. I got real excited and grabbed a sketch pad and pen. I believed I could get the image, which now plainly had a couple of eyes and a nose, to pose for me there on the blank paper while I traced its image at my leisure.

"Hey, Z, this is the greatest I've ever felt in my life!" I tried to compare notes with Z about what was going on with me just then. But Z was somewhere else himself. So, in about a minute I was back to the trace drawing I had started.

It was still there all right, but it had moved. I couldn't get it to line up, get it back into the position it was in earlier when I had started tracing it. It wouldn't stay still. I would start a line only to find the other end of it somewhere else where it just wasn't connected at all. I remember looking down at my drawing and thinking what I was drawing was looking more like a wolf than whatever it was really. I'd start again, but it kept moving around, making my attempts to capture a reasonable image of what I was seeing impossible. It just would not stay in one place long enough.

No words can describe

Then, all of a sudden, the room disappeared and I was seeing nothing but all those different colors on the water. That's all there was, just that wall of swirling color. And it was not just the colors familiar in the rainbow. It was a hundred times that; it was a thousand times that! It was a hundred thousand times that! I was looking straight into it. I was in it. I was gone!

But just as quick, like being jerked at the end of a cord back into reality, I was back! I was in the room again, and all right. Everything was all right! Everything was better than all right. I had just popped my head into another dimension and had been looking around in it. There were no words for what this was. "Amazing" didn't even come close!

I looked down at the page again. And again, I went right into the color, no warming up, just dove right in all by myself. A few seconds below the surface of reality and right back up. I didn't want to go too deep. I need to be careful here, I thought. I began to practice it. I was studying it. It was all still pretty one dimensional at first, like standing in front of a beautiful painting in a museum. But it was all painting, no frame, and no museum; just that moving million lines of unbelievable color in my head. I was in control of all this. I was learning how to fly all by myself. It was still early. The sun was just then going down.

Besides Z, I can't really remember who else was around that night. Z and I spent a lot of time in the same room, but that didn't seem to mean very much. Both of us were on trips of our own. Every once in a while, one of us would comment about some thing or a new feeling one of us was having. Like the back my neck was beginning to tighten up a little. Z told me that was from the "speed" that LSD was usually laced with. We jokingly figured that the manufacturers of this shit wouldn't want their customers going to sleep on them in the middle of an experience like this.

Falling asleep—pretty funny really. Sure had no interest in that. College life was a lot about staying awake sometimes way past when staying awake is any fun at all. During finals week, the whole campus was awash in amphetamines, reds, and black beauties. We just called them "stay awake pills". I had taken one, a black beauty, one time, and had hated the effect it had on me. I could study without the things. For myself, I had decided, if passing meant I'd have to take a hit of speed, well, I'd fail. But speed-laced acid seemed just the way to go. Don't want to miss anything you know.

Just plain Tripping

The music from the stereo set up we had was carrying me further away all the time. I wasn't worried about the world of colors earlier, but every once in a while I'd focus my eyes to a place in mid-air somewhere and go right back to the pool. Then pop back up and out, just enjoying the trip. This must be why they call it a trip, I thought. I was sure going on one every time I'd focus my mind that way. What was neat, too, was that I was pushing all the buttons, driving my mind thru the whole fuckin' universe. I could see a world of stars out there, too, if I wanted. "I could do this stuff every day." I think I had just told Z that, when out of the corner of my left eye I saw this thing start to form in the doorway between were we were sitting and the outer party room where the bar was. One second I was in the wall of color, watching the eyes and the head of the thing I was trying to draw so hard earlier in one dimension, and the next second, all that color came in on itself, coalesced I guess you say, and became a real thing right there in the room with Z and me. The wall of swirling color had kind of fallen in on itself and formed this creature that began to move on its own. It was like a universe somewhere had collapsed in on itself. Everything that was part of that dimension I had been dancing with in my mind suddenly turned into a single Fu dog.

I had not reckoned on the ability to create and transport multi-dimensional beings from one plane of existence to another. But that was what I had clearly done, and amazingly, with so very little effort.

I began to tell Z about it, but he really didn't seem too interested, saying that he had never seen any colors himself and that his trips were mostly physical sensations.

Then, it happened again, but this time without my thinking about it or anything. The dog just winked in and walked a couple of steps towards me across the floor. They weren't really steps. He wasn't picking his feet up and down. Rather, he was sliding them across the floor, like the floor was a sheet of ice. The rest of this multi-colored thick body—thick head and neck with eyes and teeth—suddenly jerked right towards me, reducing the distance between us by a third, in a single heart beat.

"Hey Z, this thing is starting to move all by itself without me having to think about it all!" I noticed that as I spoke it disappeared, but would reappear as soon as I let my eyes gaze for longer than a couple of seconds anywhere else in the room. Each time it was closer and now I could hear it breathing too. It made a low deep hum when it moved. I was more than a bit unnerved with the instant thought of having created something like this and not being able to control it. Especially since it was now clearly winking into my dimension, into my personal space. I could tell just by looking at it that it was more solid than steel, and yet it glimmered in a million colors. I knew it was what they called an hallucination. Z kept reassuring me that "tripping is like going down the world on a sliding board. . . . This thing, whatever it is, will pass. . . Just get back on the slide."

I tried that. It would not go away. I was afraid and I was becoming more afraid every second. I got up and went outside. It was already out there waiting on me. Two seconds, maybe three, no more than four unattended seconds and there it was, every time, all the time. Every speck of my being was telling me to fear this thing. It was menacing, malevolent, and it was out to get me, right here and right now.

Philosophical dilemmas

All this might seemed awful to you today! Some tripped out college student crazed with the illusion that there was this beast he had drawn from another dimension who was hell bent on hurting, if not killing him.

It was a long night. I spent it mostly by myself. Well, not by myself exactly, but you get what I mean. Nobody else wanted to be around me. Frankly, I didn't really want to be around them. I had too much I was having to concentrate on just to keep from slipping into the dog's dimension and being lost out there in the void forever. At the same time I had to stay on guard to keep the beast off me and away from my own home dimension. One second of inattention and all would be lost! Gee, maybe this stuff does deform babies too!

At one point, I actually considered taking a running jump into the concrete block wall of the outside of the Feed N Seed, thinking my death would certainly turn this shit off, whatever it was. But then I reconsidered. Being alive was the only way to fight such a powerful beast. If I died, or worse, just maimed myself or otherwise made myself so as to not be able to do proper combat, I'd be helpless to fight the son of a bitch any more, and he could just fuckin eat me, dead or alive. How's that for a quick reason in existence justification?

You have to think about all that stuff out there in the middle of the night. A lot of help I was going to get out of Z or anybody else so similarly dosed that evening. All I could do was play defense all night long. I held on until sometime around nine o'clock the next morning when the dog's energy seemed to subside. It seemed I was just a little bit stronger than it was.

Back in my bed at Jackson Courts, I remember closing my eyes, still not being able to sleep for the longest time. In my head, it was still going on. The colors and the Fu dog were now replaced by the black starry sky, and I was still feeling forward movement even as I lay there perfectly still and exhausted. I felt like a survivor of some sort of awful accident scene. My mind was damaged this morning much the way a football player sometimes feels after a real tough game the night before. But today, this day, it was more mental than physical. I was still really afraid of the dog. I had almost really lost it earlier when I was actually considering the concrete wall as a life switch to the off position. Acid hadn't helped me figure a damn thing out, nor did I feel enlightened in any way whatsoever. I just felt tired this time. I had managed a draw with the beast last night, but I never wanted to go thru that again. I decided that LSD was not for me at all.

It was two weeks before I could even smoke marijuana again without having the wall of color coming over me. My sensitivity to the effects of pot would be forever amplified, which I would still smoke for many years to come, but not without a beer or two to tone it down a notch or so where I could enjoy it. .

Today, I'm still defending the territory. But I know he's still out there somewhere, the beast that is. I've completely lost touch with Z, many others. I don't know. Given the right circumstances, I might decide to go another round with the Fu dog. I wonder what he's been up to. I bet we've have a lot to talk about. I'm sure we would.

Z bound for Nam

Classified Advertisement

FOR SALE - Brown Owsley Acid (AS in LSD)

Included in the sale of the last 25 hits Bill brought in after returning from Jonah, and then San Francisco, in April of 68. (Included is the original six pack cooler that Bateman stored the acid in, bought, maybe stolen from Bob's Bay Station at the bottom of the Maple Street hill). Bateman had saved 25 hits of the original package of 1,500, which was supposed to be destined for WGC but ended up in some truck stop in Dalton. He thought this particular issue from Owsley gave him better real time visibility on his motorcycle. The package was recently recovered from the spring that fills Tanner Beach Lake and thanks to the cold temperatures of those waters the quality of the stash is still certified to 85.1798 percent effective as delivery in 1968.--Sandoz lab reports available upon request-- [Because of time changes, for total experience in comparison with the 60's era, purchasers should take in to account factors such as weight gain, lack of circulation to key areas of the mind, when considering dosage. "S.G.", a retired educator from the Moultrie area said, "I took two hits from the get go. I didn't want to take any chances. I'm married to a wonderful husband, have three great children (two boys and a girl) and I'm so bored with reality even if I had a bummer trip, it would have been a welcome relief. But to my surprise I got off like a rocket and had the experience of some past lifetimes, or is it lack of experience with interplanetary time skip travel in recent days, that caused my family to call 911 and I got another week off while they tested. It only took me two days to come down enough to make it seem to them like I had only had a nervous breakdown or something. You can say whatever you want about Square heads but they are supportive"]

See me at the reunion for pricing----silent Sam auctions

Milo Cup Offer

If you'd like to own a mug like this one fill out the thingy below and mail it to me with a check for whatever amount you think is fair.

Milo's Coffee Cup

Name_____

Address_____

City_____State_____zip_____

Number of Cups you want_____

Amount Enclosed_____

Mail To: Milo Coffee Cup –P. O. Box 36186, Hoover, Al 35244

Book Recommendation

Left **Georgia College**, a retrospective look at West Georgia College 1964-1974. In this masterpiece of investigative journalism, **Walter Carmichael** delves deeply into the folkways and mores of the political left which characterized the majority of the student body during these turbulent times. People forget that it wasn't all just "Sex, Drugs and Rock & Roll". Remember with Walter what you forgot, what you remember, and how you learned to separate the two.

How about a cup of coffee right now?

Chapter 20

A DAY AT THE BEACH WITH AL GORE

By Bob O'Kelley

I awoke early, and not too hung over, considering that the night before; I got drunk, smoked a joint, and survived a rocket attack. I went to the outpatient mess hall and had breakfast. It helped absorb the alcohol remaining in my system.

I was in Chu Lie to see the ophthalmologist. My left eye was severely infected, but it caused me no pain. I had been living in the outpatient barracks for two days, and, as yet, no one in authority had noticed that I was there, or that I had not seen the doctor. I was only slightly AWOL. My commander back at fire base San Juan Hill had no way of knowing how long it would take to travel to Chu Lie, see the doctor and return, and I intended to make the most of it. I figured that I deserved a little R&R.

The base at Chu Lie sat right on one of the most beautiful beaches that I have ever seen. The enlisted man's beach club was only a short walk from the outpatient facilities. I was trying to enjoy myself there, but nothing I did was really satisfying. Something was missing, and I knew what it was— girls.

There were no girls on the beach, not the first one, and a beach without pretty girls is like a hamburger without meat. The company of the opposite sex was desperately missed the night before when a band played at the club. Needless to say, no one danced. But we did drink, and we drank a lot. There was nothing else to do.

O'Kelly In Front of Store 1969

The band played a mixture of rock and soul. They made the mistake of taking requests. A white guy was yelling, "Play the fuck'n Rolling Stones" directly into the face of a black guy who was yelling, "Play some modder fuck'n James Brown." It was inevitable that punches would be thrown, and they were. Just as the whole drunk place erupted into a fight there was a loud CA-BOOM. The building shook and the lights went out. Someone yelled, "Incoming!" Some hit the floor, and some hit the door, running to bunkers outside, which waited for just such occasions.

In the bunker the two guys who started the fight chatted as though they were at a Sunday school social. Odd, I thought. A fight over music seemed petty now. A hit would have killed fifty of us. No doubt, the VC knew that the club would be full. After it was over, I went back to the outpatient barracks. A joint was being passed. I partook, something I rarely did, but somehow it was in order that night.

Next morning everything seemed oddly surreal. It was one of those days when it seems as though you are not doing anything, but are watching someone else go through his life. I was walking back to the barracks after breakfast. There were sand dunes to my left, blocking my view of the beach. A soldier stumbled off the dunes and almost fell on top of me.

"Sorry," he said. I accepted his apology. Then he asked a curious question: "Are you From Tennessee? I need someone from Tennessee."

I told him that I was from Georgia. Then he said, "I guess that is close enough. There is no one else around. Would you like to meet a Stars and Stripes reporter?"

I answered affirmatively, assuming that I was to be interviewed. He told me that his name was O'Neal and that he was the reporter's body guard. I was a little surprised by this and asked, "Body guard? I didn't know that Stars and Stripes reporters had body guards." I was thinking of Ernie Pyle, the famous WWII reporter. I didn't think he had a bodyguard.

O'Neal said, "This one does. He's a Senator's son."

We climbed over the sand dune to the beach where a tall, broad-shouldered man was standing with arms folded. Four soldiers were seated on the sand at his feet. Al Gore stuck out his hand and I shook it saying, "Hello, I'm Bob O'Kelley. Did you want to interview me?" thinking maybe he was doing a story on a regular soldier's life or something similar.

Al Gore looked surprised and said, "What gave you that idea. I sent O'Neal to find someone from Tennessee."

I answered, "Well I am from Georgia .Is that close enough?"

O'Neal interjected, "He is the only one around."

Al Gore never said why he wanted someone from Tennessee, and I was not exactly sure why I was there, but I did join Gore's group on the beach. Of course, I had no way of knowing, at the time that I was talking with a future Vice President of the United States. In no way did I feel that I was in the presence of someone who should be respected. After all, he was a Senator's son, not a Senator, and he was not the first Senator's son I had met.

We made small talk for few minutes. Hoping to find some common ground in our college experiences, I asked him, "Where did you go to college?"

Gore answered, "Harvard." I was impressed and said, "I graduated from West Georgia College." I could tell that Al Gore was not impressed. He said, "Never heard of it." And he said it with an attitude, which irritated me.

It became apparent to me that Al Gore did pretty much what he wanted to do without answering to anybody. I asked him how long he had left "in country." He told me that he was going to get out early to go to Divinity School. It seems that all one had to do to get out of Viet Nam was to get accepted to a Divinity School, which he had done. No one else in the group was aware of this law. I had never heard of it. I wondered if his father hadn't got this law passed just for the benefit of Al. When I asked him if he was going to be a preacher, he only repeated, "I am going to Divinity School." I didn't inquire any further.

The conversation turned to politics. I was more or less a liberal. Most young people were in those days. Gore was extremely liberal. He ranted about his opposition to the war, and his opposition to Nixon, but when he railed against wealth and privilege, I could not believe what I was hearing, and said, "Al, as I see it, you are the embodiment of wealth and privilege. You are sitting here with a bodyguard, doing what you want, when you want, and where you want, plus you have concocted this scheme to go home at your convenience, and you have nerve to rail against privilege. Take a look at yourself."

Befuddled by my statements, Al Gore blurted out, "Well, I was raised to be President." This statement was totally ridiculous to me, and it made me even angrier. Every child in America had a parent tell him or her: "Some day you might be President." It certainly didn't make you special. I reacted in a loud voice, "Raised to be President!! What the fuck, I thought that we fought a revolution to do away with royalty."

For protection from my verbal arrows, Al Gore seemed to build a mental shield around himself. He pulled his knees closer to his chest, sat there for a minute, and then said to his bodyguard, "Let's go."

As they left, I called out, "Hey, Al, I wouldn't vote for you for dog catcher."

After he left, I decided to give up my impromptu R&R and go to the doctor. My eye was more serious than I had thought. Much to my surprise, they admitted me to the hospital.

The Art of Foster's Store

A Zig Zag Man by Allen McMillon 1970

INKLINES

Eclectic Art 1970

Michael Kuczmarski

Chapter 21

The Music

By Walter Carmichael

Walter Carmichael 1970

In the last years of the decade of the sixties, the Foster's Store music scene was the same scene that was going on from California to New York. The music had a hard driving rebellious beat and lyrics that everyone could hear but only us boomers could understand. What seemed like scattered words and chord changes to the WWII generation were the sermons of revolution to us.

Arriving in 1966 with a stack of Stones and Beatle records and dance music from James Brown, Otis, Ray Charles, and other soul giants I was ready to rock through my college career, but not prepared for the albums that would be added to that collection or the philosophies that came with them. Having already lived through the British Invasion of the early sixties, I thought I was hip to all that was waiting for me at Left Georgia.

Little did I know that over the next few years the message in the music would change from an invasion from outside to a call for evolution from within. I grew up in Jackson where the only rebel music was hidden away in the garbled lyrics of the Kingsmen's "Louie Louie", and we all showed our patriotism by singing along on the chorus of Sgt. Barry Sadler's "Ballad of the Green Berets." "A hundred men will try today, but only three will wear the Green Beret. Fighting men from the sky, men who jump and men who die," or something to that effect made us proud to be from a country who had men to waste, and bombs to kill. But over the next few years the stories from our brothers returning from a war they didn't understand changed all that along with the fashions and consumption goodies we sought.

It all started innocently enough. Ed next door in that Pritchard dorm had the first Hendrix album, which really rocked, but just what was a "Purple Haze." Later that quarter I ended up down in David's room. He was living with the hall councilor, John (a real serious guy who was in pre-med) and they gave me an introduction to the folk music of some Yankee named Bob Dylan. I was familiar and liked Dylan's electric sound on "Like a Rolling Stone," but this album was something else. My review was something like, "There's no beat to dance to, he's got the worst voice I ever heard, and I hope you stole this album and didn't pay good money for it." It took a trip through Army basic training where I learned to be a killer and some after-hour's chemistry tutoring from Bateman before I could hear the meaning in, "The times they are a changing."

That meaning has flipped on me because now I'm a parent of two college students and like other "mothers and fathers from across the land, I tend to criticize things I don't understand." I don't want to believe "my son and daughter are beyond my command" but it is as true today as it was then; so I better learn to "lend a hand" because I'm not "getting out of the way." (You know you're getting old when your own children can use your lyrics against you. Take my advice. If your children haven't stumbled across your record collection yet, dump the records or the turntable quick.)

But even though the music of the late sixties was like an underground newspaper that kept us informed about war and political events that the print and media of the air were either censoring or completely ignorant of, I tended to stick with the protest music that had a beat. And I guess that's why the Stones were always with me. After all, "What can a poor boy do, except to dance to a rock'n'roll band, because the streets of Carrollton just ain't no place for a street fighting man." And dance we did.

If I had been born with any musical talent, I'm sure I would have already died with a guitar in my hand but when God only gives you feet and booty to shake, you make lemonade or anything else the girls want. Left Georgia may not have had a football team, may not have had fraternities or sororities in '66, may not have had University in the name, but we did have girls. And the girls of Left Georgia were the greatest. I partied at a lot of colleges during those years and had great times at other institutions but I always loved, thought about, and came home to our girls. They were beautiful, unpretentious, didn't take any shit off of us, and they could really dance. Even in the later glam rock disco years of the seventies, nobody looked or moved better on top of the big speakers at the *Slimlight* than Marilyn.

I think it was in the spring of '67 that I moved into one of Dr. Cruz's houses on top of a hill out on Lovern Road. I lived with Richard, Marshall, David, Doug, and Jim. These guys and several others ended up starting the SAO fraternity, which became the Kappa Sigs. We had some great parties out there and I really liked the place because of its isolation from the rest of the Carrollton world. That's why I trusted it to another dorm mate, the Spinks, to look after it for me during the summer. Mickey assured me the place would be cared for, and awaiting my return that fall.

It was waiting all right, just like a bear trap, make that babe trap. Spinks had restocked the place with friends that defiantly weren't on the academic fast track but were a tight loyal bunch mainly made up of the Rockmart mafia. K. C., Bob, Cooper, Billy were some of them but I'm having trouble with the rest. There were so many people in and out that I don't really remember who was paying rent or just crashing there for a few weeks. I think David had come up with the name of Animal Farm after some book we were supposed to read in English that spring. But since the Rockmart crew couldn't spell "animal", they shortened it to "The Farm" and the parting really began in earnest.

Most of us were working jobs on the weekends, which put a lot of pressure on us to make up the partying during the week. Sunday through Thursday nights were wide open. I had a good tube type double amp stereo system with big speakers that was set up in the living room and never turned off. I also made a strobe light out of an old electric fan and a piece of plywood with a hole the size of a spot light in it. By regulating the fan speed you could get any kind of strobe effect you wanted. The Animal Farm was the hottest dance club disco ticket at West Georgia. It only got sort of quiet at night when the last record hit the last grove and just clicked through the darkness until dawn. Unfortunately for the rest of us, Cooper had an early class.

That spring someone stole Doug's classic 1967 Shelby Mustang right out of the yard after one all night party. Cooper wasn't taking any chances. Losing a classic collector Mustang is one thing, but the thought of losing his motorcycle was more than he could stand. So the Triumph always spent the night inside with us, down the hall next to the bathroom. For some reason Cooper got stuck with an 8:00 am class, which meant he had to be out of bed by 7:45. Every day (or most every day) he awoke, went down the hall, took the tone arm off the record that was clicking, put on "Going up the Country" wide open, and went back to the bathroom to quickly brush his teeth. If the heavy base from Canned Heat hadn't woken everyone up by then, starting the Triumph and roaring off down the hallway did. Several of us would think about getting out of bed and giving Cooper hell about his inconsiderate behavior toward the rest of us, but we never did. I didn't learn this at Left Georgia but I knew from early childhood in Butts County that you didn't come between a man and his motorcycle.

The music at The Farm was not political. It was all about the beat and dancing with those good looking girls that really knew how to shake that thing. The Temps, Tops, Tams, Swinging Medallions, Sam and Dave, Aretha and other tunes that Spinks still dances to today were at the top of the charts. Janice would offer us a piece of her heart, we would all scream along with Dixie, and at some point "Flat and Scruggs at Carnegie Hall" would come on and we'd buck dance to "Foggy Mountain Breakdown" and sing the chorus to "Martha White". Does the flour still feature "Hot Rise"? In other words, totally mindless music generated to appeal to the feet not the mind. We had a great time that fall and somehow survived the partying, the car wrecks, the gunfire, and the music with only minor casualties. The police only showed up a few times and only on one of those occasions was it an official raid complete with search warrant. But since Bad Russ was holding all the goods down in one of the old motel rooms that Cruz set up down in the flood plain nothing was found except some

missing tombstones.

Carrollton Band Possum Trot

It was still a pretty simple semi-innocent music party scene for me at that time, but it all changed fast when Bateman turned me on one day in his trailer behind The Farm. After spending most of a day and night between two car speakers on the bed playing a Led Zeppelin II eight track around and around my musical taste changed dramatically. It was time to "Ramble On". After a couple of tokes on the water pipe , Dylan's verse was magically translated into something I could understand but not put into words. And such was the language of the times. A whole new meaning for life was coming over the outlaw FM stations. It was something the government couldn't understand, stop or translate into anything that made sense to the straight heads. You have to remember that by this time the FBI had been working on deciphering the "Louie, Louie" lyrics for eight years with no success.

It's still hard to believe that opinion on the Viet Nam war flipped so fast. We went from having a right wing "Kill a Commie for Christ" attitude to a "Flower Power" and "Make Love Not War" philosophy overnight. All of a sudden communist-inspired losers like Cassius Clay, Dr. Martin Luther King, Jr. and hippie dippy leaders from the left coast started making sense. And then religious leaders from other denominations who had been in hiding discovered the teachings of Jesus and they started asking political leaders embarrassing questions like, "What in the hell are we doing in Viet Nam?" And when all the politicians and military leaders could only answer, "Well, we've got all these bombs, planes, tanks, and other great gear we've got to do something with, and if we don't kick a little ass every once and while the economy will suffer," a sudden kind of morality appeared from nowhere and everybody but Nixon jumped on the bandwagon.

I will always give the credit for blowing the cover off the propaganda the government was sending out to the returning troops from Viet Nam (especially the draftees). The truth they brought back woke us all up. However, I'll give the songwriters the credit for spreading that message and giving us anthems to march by. The thoughts behind those lyrics made us examine what was real in life. We dumped a lot of material goods that stood in the way. We didn't spend a lot of money on our wardrobes, but spent a lot of time in front of mirrors to be sure we hit the streets looking like someone who never stood in front of a mirror.

We tuned in, turned on, and dropped out. We swore to return to nature, love our fellow man (make that women in my case), and to never again return to a materialistic world dominated by right wing phonies. But in the end we are Americans and we get bored quickly. So when we hit the discos a few years later dressed in poly-something plastic with stacked dancing shoes and John Travolta moves we shouldn't have been surprised. It was great music, with a beat for dancing. And just like at The Farm, you go where the girls are and you get there looking like they want you to look.

The late American philosopher Sonny Bono said it best about us and our country, "The Beat Goes On!", whether you are listening, dancing or not.

Annual Spring Concert Stills by Walter Carmichael

Playing,

Listening

All profits gained in the sale of this DVD will go to a fund designated to do away with crash commercialism, right. ..

-The DVD Deal –

Tear this page out of the book and mail it to me, Wayne Lankford, along with twenty bucks to: Foster's Store DVD Deal, P. O. Box 36186, Hoover, Al 35244. Send four more dollars for postage and your address.

This DVD contains all the pictures on the website along with some tunes you can zone out to while you look at the pictures. What?

Name_____

Mailing address_____

City_____State_____Zip_____

Number of DVD's ordered_____

Amount $ Enclosed_____

The Art of Foster's Store

Unknown student 1970

Displaying the American flag like this for some was a form of protest. By others it was considered artful. Maybe just warmer.

Historical Photo - Foster's Store 1950's

Duffy's Sausage Truck and Man in Overalls

Chapter 22

The Poetry Pages

By various and sometimes unidentified poets

The Prescription for Mediocrity

To be friends you must sometimes toil

But rewards overcome sacrifices

When mutually conceived relations

Becomes a curing salve

The friendship which you have willfully achieved

May become non-willing unconcerned-ness.

As disinterest grows like algae

In fishbowls without snails.

And our judgmental inconsistencies

Take over and we are once again its slaves

The Cure:

 3 grams of unselfish consideration once a day

Minus 3 ounces of unjustifiable onion

Plus a smile

Add 3 cents worth of joy

Commit the moment to just being real.

Share it with a friend.

Upside Improvisational Downsides

 When you're tired and confused

Go out and beat up an old lady;

If a brother needs a helping hand

Give him a foot right in the Balls

Join society and get your head together

If it's not bothering anybody kill it;

When you're sinking in the muck of reality

Hold your breath

When you're all up tight

Run around the block till you're dizzy;

When you're depressed

Chew some bubble gum;

If you're bored

Start a fire;

When you're horny

Go out with a cripple;

When the establishment wants a piece of ass

You may as well spread your cheeks...

Unscheduled Examinations

While walking in my mind one warm and thoughtful day

I revised the edition so that it could be more easily digested.

The path leads through streams,

Fields, and flocks of birds,

Villages, forests, hills, pills, spills and doors.

This striving for identity is a ruthless haunting game.

To move freely in the vacuums of life and times

I find myself mixing a deadly brew

Of judgments, and observation

Interlinked with speculation and mindless participation

Stumbling on a rock to find

One time the other side is cool and refreshing

Observe the parasites which make up our masses.

 I remember about tripping and all that stuff.

I have no problem with using names

Like Sleepy or Wade Longham

And in my meager opinion

This somewhat adds to the flavor of the story and the time.

Let's face it we were all someone else

Back then, in every case of beer.

You make so many contacts

Looking back on what that was

As this somehow helps as

We try to understand what is

And lord only knows about what will be....

See you sometime in now or then

If not eternity.

Sleepy Jack

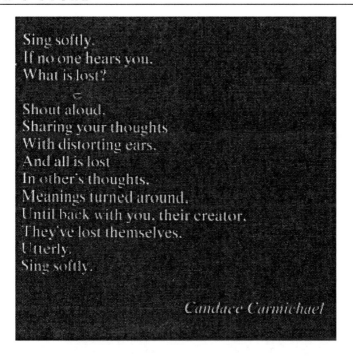

Sing softly.
If no one hears you.
What is lost?

Shout aloud.
Sharing your thoughts
With distorting ears.
And all is lost
In other's thoughts.
Meanings turned around.
Until back with you, their creator.
They've lost themselves.
Utterly.
Sing softly.

Candace Carmichael

Artifact - West Georgia College Meal Ticket

Store Mate Candee Carmichael

The Art of Foster's – From Eclectic 1971

Michael Kuczmarski

Chapter 23

Current Events II

By Foster's Store Staff

New Hominoid Discovered by College Student ?

Meet

Westgeorgenous Pabstblueribbineous

Recent photos believed taken by Anthropology student Winston Spacey.

"The Feed n' Seed is completely grown over with privet hedge and small pine trees" , says Physical Anthropology major, Winston Spacey. "I just wanted to see for myself. I'd read about the site on the web, and because I drive by there at least twice a day from my home in Bowden, it was easy, I just pulled into the lot and snuck around through a small opening between the east side of the store house and the overgrowth."

Impassable West side   **Crawlspace entry point**

Spacey tells of crawling on his belly for about twenty yards thru the dense jungle, when he noticed an opening where direct sunlight was reaching the ground. "It all just sort of opened up all at once, and there he was, just chewing on what looked like a piece of an old Frisbee. Beyond that there was the remains of what looked like an old couch and a large wire spool just in front of what must of been the ruins of the old Feed n seed. There looked to be several of the apelike creatures just sitting around doing nothing, just enjoying the day. It was then I saw what I guessed to be the dominant male ape, and just before he noticed me, I was able to snap a quick picture with my digital camera; I guess that commotion got his attention as he immediately started towards me. I got out of there as fast as I could; it all kind unnerved me."

What Spacey thought might be good subject for a term paper in his Ethnology class has turned into an event which may change his life forever. "I could probably get Grant Money all the over the place to study this ", guesses Spacey.

It was previously believed that Phil Spackman and Richard Duncan were the last inhabitants of the Feed n' seed. This, yet to be confirmed, discovery may throw that theory out the window and open up a totally new discussion as to what was going on during the last days of student habitation at the complex known generally as "Foster's Store".

Family Resemblance?

Spacey closed the interview with one very disturbing theory he says will require much inspection. "It just seemed odd to me, maybe just a little too coincidental, that this apelike guy resembled so much physically two of the stores more notorious residents, Spackman and Duncan.

Spackman   Pabstblueribbineous   Duncan

Spacey ended saying that the fact that he was only a sophomore inconsequential, stating that just because the prevailing science accepts the fact that theses kinds of physical changes would require billions of years to transpire, it doesn't mean that such changes couldn't occur de-evolutionally, given the consumptive and social habits of some of the last residents here.

More on this ongoing story as events transpire. Attempts to contact either Duncan or Spackman, have been so far unsuccessful. Investigation continues.

the editors

The Art of Foster's Store

Allen McMillan 1970

Chapter 24

The Great Coleslaw Massacre

By Allen McMillan

"The time has come," the Walrus said, "To talk of many things:

Of shoes -- and ships -- and sealing-wax –Of cabbages -- and kings --

And why the sea is boiling hot --And whether pigs have wings."

Lewis Carroll, Alice in Wonderland

On a warm, calm Carrolton day, several of the Foster's gang; Dan, Wayne, Jim, Mac, Bobo were alternately throwing a Frisbee, drinking beer and enjoying a bit of "herb." As was often the case while we relaxed, we talked and discussed . . . thoughts, career plans, ideas, girls, world events and the ever-present War in Vietnam. I'm not too sure anyone our age yet understands the war: its purpose, how it all got started, why we were there, if we were winning or losing. To add insult to injury, the media of the day didn't seem very clear on the issue either.

At Foster's, the focus was always on the activities of the moment. Bobo announced: "Let's have a Barbeque at my house." At the time he lived on the lake, had plenty of space – Bobo said he had the Barbeque covered. Wayne volunteered, "We'll make the coleslaw. How many people you think will be there?"

Bobo is Bob Abbott - eating Ice cream

"About a hundred" Bobo replied.

The day turned into evening, Wayne and I relaxed on the porch with a cold beer. I asked, "...Coleslaw for a hundred, won't that be expensive and a big deal?"

Wayne responded, "...Naw, I've made coleslaw hundreds of times. It's no big deal. We'll just be making a bigger batch."

Here we were both close to graduation; so I posed the following puzzle: "Just how much coleslaw you think an individual will eat?"

"I guess about a cup – I make some good coleslaw." Truth was, Wayne was and still is a good cook. I had no doubt the coleslaw would be good.

"How many heads of cabbage you think it'll take?" I asked.

Wayne took a long draught from his beer and looked into the distance, lost in thought. I could only imagine the mathematical equations running through that mind: mayo times shredded cabbage times Durkee's Salad dressing, plus pickles over 100. Far too advanced for me. His eyes opened, he cleared his throat, took another slug from the bottle and pronounced, "I'd say we need 50 heads of cabbage, maybe a few more to be on the safe side." Like so many things Wayne said, it made sense at the time.

Somebody lit a joint, the conversation changed and eventually we went to bed. Classes came and went as the days went by. Finally the day of Bobo's Barbeque was almost upon us.

"Hey Wayne, think we oughta do something about the coleslaw?"

"Naw, we can do it Friday night. We'll buy a 12pack, some mayonnaise, Durkees Dressing, some pickles, cabbage, and you and I can have a few beers and grate cabbage."

Again as with most of the things Wayne said, it all sounded reasonable to me.

Friday evening rolls around and we go out to buy cabbage. Now I ask you, dear reader, if you've ever tried to buy 50 heads of cabbage in a relatively small Georgia town. Cabbage isn't a much-sought-after vegetable. Unlike corn, tomatoes, beans, people just don't do a lot with cabbage. If you take a look at the national vegetable usage chart, cabbage ranks only slightly ahead of Brussels sprouts and kale. Not to demean cabbage or any other vegetable – cabbage is just not high in demand. We visited several grocery stores and markets and collected about 10 heads of cabbage.

"No worry we'll find more tomorrow; in the mean time we need to start drinkin' and fixin' the coleslaw we got." Again, it all sounded so reasonable.

Two beers later Wayne introduced me to the finer art of cabbage handling and the manufacture of coleslaw. "First, take the head of the cabbage and slam it on the counter top, like so." Amazingly after slamming the cabbage stem on the counter the stem and core pulled out easily, leaving me with a head of cabbage ready to grate. Wayne had an old, old grater, one I'm sure his parents had handed down to him. I got to work. Grating a head of cabbage is not difficult or strenuous work. Grating 10 heads, while Wayne mixed his secret coleslaw concoction of: mayonnaise, Durkees Dressing, salt, pickles, vinegar and just a few shredded carrots – is work. The beer made the coleslaw project somehow a bit more worthwhile. Six or so beers later we had every bowl, glass, container, pot, pan, tray we owned filled with shredded cabbage. Those of you who have never made vast quantities of coleslaw probably don't realize how much liquid can come from shredded cabbage – I know I never did. The liquid from every bowl, glass, container, pot, pan, tray was dripping onto the counters, tables and eventually the floor of the Feed & Seed kitchen. Luckily we were running out of beer, cabbage, bowls, glasses, containers, pots, pans, and trays. So we refrigerated what little we had. I began to think things weren't looking so good. So we went to bed with the words of Scarlet O'Hara: "...Tomorrow is another day."

Regardless of how I felt, we had to deliver – we had promised Bobo enough coleslaw for 100. It's hard to sleep when you're having difficulties meeting your obligations. Thanks to Wayne our obligation was coleslaw.

We got up pretty early, I'm just guessing about 10. Wayne and I began our quest for cabbage by visiting every small grocery, truck stand, bait shop and store that carried food of any type and, believe it or not, finally got 40 more heads of cabbage. We even had a few extra thrown in that "might be getting' some age on 'em." At one place the proprietor, an old man, looked Wayne square in the eye and asked "just what're you boys doin' with all this cabbage." Wayne answered, "Coleslaw."

When we left the storeowner had the strangest look on his face. What in the world were these two long hairs doing with that much cabbage?

We got back to Foster's just in time to get a frantic phone call from Bobo. "Where's the coleslaw? People are starting to gather and we're startin' the grill."

"Don't sweat it, we're almost on our way," Wayne lied.

"Mac, how fast can you grate this stuff?" Having no previous point of reference, this question was indeed difficult. If I could do one head of cabbage in five or so minutes, I figured I could do about ten heads of cabbage in an hour. At that rate Wayne and I could be finished in a few hours with the remaining 40 heads of cabbage. "Not good enough, we gotta get this coleslaw thing in high gear. We'll pace ourselves, every five heads of cabbage we'll stop and have a beer." That was another thing Wayne was good at – motivation and organization. We had a plan, two graters – we'd borrowed another one from Candae Carmichael. We had the purpose - coleslaw for 100. We had the ingredients – Wayne and I had just made the largest single largest Carrollton purchase of mayonnaise, Durkee's Dressing and sweet relish pickles.

We went to town. It was amazing: we were shredding cabbage in less than five minutes a head, and in some cases we were breaking the two-minute mark. Looking like two skilled Ginsu Masters, we had shredded cabbage everywhere. The kitchen table was completely covered, heaped and mounded with shredded cabbage. The counter tops were three feet thick with cabbage – we had completely run out of room we didn't have anywhere to put the shredded cabbage. For the first time in my life I saw fright in Wayne's eyes – the clock was ticking – Bobo was waiting and - our reputations, all be they shaky at best, were at stake. Precious minutes were being wasted, Wayne was thinking – the phone rings. "We gotta have the coleslaw, we're ready to put the chickens on and they won't take long – get your ass and the coleslaw over here, NOW!"

Up until that moment I had never experienced the urgency or importance of coleslaw. The floor was at least an inch thick with cabbage juice.

Wayne came alive. He thrived under pressure. He ran outside, to the barn adjacent to Foster's Store returned dragging an old plywood backstop, he quickly covered the backstop with plastic garbage bags and began heaping the shredded cabbage on top. That act freed space on the counters and kitchen table, we began to shred like mad. With concentration and focus, we were coordinated and orchestrated in purpose.

Wayne began to mix his secret ingredients: shredded cabbage, mayonnaise, Durkee's Dressing, salt and sweet relish pickles. I looked around and all you could see was mounds and mounds of shredded cabbage and gallons and gallons of cabbage juice everywhere, it was dripping from pans, through cracks in the table, from counters onto the cabinet doors and all of it eventually onto the floor. How could you mix this much stuff? It would have been tough with a commercial mixer. In my mind we were facing the impossible.

Wayne added some boards underneath the plastic covered plywood for support and began building the biggest mound of coleslaw ever made in any home kitchen. He added jar after jar of ingredients a few pounds of salt. Wayne employed a skillet rather than a spoon and began mixing. To this date that was the biggest food mess I've ever experienced. We were both covered with coleslaw. Depending on where you stepped, the floor was either real sticky or real slippery. It was almost impossible to walk.

Upon completion we both took a moment to share the pride of our masterpiece. If you were focused on just the coleslaw, that's all you saw. Anyone else would have wondered what these morons had to smile about. A quick purview and you had to wonder if Laurel & Hardy had just left "this fine mess."

We had to get to Bobo's and quick... what's a Barbeque without coleslaw? Wayne's idea was to carry the coleslaw using the two planks under the plastic covered plywood like a stretcher out to the car. Do you have any idea what that much coleslaw weighed? We couldn't even begin to balance it, much less lift it. No panic, we had more garbage bags, we began filling garbage bag after garbage bag with coleslaw. I backed up the purple Chevy as close as I could get to the Feed & Seed. We began carrying the garbage bags of coleslaw to the car. We quickly found that very large bags of coleslaw are unwieldy. The bags were stretching and beginning to break. By this time the coleslaw and cabbage juice were seeping everywhere throughout the Feed & Seed.

Wayne got a wild, crazed look and took off running toward Mr. Foster's house returning with Mr. Foster's wheelbarrow. We loaded that baby with as much bagged coleslaw, as it would hold. Some how we got my trunk filled with coleslaw and took off to Bobo's.

We arrived at just about the perfect time. We pulled up as close to Bobo's kitchen as possible and began scooping coleslaw out of the trunk into any bowl, glass, container, pot, pan, or tray we could find.

Bobo was outside grilling the chicken in some kinda wire frame contraption. There were a couple of kegs of draft beer and the chicken was just unbelievable – to this day I don't think I've had chicken any better. We ran out of chicken and coleslaw that night. Luckily the beer lasted much longer.

It took us days to get rid of the remnants of cabbage and coleslaw from the kitchen. We ended up just hosing that half of the Feed & Seed out. It was a mess all right, but for a moment it was a masterpiece.

Ask the Spirit Dude

Dear Connected One,

I seem to remember a rumor sometime around 1974 that one of the guys what lived at the store had a bit of a breakdown and moved to Atlanta for a while. I heard he had a really unique system for picking up babes. You know any thing about that?

MD Freak

Dear MD,

You must mean Walter. Yea he was a good boy, but a little strange. In order to overcome his shyness he developed a ventriloquism act with the stuffed head of a polar bear. He was also some kind of mind control expert. He and the bear head could make the chicks do anything. Their favorite thing was to make them think they were monkeys. People would throw peanuts at them and these women would scoop them up by the handfuls and eat the shells and everything. When Walter's medication finally kicked in, he quit the street circus troop he was a member of and became a disc jockey.

Walter and mind control subject.

Picture taken prior to successful medication program.

Support Your Team!

THE GREEN JAY RUSHERS

Chapter 24

✻ Headquarters ✻

By Wayne Lankford

In 1968 Sid Shortt opened a retail store at 401 Maple Street in Carrollton. Right on the main drag thru town, out in front of everybody, and in broad daylight, *Headquarters* opened its doors for business. The name of the store was a not-to-subtle title for a business, whose main customer base would be individuals, who, at the time, were referred to often and collectively as "Heads", short for names like, "Acid Head" or "Pot Head".

Yes, it is true, you could buy all sorts of clothing there, shirts and bellbottom jeans, men's and women's attire of the day, the latest in "hippie" fashion and all the clothing accessories you'd need to get that "with it" kind of feeling.

But a lot of Sid's customers were seeking out items not sold anywhere else in town. **Headquarters** was a **Head Shop**, first and foremost. For Hash pipes, water pipes and especially high quality rolling papers, Headquarters was the place to go. In Carrollton, it was the only place to go.

Marijuana rolling paper with peace signs & flag   Standard Zig-Zag

Today, selling these items is illegal, of course. Back then however, it was just frowned upon, and there was nothing legally anybody could do to stop it. At the time it was widely believed that the **FBI** kept the place under 24 hour surveillance. I always felt like I was having my picture taken if I even drove past the place, and I wasn't the only one.

Girls shopping for bellbottoms 1971

Recently, I asked Sid to estimate the number of single cigarette rolling papers he sold while the place was in operation between the years 1968 to 1973 when he converted the building into what it is today, ***The Maple Street Mansion****. "Certainly in the tens of thousands", he recalled, adding, "most of my customers for pipes and papers usually entered in thru the side door and bought cases of papers at one time, just to avoid having their pictures taken so many times by the FBI."

Sid & Doug Gill, as Paraphernalia Dealers

Doug, you might note, once played football at Georgia Tech.

If at the time Ed Tant was the number one threat to the safety and sanity of the good people of Carrollton because of his controversial views appearing in the School newspaper, Sid Short was number two. (Some might dispute my ranking system) There Sid was, the pied piper of Carrollton and WGC, playing a tune that was irresistible to most of a generation. Getting high was a political statement as much as anything else and Sid was pounding the drum every day from Headquarters.

Sid Shortt, Headquarters front porch 1971

If somebody wanted to, they could write a whole book about Sid and his success in life. All of us are shaped somehow by our circumstances and the people we meet along the way. Back in 1968 there was a whole town full of people who wanted him to fail and maybe that's how best to describe Sid Shortt: He sure disappointed a whole lot of people, just by being successful.

Some History about the building from Walter Carmichael

The mansion was built by L. C. "Mr. Cliff", Mandeville, founder of Mandeville Mills. L. C. gave most of the land for the college.

The home had the first phone system and running water, thanks to a copper water tank in the attic. First telephone system started by Mandeville and his partner a Mr. Chaney.

When L. C. Mandeville built his mansion on Maple Street close to his textile mill, he couldn't have imagined what his home would end up housing, or that it would be owned by someone like Sid Shortt, who would be selling items that put the business, customers and owners on the most wanted list. WC

Free Advertisement

Sid now in Helen GA

Go see him.

In memory of a friend of the revolution.

Chapter 26

New Foster's Store Coverage Continues

By The Staff

Church leader presents opposition to planned **"The New Foster's Store Mega Complex".**

Scene of chaos ensues.

A news conference was held this evening at the proposed site for the "New Foster's Store". Jacob Legg, Pastor of the **Church of the Cleansing Fire,** made an opening statement and took a few questions from reporters. Along with Pastor Legg a few of his supporters held lit torches illuminating the scene out in front of the now infamous and all but abandoned and overgrown site, just west of the U of WG campus.

"It's gone far enough! I am here tonight to let the world know, in no uncertain terms, that my followers and I, inspired by the only true God, will not allow this once den of inequity to raise its ugly horned head again."

Wearing a black robe complete with an embroidered red and gold flame sewed to the left breast side, and while standing on what looked like an empty case of returnable Pabst Blue Ribbon bottles, the Reverend Legg continued. "As soon as I read of the proposed stock offering in the Wall Street Journal from my home in Montana, ("my fortress of oneness") I knew my mission was clear. I should return here to Carrollton, to West Georgia, and offer my leadership to oppose this vile new venture."

Legg then provided some history about himself, and we soon learned that he also once attended West Georgia during the days that Foster's Store was in operation as a place of residence for college students. While he was doing that, a couple of his black robed supporters were passing among the crowd placing stickers, with either the word "fire" written in flames, or a single red and gold flame on the chests and backs of the gathered group of about 10 individuals, mostly media. From there, they then moved along to the front of the now abandoned store house and covered the door and windows with a similar sticker, complete with a toll free number for "donations". The donations, Legg offered, were to combat the ace legal team of Gungii, Clapsaddle, & Obberwolfer, that the New Foster's Store developers had put together in order to "disguise the real purposes of this "work of the devil himself". "Organized Blaspheming for profit is not a condonable enterprise", he added.

It was about that time that this reporter noticed a number of what looked like similarly-robed middle aged females setting up tables and spreading out small silver and gold pins and necklaces, each with a center piece of ruby colored glass spelling out the word "fire", or pins and earrings similarly adorned with red flames. I could see too that a booth was quickly being erected that had at its apex, a large neon flame that clicked on and off, lighting a display of books and audio tapes, all authored and produced, I learned, by Pastor Legg.

Just then, about at the same time they seemed to be finishing the adjacent "Swords of Light" and the "Food for Mighty Warriors" booths, the first of five tour busses arrived. The next thing I knew a Cable News helicopter was landing in the middle of the Bowden Road and a reporter was pushing his way, microphone and cameraman in tow, to the front of the crowd, where he too steps up on his own empty case of Pabst Blue ribbon bottles and begins questioning Pastor Legg. I couldn't hear a thing he was saying because at the same time, a band was beginning to play a kind of hard rock, hip hop rap version of "*Nearer My God to Thee*", while some guy who identified himself as an associate producer for *a major nightly news show*, inquires if I can be available as a guest for a "live" satellite hook up interview for this evenings show? The guy then hands me a press release, from Legg and *The Church of the Cleansing Fire*, in which Legg's spelled out a ten points summary outlining his movement's fervent opposition to the proposed building plans for The New Foster's Store. Lights are flashing from digital cameras taking stills of the reverend and a huge beam of light from one of the circling helicopters above is illuminating the entire scene.

All this, and then, about every police car in town pulls up and I notice a very calm Butch Gungi, lead attorney for the Bond Issue and the development board, along with the Chief of Police and District Attorney. Together they all wade into the throng of reporters and black robed and now electric (battery operated I'm guessing) torch carrying supporters as a police lieutenant hands Legg an order to "cease and desist" his "unlawful assembly".

Suddenly, there is the sound of an explosion and huge fireball spreads out and upward just about fifty yards east of the crowd's location. I can see someone has erected a bon fire with an effigy of Mr. Foster himself along with a scaled down version of the main storehouse atop the growing flames and now spreading among the wood pile below. About half of the robe wearing tour bus crowd, I estimate at about a hundred people, have formed four circles and are marching around in opposite directions, the pile of growing flames right next to the highway, chanting, "Praise the Lord, Kill the monster, Praise the lord, Kill the monster!" Kind of showy I suppose, but all pretty upbeat really.

There's a little pushing and shoving between the police and the *Church of The Cleansing Fire* people, but Reverend Legg, now equipped with a megaphone, extorts his supporters to be lawful, directing them to re-board their buses and meet back at the motels they've rented over in the Douglasville area. Legg makes one more statement saying "Our work is done for the night, but our mission is clear".

I see Butch Gungii is now walking back to his limo and I run after him to get his reaction to all this. "Hey Butch, what do you think about all this?" Butch pauses as he's about to enter the car, a smile beginning to grow across his face, which is still being illuminated by the flames of the bonfire, "You gotta love America," is his only comment.

The advance guy for the nightly news comes up to me with a sad look on his face, "Well, no remote tonight, maybe if we could've of gotten those guys in the robes to set the actual building on fire we would have had a chance for a small piece of "air-time", but they won't go for it, usually, if there's no blood, there's no story. Maybe, if they had clued me to the exploding bon fire?" I shrugged my shoulders in agreement and regret, adding finally, "Well, tomorrow is another day in Georgia."

"You got that right Scarlet!" is his only reply. I guess we all will just have to stay tuned. "It's just getting started", I mused to myself as I got in my car and pulled away. Then I wondered a bit further, "You suppose there really is a family of ape-like creatures living back there in the Feed N Seed?"

Historic Picture

History raising its head and a bottle of bourbon at the same time. Reason for fear?

Pre Tams Party Jackson Courts

Book Recommendation

The Complete Book on How to Teach Dog Meditation - Communicating with one's inner being is just the first step in finding your path in the universe. Everybody knows that. But what if you want to take your dog? Are you seeing the light? Well, **K. Allen McMillon** seems to have, or at least that's the gist of his theory put forth in this instructional How To Book. I found his stream of consciousness writing style somewhat troubling at times but my response was simply Pavlovian I'm sure. If you are interested in trying this with your own pets, you're advised to start them when they are Jung. The course time to complete canine harmony is about ten years. Plug that in your Day-timer and you're there.

The Art of Foster's Store

Half a Target and Some Blurry Spots

1971 Poster Art by Bill Harrell

Eclectic Poetry- from memory

What's that click behind Your Eyes?

All I ever wanted was to have you laugh with me,
but you never even turned you kaleidoscope eyes to me
anymore, baby.
I'm all cut up and empty from throwing myself against
your sparkling teeth, from trying to get out of the box
where you keep me.
But you never heal me anymore baby.
Why don't you ever answer your phone anymore baby?
It just rings and rings and rings and rings.

Mary Jo Muse

Chapter 27

Just Remembering Foster's Store

By and from a few old store mates

From Mark Pitstick

Mark & Shelly exiting Candee's place under storehouse

I lived at Foster's in the early 70's along with Chip Perdue and Frankie Shelly. I lived there again a couple of times over the next two years.

I remember that particular weekend well (when this picture was taken) because I hit a tree with Walter's car. I was trying to drive home from a Farm party that we had all gone to, only I was *SO* inebriated. Walter had thrown me his car keys about half way through the party and told me to drive his car back to the Store for him. He had hooked-up with some female friends and realized he wouldn't need his car. When my girlfriend and I finally left the party in Walter's car I promptly backed into a tree, denting and scratching the side of the car.

When I arrived at the Store I decided to leave a note on the car explaining what I'd done, that I was sorry and would pay for the damage. I was still in bed the next day around noon when there was a knock on my bedroom door. It was Candy Carmichael (she lived in the small apartment under the Store) and she began to tell me in a serious tone that she'd seen the damage to Walter's car. She then told me that they'd already had the damage appraised and that Walter had headed back to Atlanta. I then asked her what it was going to cost and she told me that it would cost like 400 bucks. By this time I'm wide awake and sitting straight up. I said something like, "Holy shit …!"

I look back up and see Candy laughing so hard she's bent over.

After a good laugh, I asked if Walter was mad with me. She told me heck no, it was an old beat-up car and he said another dent wasn't going to hurt anything.

Mark Pitstick and the crew

I had some great times at Foster's and still remember the wonder of lying on the floor in the music room, being high and looking up at the spots on the ceiling. If you looked long enough you realized they formed into a kind of pattern that only someone in an altered state could understand. There was also a small hole in the ceiling that housed a picture of Stanley Kubrick looking down at you. This was a very heavy place.

Mark Pitstick, Frankie Shelly, Chip Purdue,

Speaking of Stanley Kubrick,..

About 1971 Stanley Kubrick came to West Georgia to speak. I went to see him. As I remember it, Kubrick's topic was "The Future." I can still see him standing up there behind that lectern in one of the larger lecture halls in one of the newer buildings. Kubrick talked for about half an hour about what life might be like in a hundred years, a thousand years. He was sharing his vision with an audience of about fifty. I was sitting in the back of the hall when this guy in the front raised his hand to ask a question. He's angry; he wants to argue, start a fight—as I remember his tone and demeanor. He asked his question like "Hey, you idiot!" He didn't say those words, but that was his tone. "If there won't be any jobs in the future, if we won't have to work, what the hell are we going to be doing all our lives?" He was pissed off.

Do you know how sometimes you go to a large lecture class and the lights seem overly harsh? I remember Kubrick's forehead, almost white under those spotlights pointing down to him from the ceiling, the rest of the hall in dimmest light, that contrast: that shining reflection from his skin and behind him the blackness of the empty stage. I remember him taking a deep breath, shrugging his shoulders. Then a pause, a real pause.

I could sense exasperation suffusing his whole being, his eyes looking blankly out over us all and to the back of the room. Another deep breath. Then he moved from behind the lectern and walked out to the edge of the stage towards the guy who'd just asked the question. He looks right at him, right straight down to him, now away from the microphone and fully aware of that, in a voice loud enough that even I in the back of the dark room can hear.

"Well maybe, just maybe, if we don't have to spend our entire lives working to maintain our shelters and feed ourselves, maybe, maybe then, maybe at that time we will at last have enough time to finally get down to the real business of what being a human being really is."

The real business of being a human being: that's a thought I've never lost. I remember putting that picture of Kubrick up in that crack in the ceiling in the womb room. Yeah, I remember that. Foster's Store was a very heavy place.

wl

The Art of Foster's Store

Allen McMillan 1970 *Eclectic*

Neighborly

Mr. Bristol moved across the hall from Mr. Bender on the second floor of the old apartment house.

To show that he wanted to be a good neighbor, Mr. Bristol, on the first Wednesday, swept the whole hall and all the way down the stairs.

To show that he wanted to be a good neighbor, Mr. Bristol, on the second Wednesday swept the whole hall and all the way down the stairs.

This went on weekly for about five years. Then one day, a Thursday, Mr. Bender came home and the stairs and hall were dirty and he went into his apartment and got his shotgun and went across the hall into Mr. Bristol's apartment and said, "You lazy son of a bitch," and with that he blew Mr. Bristol's head into tiny pieces and then he swept the whole hall and all the way down the stairs.

Walter Carmichael

This next chapter might seem out of place to some. Nathan Barfield never lived at Foster's Store, so why include anything about him in this book? I guess the answer is that his name just kept being mentioned by former store mates. Nathan died a few years ago. It was very sad and many people miss him. The thing is that there are probably enough Nathan Barfield stories to fill a book. Maybe somebody will see this and do that. Maybe that's the real reason he's mentioned here. I don't know.

I guess the same goes for Bill Bateman. But Bateman did live at Foster's Store, at least for an instant. Like Nathan, Bateman choose a path different from the rest of us, but not different from paths others were taking all over America at the time. These two guys are descriptors of lifestyles that can have deadly effects. Alcohol destroyed Nathan Barfield. Bill Bateman destroyed himself another way.

Maybe the way to read this chapter is forgetting if you can that these are single individuals. Think of them as *alpha* and **beta.** They just happen to represent more than what they appear to represent. I don't know again.

Chapter 28

The Good, and the Bateman

First, About Nathan Barfield

By Richard Hurt

Nathan Barfield   1973

Bill Bateman   1968

The first time I saw, or should I say heard, Nathan Barfield was in the summer of '69 at The Farm. I remember having to park out in the pasture because the place was so crowded and then hearing the band and trying to get into the living room that was so packed I couldn't even see the band. Everyone was watching the band and no one was dancing. I couldn't see the players but I could hear the guitar and all I wanted to know was, who is that guitar player? Eventually I got close enough to see Nathan wailing away on his gold top Les Paul and just mesmerizing everyone. The house stayed that way until the band quit playing.

The second time I saw him was much more intimate. It was in the basement of The Farm and it wasn't nearly as crowded. There he was with Johnny Davis, Farm brother and younger brother of Duane Davis on Hammond B-3, Mike Green (now retired president of the Grammy's) on sax, James Street on bass, and a drummer whose name I can't remember. The band was *Shallowmar* and they were really good. I stood and watched the entire set without moving and just couldn't believe a band this good was playing in the basement of The Farm on a Saturday night when half of West Ga. College had gone home to Atlanta and elsewhere.

I have so many memories; I remember the first time I ever played a gig with him. It was 1974 and he was working in Terry Bonner's "Sweetwater" leather shop right off the square behind the Green Lantern.

I was tired of playing drums and just beginning to play guitar but not good enough to play out, and I would occasionally go down to the leather shop and get him to show me some licks. Eventually I got pretty good at copying him, but then he would play something fancy and blow me away. Once after doing this he smiled and said; "You never catch up." How true.

Nathan knew how determined I was to be a guitar player and instead of badgering me for switching instruments like most everyone else, he asked me to join his band as a percussionist/harmonica player. My first gig not on drums was at the Moose Lodge and I believe the name of the band was *Fat Fox* with Joe Kent.

Having never played any instrument but drums at a gig you can imagine how excited and nervous I was. We played several gigs after that and I loved not being behind a set of drums and actually being able to play some melodies on a few songs. Because at the time he asked me I was still not playing the guitar, his invitation did a lot to bolster my confidence in playing something besides the drums. I had learned to play harmonica from Bob Cason, an old roommate who was real good, and lucky enough to be asked by Nathan to play some gigs.

In the summer of '74 I was a soundman for a few months for *Rocket* which consisted of Nathan, Ricky Fowler, Don McWhorter, Russell Daniel, and a keyboardist named Doug whose last name escapes me. I remember a road trip to some gig in Alabama when I was sitting in the back of the van and playing harmonica. At some point, Nathan, who was sitting in the front yells back at me: "Damm it Richard, quit playing that harmonica! You sound like some old drunk blues guy!" Everyone broke up laughing but I was humiliated. Later I realized he had given me the best compliment possible.

Nathan was quite an influence on me from the first time I saw him at *The Farm* in 1969, wailing away on his gold top Les Paul, right thru his stint with Ziggurat when he would sometimes get so outside he'd sound like Steve Morse on acid. In 1984 he formed the band *NightWing* with Steve Smith on drums, James Hornsby on vocals and Marty Lovorn on bass while I was playing weekends at a biker bar on Lawrenceville Hwy. Nathan and Steve and their soundman Terry came by one night and asked me to join the band and I've always regretted not doing that. I had a cushy gig where I didn't have to move equipment and a short drive and thought that's where it was at. I later realized that *Nightwing* would have been one of the best bands I'd ever played in. Nathan was always way ahead of everyone else in talent and I think he was a little disappointed that his talents had never been discovered, but that seems to be the norm in the record business. He is sorely missed musically and personally.

Richard Hurt

From Walter Carmichael

Nathan Barfield (THE GOOD)

The last time I saw Nathan and heard Nathan play was at the Mansion in 1993. Richard Hurt had invited me to an annual event sponsored by friends of the late Steve Smith. They organized themselves under the name of the *Zachariah Foundation.* Different bands and musicians played at these events over the years and donated over $50,000 to different charities.

Nathan on campus circa 1970

During the West Georgia years I had heard Nathan perform with different groups, mostly made up of Carrollton musicians or students from the college. I considered Nathan a friend although I can't say I really knew who he was. In conversations with me he struck me as a private person who guarded himself against others getting in his space but he may have just been guarding himself against me.

He was a good guitarist in those days but the one I saw at the Mansion that night was a great guitarist. Richard and others at the event informed me that Nathan had been a professional all those years in between and showed up for the event every year with his band *Iron Horse*. As they say, practice makes perfect.

Mickey Spinks and Steve Smith, right, with dates

I remember that Iron Horse was a solid band and all enjoyed their set. I really don't remember what they played but they played it well with a lot of energy. But I do remember that at some point Nathan came out alone and played solo. I think it was held around the Fourth of July but it may not have been. But for some reason he played a semi-Hendrix version of "The Star Spangled Banner" and it just knocked me out. Number one, I was surprised to see him on stage alone.

He never really struck me as a person who wanted the solo spotlight on himself, although when you play lead guitar that's what it's all about. Later in the evening, we got together and talked for a while. I came away knowing nothing more about Nathan that I didn't already know, which as I said was nothing.

Later in the year we went to the Georgia Music Hall of Fame Award Show and ran into **Mike Greene**. I told Mike that I had seen Nathan perform a few months earlier and that he was playing great and added that I was surprised that he had continued a music career for all those years. That life is so tough off stage, especially when you have to deal and live with a bunch of musicians in a band. Greene responded with,

"What else could Nathan Barfield do?" Hey, don't ask me. I never really knew the guy.

Nathan Was a Friend

By Roger Hornsby

Nathan was a friend though I couldn't say a close one. But, hell, how many close friends can any of us say we have? He was a guarded fellow, as some may recall. It took a while to see through the façade of hardness to a genuinely good, honest heart that lay underneath.

I'd heard Nathan a time or two and recall being impressed with his playing, but my first recollection of one on one with him was when he worked for Neil Ballew's music store in downtown Carrollton. I had just bought my Gibson ES-335 and could not get it to tune up to suit me. A couple of others had tried without success to help me out. Nathan took pity on me and spent a good deal of time helping me get the lady where she sounded acceptable to my ears. I really appreciated his effort and knowledge and our relationship had its beginning.

We never played in a band together, just an occasional electric or acoustic jam. But over the years we would take in watching each other's group perform and offer praise, support and constructive advice. And numerous times our band Zachariah would share the bill with his Iron Horse for the Zachariah Foundation's Freedom Jam. (That group has raised over $100,000 and still counting in honor of Steve Z. Smith) I thought frequently about getting him to help me with my amateur guitar playing but never seemed to get past my laziness to do so.

Our biggest connection, believe it or not, was in the realm of residential construction. I made my 'real' living as a carpenter/contractor and on two different occasions Nathan filled in as my 'right-hand' man. The first was on an oriental style retreat for a therapist just outside Carrollton. I had my doubts about how it was going to work hiring a lead guitarist but I was in a real need of help and Nathan was the best I could come up with. If you knew Nathan picturing him in the hot sun doing heavy lifting, sawing and hammering all day would not be easy. He was a musician to the core. But he never disappointed me. He was loyal – on time and gave his all every day. He truly gained my respect because it was obviously not easy for him. We were working this job together when Steve Smith passed away. That bonded us even more.

The next occasion I was again in need of help building a house and Nathan needed money as well. I recall us bickering on his wage. I finally offered him $12/hr and he got a kick out of razzing me – saying he would have done it for $10. He knew me and I knew him well at least on this one level. I appreciated him being there when I needed him.

I last saw Nathan just a couple of weeks before he passed over. It was in Home Depot. As most usual I was on a tight schedule – rushing there for some supply and trying to get wherever it was I was headed next so that I could be efficient. I passed Nathan with his skinny white legs protruding out from a pair of shorts. He, of course, was in the opposite situation with no place he needed to be. We shook hands and spoke briefly – then I excused myself and hurried away to some task that holds little or no meaning in the long run. If I had only known I would never see him again....

I know this world did not live up to many of the dreams that Nathan had – that at times they were so close... only to slip away. But I hope he knows how he touched me and that I have really good feelings whenever his memory passes through.   Thanks Nathan.

The Art of Nathan Barfield

Back Cover of Eclectic Fall 1970 by Nathan Barfield

Then there's Bill Bateman.

I know Bill was around West Georgia and Atlanta a lot, but I'm not really sure if he was ever enrolled. While researching this book I discovered the most amazing thing! Bateman actually lived for a time at Foster's Store. I got this receipt out of Mr. Foster's receipt book. He was there.

To those who never saw his halo, never heard his laughter after he cut you down, he may appeared as a dark figure racing through a darker night. He was cast in the role of a drug dealer; the times demanded someone to play that part. We knew all that, but he never sold a single thing to anybody I ever knew, nor did I ever see him ever use any drugs, of any kind. We played football every Sunday afternoon in Chastain Park for a couple of years at least. I wanted to leave this next piece out of the book. But we all need to be reminded that even in times of madness and war, man's greatest battles are fought within over one's soul. People like Bill were around and are around. Maybe you knew a Bill Bateman? Maybe you just thought you knew him.

But here goes anyway. A partial portrait of,.......................................

.

Bill Bateman (THE BAD)

By Name withheld

Bill was one of those guys in life that always made me wonder 'where did I go wrong?' Here's a guy without a degree, who never works yet lives a lifestyle I can only dream of. I have a few Bateman stories that are so unreal, I won't even bother telling them.

Because of Bateman I have:

* been interrogated by the F.B.I.

* been interrogated by the City of Atlanta Police

* been interrogated by Fulton County Police

* been handcuffed by the Atlanta police

* spent an evening with Al Kooper

* met Ted Nugent

* met Vanna White

* met Sid & Marty Krofft

* saw an X-rated puppet show performed by a puppeteer who worked with Sid & Marty Krofft

* had the same puppeteer explain the future of X-rated puppets as the next "entertainment frontier"

* had my ass saved by Bateman brandishing a loaded weapon (it was his fault to begin with)

* risked my life by Bateman brandishing a loaded weapon on more that two occasions

* avoided arrest, once by taking a U-Turn on Peachtree doing at least 90 miles an hour

* looked under my bed to find a suitcase filled with cash and over 1 lb. of cocaine

* been to parties with the likes of people I could have never imagined existed

* met and had a long discussion with a pimp

* met and had a long discussion with a hooker

* met other countless characters, either of note or notorious

Please don't use my name. Perhaps asking others to add to the above list, much like the "Auto Bahn" list on the bathroom wall at the *Place on Paces* would better profile the life and times of Bill Bateman. To this day the man is an enigma, I never really knew him although, I did get close on a couple of occasions.

By Walter Carmichael

A few words here about the late Bill Bateman (if that was his real name). He didn't have to die to be called the late Bill Bateman because he was always late. He was always arrogant, spiteful, conniving, disrespecting of authority or disrespectful of those who were respectable of authority. And those of us who spent time with him always left with the same question, "Why in the hell am I spending time with this guy?"

Bill with Malamute pup "Thunder"

Spending a night partying with Bateman meant that you put your life, reputation, jail time, family relations on the line. But from the first time you met him all of that was understood. So you had nobody to blame but yourself when things went bad and things went bad with Bill every night. Making the decision to hook up with him was like saying, "OK God, I'm putting it all on the line here; take me if you want me."

There are so many stories from so long ago I could throw in here to make the point but those of you who knew him all have your own stories and I'm sure you've got stories wilder than mine. The wrecked cars, flunking the draft physical, drug deals gone bad, lovers gone bad, fights gone bad, shootouts gone bad, Bill gone bad. But living on the edge with him at least made you feel alive—real alive.

Example number 1: Bateman and I walk into Grant's Lounge late one night to hear some of the Macon bands jam with their magic music. (Grant's Lounge is a black club where all the Capricorn musicians and Capricorn want-a-be's came to be seen and play.) It looked like a real rough place but Mr. Grant always kept a tight lid on the bar and there was very little trouble there.

Bateman walked in with me close behind. On the way back to the grill part of the club he arrogantly walked passed everyone giving them the evil eye. (Bateman always made sure he was seen more than anyone else.) Arriving at one of the tables in the back in full view of everyone, he picked up a loaded ash tray (remember ash trays?) and dumped it on Grant's floor saying loudly, "Grant's Lounge, the same old fuckin'dump it's always been." While I'm checking for the nearest exit, Bateman gets into some kind of friction with Grant's daughter Cheryl over the order and seems a little pissed that we've been there almost five minutes and the bouncers haven't tried to throw him out.

That reminds me of another Macon story. I need to ask Mann about it. They loaded up in VW bug and headed to the Led Zeppelin concert at the coliseum. Outside of Macon they had a flat. I think the car belonged to Bill and of course had no spare, no jack, no nothing except a head full of acid; but somehow they managed to make it to the show on time. I forgot who they ripped off to accomplish this but it was quite a story. I can't remember them all.

The first time I remember being in Bateman's presence was at Jackson Courts. Some of us were hanging out and somebody said, "Lookout, here comes that asshole Bill Bateman." This was during the straight head years and Bateman had short hair and an athlete's build. It was rumored that he was some kind of big time football player that was going to play for the Bulldogs but got injured. This was just one of the thousands of rumors about Bill heard over the years and maybe some of them were true, but you never knew. You always felt that he was behind about 90 percent of the rumors. You bring up a lot of bad points about Bill, but you had to give him credit for being an excellent self-promoter.

By the time I got back from active duty with the Army in '67 things began to change and so did Bateman. When I ran into him again he had let his hair grow long and gone to the Left Coast look. The people in Carrollton thought he had the Hippie look but Bill was never a hippie; he was too mean for the summer of love thing.

By that time Bill had taken on the lifestyle of a star. His motto should have been, "I don't want to be a rock star; I just want to live like one." And he did. We had some great times back then. Partying all night, riding motorcycles wide open through the night and engaging in other emergency room types of activities. I know that Bill was around West Georgia for quite a while, but I'm not sure if he was ever actually enrolled. He never talked about going to class but he could have. If he did he would be too ashamed to admit it and would have kept it hidden from us.

Bateman's mother must have dipped him in the same pool that Achilles' mother used because he always seemed to slide by the law and death. I mean this was the kind of guy that any policeman would love to bust and beat up on the way to the station, but he was always too fast or too passed out. The narc's couldn't set up a deal because his own customers couldn't even set up a deal. If you fronted him the money he defiantly wouldn't show up on time with the goods if he showed up at all. The secret to doing business with Bill was not to do business with Bill.

This brings up the story that happened outside of Richard's Nightclub in Atlanta. Bateman left to get something and when we found him in the parking lot, he had been beaten up by a client and he was pretty pissed, not because of his injuries but because the guy had taken his Rolex. At that time I didn't even know what wearing a Rolex meant. In later years I learned it was a very prestigious watch that did everything but keep time. So it was perfect for Bill.

We lost touch for a couple of years in the early seventies. Bateman had moved from the Hippie Dippie scene of the sixties into the New York cocaine club scene that was just blooming around Atlanta. When we hooked back up he had only expanded his rock star scene. He always had big hair, nice apartments or houses with plenty of expensive furniture and a nice fast sports car. And of coarse he always had a pretty, foxie, hip girlfriend that he delighted in treating like shit. The girls didn't seem to mind too much because he didn't treat them any different than any of the rest of his friends. Some said his money came from drug dealing; some said he was from a rich family who made their money out of white clay; some said he just ripped people off for a living. Some, like me, just kept their mouths shut and enjoyed him for what he was. What was he? Since I never asked questions, I never found out.

Over those years his luck ran out with the law and I would occasionally over hear conversations with lawyers about some bust or another. Bateman's attorney probably wasn't one of Atlanta's best, probably was working with the law but he had a great name—Roman

DeVille, or at least that what he told Bateman his name was. But good lawyer or not, to my knowledge, Bill never served time.

Story number what ever it is: This is the story I've been trying to get to because it's a classic tale of a night with Bill. We got in touch for some reason and he invited me up to a nice new home somewhere close to the new mall at Ashford-Dunwoody. He was living with an upscale oriental chick and an Alaskan malamute dog called Thunder. This was before he got into the Porsche cars he loved and he was driving a tricked out Triumph TR 6. He usually didn't like to hit the club scene until 10 or 11 and that's when we left that night under the influence of several something's.

At that time there was still some kind of happening scene in Underground Atlanta and we ended up there to hear some band at Sgt. Peppers. Bateman acted just like he did at Grants. I think he was upset because some of the band members had bigger hair than him and he wasn't getting the attention he deserved, so we left. Somewhere wandering around Underground between Piano Red's place and Lester Maddox's axe handle store we ran into this big, black haired, dude from New York. It may have not been New York but from the way the guy spoke he was definitely some kind of Yankee. Bateman and this guy seemed to have had some former kind of business association and had somehow remained on good terms. The Yankee had a bag of Reds, which he and Bill snacked on for the rest of the night. I didn't get into those downers because I knew I would just go to sleep but the Yankee and Bill seemed to speed off of them.

At some point they got bored with pissing people off in Underground and we left. For some reason the Yankee went with us, which was a little tough. I was already worried about Bill's high speed driving on Reds and there were only two seats in the Triumph. Bill drove, the Yankee rode shotgun, and I had a half a cheek on the Yankee's seat and half a cheek on the console. We roared off up I-75.

In those days there was an exit off of the expressway at the Varsity on North Avenue. Just after we passed the exit traffic was stopped for some reason. There was an 18-wheeler stopped dead in the road in the right hand lane. There were only two lanes and the left lane was packed with cars slowing down. Instead of waiting (waiting wasn't one of Bateman's strong points), he gunned it. I can still remember seeing the back end of that truck getting closer and closer as we were under full acceleration in second gear. As Bill hit third he swerved to miss the truck at the last second, but there was no place to go. Bill couldn't see that all the traffic had stopped in the left lane and although there was a spot for him, the car in front of that spot was parked waiting on a wreck to be cleared. At this point I'm saying the same prayer I used at this time of night whenever I was out with Bill. It went like, "Lord if you will just get me out of this one, I promise I will never have anything to do with the Devil's disciple again," while the Yankee is screaming, "YEA, YEA, YEA!" It was like being in a car wreck and a Beatle concert at the same time.

Bateman put the Triumph into a four-wheel skid but there was no way to miss the car in front but he did. He swerved hard right and found just enough room to squeeze in between the 18-wheeler and the four door Fred Family special who was stopped with the kids. It was pretty dark but I can still see the wide-eyed white eyeballs of the passengers in the other cars staring at us. I'm thinking that we needed to let the top down (since we couldn't open the doors jammed between the vehicles) and get out and start apologizing to people before the cops got there.

Bateman had a better plan. He started blowing the horn, raising hell out the window, and insinuating the whole thing was the fault of the other drivers on the expressway. This intimidation got the car in the right lane in front of the truck to move up a bit which let us back in the right lane, which did us absolutely no good since the traffic was stopped. We were just beyond the North Ave. bridge and had nowhere to go, nowhere legal anyway. Bateman floored the Triumph again and roared off to the right. At that time there was also an entrance ramp coming down from North Ave. and there were several cars stopped waiting to move when the traffic cleared. Not wanting to cause any imposition on the waiting cars, Bateman took off across the grass and headed up the hill towards the Varsity. About twenty feet from North Ave. Bill bounced over the curb onto the entrance ramp, going the wrong way of course. He did exercise caution at this point and blew the horn wildly as we exploded onto North Ave., going the wrong way once again. Bill did find time to shoot a bird and cuss some guy in a pickup truck who gave him a bad look after he had to squeal to a stop, spilling his Varsity Orange all over everything in the truck. All of this, still to the chorus of the Yankee still screaming, "YEA, YEA, YEA!"

It's two or three o'clock by this time and the Yankee and Bill agree that it's been a pretty slow night; so they decide to head back home. Somewhere off of Peachtree we hook up with some winding kind of road through a neighborhood of nice homes that Bateman delighted in driving like a road course. When we arrived home my asshole had tightened up so much I had to pry it off the console. I had had enough. After carefully locking the bedroom door and saying a prayer of thanks I drifted off mentally setting my internal alarm to wake up and be out of the house before Bill awoke and started it all over again.

Now you might think I just pulled out the most sensational Bateman story I could come up with, but it wasn't. You remember some wilder than that, don't you? I could tell some here but there might be some juveniles reading this whose mother didn't dip them.

The last time I heard from Bill was in August of '82. He called to say he was coming to my wedding. But he thought better of it and didn't show up. Out of respect for me, I guess he wanted my bride to be the center of attention on that special day. Some time later, Marilyn called and said he died. He injured himself on the inside where his mother couldn't dip and slipped away. Marilyn went to the funeral and said that was the coldest family she had ever been around. I wonder why? It's probably because they knew him best. And they knew he might be in that casket or it could just be another one of them Bateman deals.

Bateman: the last days? (Maybe)

Hanging out with George and Ron in the mid-seventies around the Place on Paces we developed a Wonderful Wednesday tradition of eating Mexican food for lunch up on Buford Highway. El Torros was the first place we knew of where you could get good salsa and what they said was traditional Mexican food, which was as traditional as they could make it for the American market. Like Oriental, Italian or whatever, they came up with a formula for American taste buds that has worked big time and now you can find Mexican even in small towns where only a few years ago the citizens of those towns felt cosmopolitan when they landed a Tastee-Freeze.

My continuing search for good Mexican over the years eventually lead me to El Azteca in Morrow and a friendship with the owner Gus and the top southside bartender, Lisa. But it was Chavo's sauces and real traditional Mexican dishes that always brought the family back. So I was very pleased when I heard that Gus had sold the Morrow business and moved his show to Rock Quarry Road off of Eagles Landing Parkway in north Henry County. Since the move, I've become a regular customer on my trips north, arriving most of the time between 1:00 and 5:00 in the afternoon. I always go straight to the bar room because I know Lisa will turn me on to the best specials of the day.

No matter what time I show up, it seems that I always run into one of the south side's top defense attorneys, Lee Sexton and one of the south side's top investigators, Wayne Boling. I kid Gus that he should be getting office rent from these guys because of the business they get done at the end of the bar.

Coming back from Atlanta one afternoon in November, I felt the Azteca Jones coming on and stopped by. On my way in I run into Wayne and Lee at the door and tell them, "Hey, I'm glad you guys got the memo about the meeting today and I appreciate you coming." We assume our usual places and since Lisa is not working I ask Gus, "What's good today?" He advised me to try the meat loaf sandwich, which I did even though I hate meat loaf. Thankfully the sandwich was real good. I guess that's because Mexican meat loaf doesn't taste anything like what mother used to make.

Anyway, none of that has anything to do with the subject of this story, it's just the set up of how we got there. During the meal they ask me about Jackson attorney, Richard Milam, who is now the DA for the Towaliga Judicial Circuit. I knew Richard from teenage dances in Griffin but really got to know him at West Georgia when he lived on the floor below us in the dorm and later we lived together at the original Animal Farm with a bunch of guys from the original SAO's. I told them that Richard was doing fine and that we had played tennis together that morning. They said they didn't know Richard played tennis and asked about his game. I said he played tennis just like he played middle linebacker for Griffin High.

That's when Wayne said he didn't know Richard played football for Griffin and commented that they must have faced each other on the field because he played for Forrest Park. Upon realizing that he and Lee were Forest Park natives, I posed the question, "Did either of you guys ever know a guy named Bill Bateman?" Wayne said, "Oh yes, he grew up right around the corner from where I lived, even though he was a few years younger." He then added, "As a matter of fact, Lee was representing him when he committed suicide."

In Earlier days, just another partier. Who Knew?

This really got my attention, because I had been trying to find out exactly what was supposed to have happened in Bill's final days, with no luck. The people that were around Bill at that time seemed to have died, disappeared, or are in hiding from people trying to find out about his last days. I don't blame them.

I relay to the guys at the bar, that I had not heard the suicide story but had heard several other versions. I asked Lee how he became Bill's attorney. He said Bateman hired him to help him out of some kind of drug bust that happened in Hollywood. (Where else would Bill want to get busted?) Lee said, "If he hadn't died we were going to fly out to L. A. that Monday morning to try the case." He said that when he contacted the prosecutor from the county's DA's office he was told, "You're client is going to prison today." To which Lee responded, "I can guarantee you my client is not going to jail today, unless you can get his body from the funeral home."

Lee then asked me, "Do you know who the prosecutor on the case was?" Now if you knew (or know) Bill you would assume it would be the most "Holly-woody" media DA of all time and of coarse it was. Before I could answer Lee said, "Marcia Clark." This was decades before the O.J. thing but Bateman always had an eye for spotting young talent, especially in women.

I ended the conversation by asking Lee who ID'ed the body. He said he didn't know. I finished the meat loaf sandwich and complemented Gus about how good it was. He said the secret was mixing beef with pork. So the afternoon ended with some questions answered and other questions left open like, "Just how much pork?"

WC

Classified Advertisings

Need to talk to you about Bill.

Walter C email me

Classified Advertisement

Searching For Humanistic Students:

Smoking

Mike Arons Impression 1972

- West Georgia College Psychology department was modeled by Dr. Mike Arons student of Abraham Maslow.

- Maslow's humanistic approach was widely rejected by behaviorism.

- Humanistic psychology is centered on the gestalt of the human mind.

- Experiential is a key word. The study of our experience of the world, while being in the world. One can not be separated from the world. Mind and body are one. Yin Yang.

- The department rallied around the personal experiences of its students.

- Mind altering drugs were of particular use to expand consciousness.

- Freedom to experience is a large part of humanism.

- Phenomenology or how we see ourselves in the world is perspective.

- Dr. R.D. Laing, a prominent British psychiatrist put it this way.

- "I see you. You see me. I see you seeing me. You see me seeing you. I see you seeing me, seeing you. You see me seeing you, seeing me seeing you...You see me seeing you seeing me, see you"....etc, etc.

- Define no limits, psychosis does not need treatment, it needs to return from the other side of reality…a trip….an experience. One can only go crazy if one is allowed to do so.

- Dr Arons often made daily decisions by turning left rather than right.

- Roosevelt U. in Chicago, and Saskatchewan are the graduate schools to attend,, and Western Kentucky U.of all places. WKU is clinical humanistic oriented.

Mike Arons

- Bob Masek, Henry Moore, Mike Arons, Hector Saravia were of a few profs in this era.
- Bob was a true friend of mine. He died young of cancer. I loved him.

- We sat in groups. We talked. We wrote. We smoked a lot. We always were eager to open Pandora's Box…..what could be inside?

- Experience consciousness sums it up.

And I did for many a pleasant journey.

Contact:

Steve Aderhold
adtaf@mindspring.com
Atlanta GA

Announcement to the Public!

Initial Public Offering!

Foster's Store, Inc.

IPO

50,000,000

**Shares of Common stock
@ $25.00 par value**

Available at Market opening soon!

Exclusively offered by the firm of:

Gungii, Clapsaddle &
Obberwolfer
Atlanta, Georgia

The times they were a changing,..

Bob Abbott just back from Viet Nam 1968 at WGC fraternity party

and so were we,...

Bobo at Feed N Seed   1972   at Student Center

Chapter 29

Remembering the Green Jay Rushers

By Wayne Lankford

I guess it was Dan O'Conner who spearheaded the organizing of the Foster's Store flag football team that year, 1970 I guess it was. I remember him just saying that I was on the roster, and the first game would be in about a week. He would get us a game schedule as soon as it was released.

We were in the student center at the time, sitting down over by the pool tables. I remember being there and watching Wylly Willingham, as usual, running the table for about the third time in a row against David Etherdige. It almost had to be a Friday because I had just begun leafing thru the school newspaper, *The West Georgian*. Dan's telling me who he signed up as players. I remember Bob Abbott's name being highlighted and thinking we might actually have a chance to win a couple of games when I notice the *Intramural Game Schedule* is staring up at me from the newspaper.

"Hey look, here's the schedule!" I say, as at the same time I'm rotating the open page to where Dan and I can study it together. I'm scanning the thing searching for a listing for Foster's Store, but I'm not finding it.

I ask Dan, "When did you sign us up? I don't see us listed?"

O'Conner, with a what they used to call a "shit eatin grin", looks at me and then at the newspaper and points his finger down the page, sliding it slowly until it comes to rest just above the team name, The Green Jay Rushers. "We're the Green Jay Rushers this year!"

I'm just like speechless. I feel like all the air had just been kicked out of me. I can't believe this! O'Conner has put together drug and pot smoking slang to make the football team name. And I'm on the fuckin roster - my name is spelled out on the list of players who smoke green and yellow joints and get a big rush out of it!

"O'Conner! Dan! Did you forget that smoking pot is against the law? Haven't we had enough attention without hanging a sign out in front of the Store that says that everybody who lives here is a dope smoker and is really just biding their time till they get busted and get sent to prison because they're so fuckin stupid?"

Dan is not even the slightest bit concerned. He leans back in his chair accusing me of worrying too much. "You need to lighten up about all that. Hey, if we get busted, we get busted. What's the sense of worrying about things we can't do anything about?"

I am sitting there in awe of his logic; how Dan could be so stupid, and how I could make such a bad choice about ever being his room mate in the first place, when I think it was Bob Heflin, senior class president, walks by, shacks his head negatively and laughs as he points at me and says the words, "The Green Jay Rushers".

I guess I got over it - but not really; but what could I do? I know all of us at the Store in those days loved to play ball. During the fall and much of the winter months you could see us out there in the yard in front of the Feed N Seed playing football practically every afternoon, sometimes playing until there wasn't even enough daylight left to see the ball.

Actually, I always thought that smoking marijuana went very well along with a friendly game of football or basketball, horseshoe pitching or whatever. As the Green Jay Rushers, we were a team and pretty much of one mind about all that. Winning was important but it wasn't everything. I remember at about a third of the way thru the season checking the paper and seeing we were in second place in our division. I suppose we were better than most of the Dormitory teams at least and equal to many of the *ad hoc* teams like our own. We knew we were no match for the big frat teams, but we weren't all that bad. I still can recall a couple of especially memorable losses.

Frank Brown was a great Rusher.

Before we even lined up against the *Black Student Alliance*, none of us had any doubt as to what the final outcome would be. I think BSA could have scored a touchdown on every play if they had been inclined to do so. They had a quarterback who could throw the ball a mile and guys who could run circles around us. It was a game where nobody was in any hurry about anything. They probably outscored us by five touchdowns, but it could have been more. They were a great group of guys. It was just real obvious to both of us that we all were out there that day because we loved football, all of us. That was the way we played it. That's the way we always played it.

Another afternoon I remember playing against one of the Frat teams and being the recipient of a very nice crack back block. It hurt, and it was totally unnecessary. The play was on the other side of the field from us and moving down field when I got hit. We were so outmatched! Didn't these guys realize who they were playing and what condition we were in? I mean who needed such violence on the football field? All of us Green Jay Rushers sort of turned down our enthusiasm a few notches after that, a protest without protesting the game formally. Except maybe for BoBo, who had lost his volume control where it pertained to football a long time ago. BoBo believed he could beat those guys all by himself. He was like that. Most of the time when we played a team so much superior to us, both teams usually managed to play and have a good time, more like a practice scrimmage than real games that counted. But after a couple more games with frat teams who wanted to win at any cost, we decided to prepare a little differently for such games.

I think I had an afternoon class that quarter and usually never got back home until about three o'clock. It was a game day. The usual set of cars was parked along with other teammates' rides who maybe didn't live at the store right then, but were still on the team. There was nobody outside as I walked down the hill to the Feed N Seed. As soon as I opened that big red heavy front door, a huge cloud of marijuana smoke fell on me like smoke from a cannon, deep from the inner darkness of the place. I waved my arms in front of me as I ventured past the front room into the den to see the rest of the team, all suited up and ready for the game, cleats, headbands and everything, just lounging around everywhere and passing one of those big Bob Marley pot-filled cigars around the room. The word "forfeit" would appear in next week's results page. Never was I surer about anything. And I was just as sure that there would still be a game played that afternoon by the Green Jay Rushers. In a few minutes, there we were, already chosen up sides among ourselves, playing ball right there on our own turf, Foster's Store.

We had a least two other forfeitures that quarter, but we showed up to play most of the time. We'd take turns playing different positions. If one day what O'Conner was trying to run wasn't moving us, he'd suggest somebody else be quarterback for a while. We took turns playing the line and the backfield. I remember Walter Carmichael showing up one day to play in cowboy boots. He volunteered to run the offense as the quarterback a while. He did a good job that day too! The big play that day was the one where you do a quick substation, but not really. You have all the guys and your friends all get together on the sidelines to form a crowd. You send somebody out of the game but not all the way. The eligible receiver will just stand there barely in bounds, right next to the side line with all these other people standing around him. At a glance, it looks like he's just another spectator. Even after the ball is hiked, the "live" receiver will stay in place until the rest of the players are all faked to the other side of the field, at which point the receiver runs all the way down the field and will usually be open for the touchdown pass. That was Walter's favorite play. Pretty funny stuff when it worked.

I remember another one of my favorites. It wasn't planned at all, it just happened. I was a kicker in high school so I usually kicked off and kicked extra points and field goals. My most memorable moment from those days was an extra point I kicked. There was a road right next to one end of the field. When you scored on that end, if the kicker had any leg at all, he could end over end it up and thru the goalposts and further over the whole roadway. It was common to see the ball go in the street and further. One day, we had just scored and I was standing there with the teams lined up and ready to do the extra point when I notice a campus truck, a big flatbed, headed down the hill, about to pass right behind the goalpost where I'm kicking.

If I time it just right, I think to myself, and right then I call the signal to hike the ball, O'Conner sets it up and just at the right moment and with just the right amount of force, I kick the ball up and right thru the center of the goalposts. I see it, it has a chance, the truck is almost there as the perfect end over end football starts its downward arch and right into the center bed of the truck, bounces around a couple of times and is carried off by the truck, the driver unaware that he has our game ball. I even got cheers from the opposing team.

I'll never forget the Green Jay Rushers. What a great name for a football team. Don't you think? That O'Conner, I must admit, he was some kind of a genius.

Rushing Practice

Dan O'Conner in hat with other Rushers

Book Recommendation

Remembering The GreenJay Rushers, **Football Plus Marijuana or "Everybody Go Long"**

Intramural Football Left Georgia Style

They didn't have customized jerseys or lot of fancy plays, but the guys from Foster's Store came ready to play. They were as surprised as anyone when they actually won a few games. It must have been unnerving for their opponents to have to line up across the ball from a bunch of long haired glassy eyed freaks. "Yellow 44, Green 17, I think I'm having a Flash Back from last night's Acid trip,. Hike!" These were the kind of audible that unnerved many a well drilled Frat team. This was a team with a lot of talent. Too bad they seemed to be penalized so often for delay of game. For this one, go Left.

The Art of Foster's Store

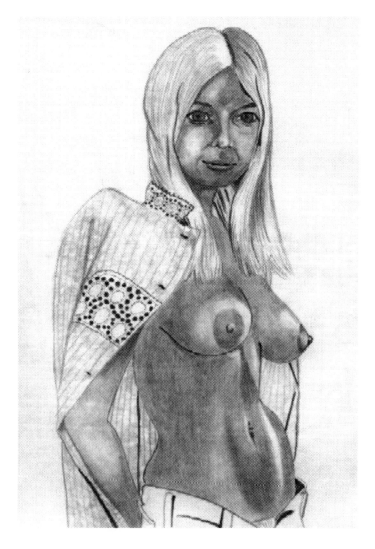

Pencil Drawing by Allen McMillon 1970

Chapter 30

A Fictional account

UFOs disguised as Propane Tanks - Worldwide Phenomena Exposed

By Wayne Lankford

As told to Wayne Lankford by L.R. Foster, Carrollton GA, October 1969

What appear, to most of us, as harmless looking propane tanks are actually space ships from the planet Mars, theorized Lounie Foster, longtime Carroll County resident and former proprietor of Fosters Grocery, Feed and Seed. Mr. Foster contends that, these benign looking vessels are actually cleverly disguised interplanetary vehicles, malevolently designed to infiltrate our planet, and for now, just lay dormant, awaiting signals from a mother ship. "The propane breathing Martians, " Foster muses, "are just waiting to take over the world."

He points to the fact that these small space ships are spread out all over the countryside and make a perfect avenue for these aliens to launch a "surprise attack" on "ignorant and puny humans". Mr. Foster reports that many a night he has witnessed the diminutive space travelers "flippin the lid" and unscrewing the tank top from the inside and then "spreading like rats" along the ground behind his Bowden Road residence.

Attempts by this reporter were unsuccessful to discover any creatures myself, either inside the suspected tanks, (spacecrafts) or outside about the ("landing zones") surrounding grounds. Foster contends that, for now, the aliens need to stay very close to their propane supply but contends strongly, that this won't be for long. And another threat exists, so adds Mr. Foster, looking up over the propane tank towards the adjacent pasture. "See those Hay bales?" He adds, "They just look like hay bales; actually they're space ships from Venus."

This is where I felt like I had to interrupt and conclude the interview and point out to Mr. Foster, "Mr. Foster, see those empty beer cans? Well, that's what they are, empty beer cans?"

You decide. Is any of this real?

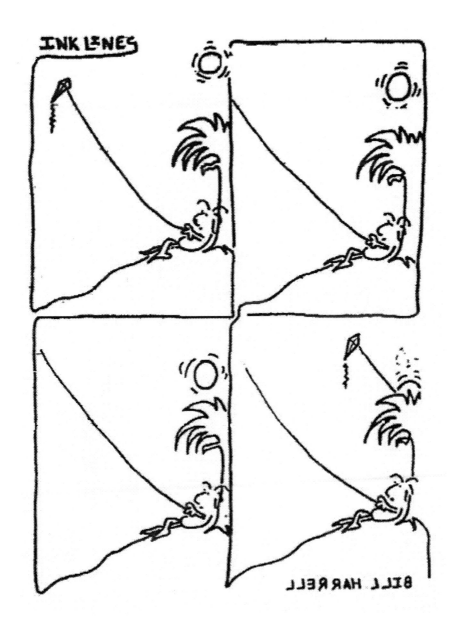

Speaking of UFO's.

Office of the President
Carrollton, Georgia 30118-4500

October 20, 2005

Mr. Wayne Elliott Lankford
1945 Mountain Laurel Lane
Hoover, AL 35244-1113

Dear Mr. Lankford:

It was a pleasure to read about you and your newest book in the current issue of *Perspective*. As a successful author and University of West Georgia alumnus, you are a fine role model for our current undergraduates. I can only hope, however, that our students will choose to emulate your hard work and literary accomplishments rather than the antics of their predecessors at Foster's Store.

Congratulations on your newest book. I hope it is a resounding success and is followed by many others.

Sincerely,

Beheruz N. Sethna, Ph.D.
Professor of Business Administration, and
President of the University

Tel 678-839-6442 • Fax 678-839-4786 • bsethna@westga.edu • www.westga.edu
The University System of Georgia • Affirmative Action/Equal Opportunity Institution

Student Killed In Viet War

PFC William Cotter Ray, 23, who had been in Vietnam less than a month, was killed in hostile enemy action on Thursday, Nov. 6.

Ray entered the U S. Army in January, 1969. He arrived in Vietnam Oct. 12. Death came for Ray just three days after he was assigned to the Fourth Infantry Division at Pleaka, Central Highlands.

He was a native of Marietta, Ga., and graduated from Marietta High School in 1964, Reinhardt College in 1966, and West Georgia College in 1968. He was a business major, and lived in Aycock Hall and later in South Park Apartments.

He was engaged to Donna Pruitt of Marietta, and they were to be married when he returned from Vietnam.

Of course Bill here won't be making a statement today. He's dead, you see. Along with close to 60,000 other guys who got killed in Vietnam.

This next chapter is supposed to shed some light about having to worry all the time about whether or not you might have to go over to the other side of the world and do some things that you weren't too crazy about, like getting killed or killing somebody else.

It's really funny stuff!

So is a lot of insanity to some people.

It was everywhere you looked, even the school newspaper

This is page number 310. I have nothing to say here. I wanted to leave it completely blank, but thought better of that notion realizing that some people might bitch and complain about white space in the book.

So this is your space, I give it to you freely. It is the only free page in the book. Look at all the empty space you own now!

What do you see? I'd like to know. email me wayne@fostersstore.com. Put "what I see in the space" in the subject line. Or just mail it.

Chapter 31

The Draft - Part 2

By Wayne Lankford

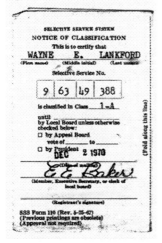

My Draft Card

1-A
Classification

I think my number was 62.

This lottery thing, it was insane! Think about it. Think about a drawing at work or somewhere, a "names in the hat" thing. Now think about 365(plus leap year of course) names representing every man between the ages of 18 and 25. Not every person, just every male. My father once remarked to me that "if they started drafting people at age 50 we would never go to war". If they put politicians' names in the hat, I just bet you these fuckers in Washington could find another way to eventually solve things. Carpet bombing is just too fucking easy. Fuck. There's the word. Fuck it! Fuck it! Fuck it! Fuck it a thousand billion fucking times.

Tell me: are you one of these people who think that using the word "fuck" so obsessively is obscene? My guess is that, if that's the case, you probably never knew anybody who went to Vietnam. You probably believe that we as a country, The United Fucking States of American could do no fucking wrong. If that's the case, I know some people who think you're fucking nuts.

I don't know, but at the time I got my number, fucking number sixty-two, which translated for me particularly, "Congratulations, you get to go in the army and probably to war and get your fucking ass shot off." By that time I had a real fucking good fucking idea as to what all that meant. Shit is a good word too! Let's don't forget shit! Fucking Shit! Fucking sixty fucking two shit fuck! "I'm fucked"!

My brother only spoke to me one time about Viet Nam. He was there during the Tet offensive. My brother was an Eagle Scout. He married a Colonel's daughter. He was what they used to call, "Gung Ho". He was going to be a career man. He knew volunteering to go to Viet Nam after graduating from Military school would help his career. He ended up in the Medical Corps. Then one sunny day he's walking along with his rifle company, showing a new medic the ropes when they come under attack. A bunch of guys wearing black pajamas pop out of the tree line and start trying to kill everybody. Oh look, they have rockets too! How about that! Look! There's a guy with his guts hanging out. I guess I need to attend to him. Let's see, how to get all these guts back in to where they're supposed to go? But what's that guy doing over there? It looks like he is pointing that rocket launcher right at me. This is really difficult. If I run away right now, this guy who I'm giving aid too will surely die. If I move my hand away from this broken artery before I can clamp it, he will bleed to death, but if I don't move right now that rocket coming at me will kill both of us. Such a dilemma. There should be more time given to think about things during wars. But right then there's that puff of white smoke from the rocket launcher. What to do, I've already puked right into this guy's open chest, and he's still screaming, when out of nowhere another guy in my company comes to the rescue. He probably should've turned left and started running instead of right. I guess he didn't see the guy with black pajamas shooting a rocket at us, because he ran right into the path of the rocket, and in one big explosion, he was gone. I mean, except for his boots. They were right there where he used to be, empty, smoking.

The guy with his guts blown out lived. So did my brother. They were pretty lucky. Don't you think? All I knew was that after that, I really didn't want to hear any more war stories about Viet Nam. But of course you couldn't avoid that. This war was televised, and unlike previous wars, the veterans of it were all around you. I had one friend, Bobby Knight, who had lost a leg. He was a medic too. He was carrying a wounded guy back to his line when he got shot. I remember he said it was at night. He said that sometimes when some guy would be dying in his arms, they would ask him to call his parents or his wife and tell them that they loved them. I asked him if he ever did that. He said that he never did. He said the worst thing about having an artificial leg was that he had to pee a lot more than before he lost his leg. We were playing golf one day, I remember him laughing when he hit the ground on the driving tee. He swung too hard at the golf ball, lost his balance and fell down. It was hilarious. We had played football in high school together.

Fuck. Fuck, Fuck, Fuck.

I was living at Foster's Store when my college deferment ran out. It was only good for four years. I still had a couple of quarters to go before I'd graduate, but I wasn't thinking about that. All I could see was the letter from the Selective Service, the Draft Board, ordering me to appear for my physical. Five years earlier I had to take a Physical in order to play football. I could not believe it! The Doctor said that my blood pressure was too high and that the only way I could play sports my senior year was to get a note from my family physician saying it was OK with him. I did that and I played football and was on the track tem my senior year. During the next four years whenever I went to the Doctor, there it was, my blood pressure was always a little high, but sometimes it was completely normal. When I got my letter to go to get my Army physical, I called my Doctor and asked him if he would write a letter to the draft board. He said he would and sent it to me to give to them when I went in for the physical. All it said was that my blood pressure was this or that on these dates. I wasn't that much higher than normal. I didn't know what was going to happen. The letter didn't say anything about me not being physically fit enough to serve in the Army.

I remember showing up at the place where you had to go to take your physical. For me, it was on Ponce de Leon Ave in Atlanta. First they pointed into this kind of a classroom with desks and told us, no ordered us was more like it, all to sit down. This little shit of a sergeant or something gets up and while looking someplace else orders us all to take out our driver's license and place it on the top right hand corner of our desks. Then he orders us to copy the address that's on the license on to the blank form that's on our desks. I had moved a couple of times since I got my license so the address where I lived now, Rt 7, Box 39, wasn't on the license. I raised my hand and told the guy that where I lived now and what was on the license weren't the same. I started to ask if he wanted me to put my current address instead of what was on my license, since it was wrong, but he went a little nuts and walked over to me and right there, leaning down at me, almost yelling at me like I'm a stupid idiot or something, "Well, If you don't have the correct address on your license then you can't copy it down then can you?" I left it blank. He left me no choice.

Fuck. Fuck. Fuck.

The whole thing moved quickly from the classroom setting to where you find yourself in a long line moving thru a number of rooms or areas where they test your eyesight and everything else. Everybody's in their underwear. Mostly it's very quiet. At some point I notice a group of three or four guys sitting in a corner, one of them is shaking all over like he's cold, another one is almost asleep and another one is looking right at me with his eyes as black as saucers. I ask the guy who's taking my blood pressure what the deal is and he tells me that "those guys have been here a couple of days, and that they'll stay here until they come down from what ever drugs they've taken believing they would get them out of this."

I'm taking a deep breath as he is taking my blood pressure. When he's finished I stand up and tell him that I have this letter from my Doctor and I don't know who I need to give it to.

He asks me, "What's wrong with you?"

Fuck. Fuck. Fuck. This guy just took my blood pressure and he is asking me what is wrong with me. I am fucked!

"You can give it to me" is all he says and places it aside and goes on to the next poor fucker behind me.

From that point, the physical deal is about over. They collected urine specimens and then we got dressed and went back into the classroom we'd been in previously, where another army uniformed dude, an officer this time, comes in to tell us that if we are ordered to report for duty we better not try to run away because they would come for us, they would find us and we would be thrown into prison for at least two years. I'm thinking about how far it was to Canada and so is everybody else. It's 1971. This guy says that if your number is lower than 242 or something and you've passed the physical this morning, you should receive your report for duty notice in about 90 days.

Let's all say it together, fuck, fuck, fuck! Shit, I'm shit!

To say I was a bit depressed was an understatement. It wasn't about fear right them. It was just about shock. It was about endings. These guys didn't give a shit about my letter from my doctor. They didn't give a shit about anything, why would they, they were already in the fucking Army. I didn't know anything about anything any more. That's the way I felt right then. My head was hanging as I walked down the stairs to the entrance area and out the door on to Ponce and the daylight.

How long would all this take, I thought to myself? Then it occurred to me that the guy sitting in that glass enclosure, maybe he would know; so I went back inside and asked him when people usually got their letter to report for duty? He just said the same thing the officer guy had said about if you passed your physical it would take about 90 days. It occurred to me to ask him how long it would take to find out if I'd passed the physical. So I did.

"What's your name?" He asked quite simply. He asked me just like he already knew. There this guy was sitting at a desk with a single telephone behind one of those big glass windows with a little round hole in it you could talk through. This guy already knew my fate.

"That's Lankford, with a k,.. l, a, n, *K*, f, o, r, d."

"Yea, here you are. You failed. You have high blood pressure." As matter of factly as anybody had ever told me anything in my life, that's how he said it. And just like someone had passed the salt after I had asked for it, all I said was, "Ok, well, thanks" and turned left toward the doors and the street when it hit me. I needed to make sure.

I walked back up to the window and asked, "What does that mean, that I failed?"

"It means you failed, you can't be drafted!" He was emphatic now.

I just had to be clear on what he was saying and what I was beginning to realize were the same thing. "What if I want to join the Army right now"?

Getting exasperated now, he raises his voice a little, "You can't join the Army now. They won't take you. You failed the physical".

"Do you mean I'm not good enough to be in the army?" I implored further with him.

"That's right, you'll never be in the Army, or any of the armed services." he replied.

I turned back towards the street, muttering things like, "well that's a hell of a deal, not good enough to be in the army" and stuff like that as I walked thru the double glass doors and down the few concrete steps to the sidewalk to an empty Saturday morning Ponce de Leon Avenue.

At the end of the block I let out a yell so loud that I'm sure they heard it about fifteen blocks away up on Peachtree Street. I was free! The sky was blue, at least for me.

What a Happy Guy Looks Like!

Classified Advertisement

Viet Nam era combat blouse - I seem to remember **Ron Lightzy** giving me this one day down at the Feed and Seed. After 30 + years, maybe it's time to get it back to it's rightful owner. Or, I'll take best offer. Has "*Glover*" name tag and "Airborne insignia on left sleeve. I cut the sleeves off during a Willie Nelson concert sometime around 1978. wayne@thebikepath.com

Bill Harrell's undefeated Army

Foster's Store

Milo's Poster may be ordered on line at www.miloville.com.

Chapter 32

Animal Farm

Preface by Wayne Lankford

Back in 1966 or so, about the same time that Ethel Foster was deciding to turn the old store into living quarters for college students, there were others who believed that the general party atmosphere might be improved upon by the addition of a few social fraternities and sororities. Sometime along spring of 1968, still my freshman year, I remember somebody coming up to me on campus and asking me if I would like to pledge his fraternity, the Cavaliers. I remember thinking that it was nice to be invited into such a thing, but I recall almost exactly my response.

One of the things that appealed to me most about West Georgia was not so much what it was, but what it was not. While in high school, starting in my junior year, I started going to fraternity parties around Atlanta at Georgia Tech, at Georgia State, Emory University, I even made partying road trips to frat houses up at the University in Athens. Make no mistake: I believed that these were my kind of people, and I felt certain that pledging a fraternity somewhere would certainly be in my future. And then something real strange happened. I found myself at a party on a Wednesday night at Jackson Courts while I was still a senior in high school. Now this was no *Kappa Sigma* keg party like at Georgia Tech: there was no famous name band playing or really much going on besides a bunch of people, males and females, all hanging out together and having a good time. There was just something really "laid back" about it. It was small-scaled, simple. There was an air with these people quite different from the air in Atlanta or the atmosphere at a Pike party in Athens. It was just people being themselves and everybody was the same. There was no branding. Everybody was welcomed into the partying fray as a brother or sister. West Georgia to me was what it wasn't more than what it was: cleaner, simpler, a place where I could feel at home as who I was already.

I made a few more trips to Carrollton before I ended up there as a student. West Georgia was the only school I even sent an application for admission. So I remember very well my response whenever someone approached me about being in a fraternity. I'd just look around, turn my head all around and up and respond with something like, "Man, why would you want to screw this place up with a bunch of fraternities?"

The thing was that when I was in high school, I thought fraternities were great, but by the time I was in college, I was already bored with them. They were too big, they had all matter of silly shit attached to them: pledging, big brother-doms, little sisters, sweethearts, hell weeks and just a bunch of downright fearful things like blackballs and councils, you know, organization and dues. And it just got sillier from there.

There were teasing pitches. After you graduated and went looking for a job, former frat brothers would all be high in the big corporations and able to help you out finding a job. They could provide references. Because of the worldwide reach of the brotherhood, you would be able to find friends all around the world. I guess all that's true, but for me, it just had no appeal whatsoever. That whole sales pitch was about fear: without being in a fraternity, you run the risk of being alone in the world, friendless and without your friends to help you out you will end up as a failure.

I was simply me. I was not a me that had to be a part of something bigger to exist. I could exist if I were not this something-more person because of kinship to a fraternity. I did not really need that kind of help. I really didn't.

I don't mean to come across as critical of frats in general. It's just that they aren't for everybody. I just happen to fall right in to that "not for everybody" group.

So, out of nowhere, the Animal Farm comes along. It appears to me, from what I begin to hear about it, that it's just another want-to-be fraternity.

By this time I'd dropped by a few West Georgia frat parties and always felt that out-of-place feeling. One night I showed up with a date at a Farm party and was most pleasantly surprised. This group was not like a fraternity at all. No, these people were crazy. These people were not here because of what they might be able to do for each other ten years from now, or because they had to be there, or because they wanted to be popular or had some hidden political agenda for the future—motivations so obvious when present and just as obvious when they are not. Just think about that. No, the Animal Farmers were there because they all were living in the present. There was a keg party going on. There was music playing. I remember standing there with my date and . . . Well, I remember a lot about that night, but that's another story for another time.

You should know that I personally never joined the Animal Farm, but many a Foster's store mate did. There was a commonality of purpose that fit real well with the Foster's crowd. No purpose is so clear sometimes and such an admirable goal. You got all that and more with the Animal Farm.

So, what follows then is a brief history of a place that, like Foster's Store, ain't there any more.   We include it because the Animal Farm was part of the fabric of West Georgia during the time this book records.   One could write a whole book about the Farm.   Maybe somebody will someday.   For now, right now, here's Mickey Spinks.

Farm Group Picture 1969

The Animal Farm

By Mickey Spinks

It was spring quarter 1968 when the seeds of what was to become the Farm Brotherhood were first sown. I was living in Jackson Court Apartments. Now Jackson Courts was OK for most of us, but after a while the boundaries that were in place to curb in the extreme parting crowd became much too confining and many a Jackson Courts camper soon longed for the real freedom that was, that had to be, "out there somewhere!"

Off campus living, that would be our destination. With a place out there, that I'd be able to leave all this heat and inconvenience, increasingly more uncomfortable as was the aftermath of every little party we'd thrown. I was tired. All of us were tired of the Carrollton Police dropping in always so unexpectedly because our partying noise level disturbed some, particularly the apartment management in the person of Coach West.

Yeah, Coach West. What a piece of work that guy was. He had no sense of humor about anything. He may have invented "finger pointing in your faced pissed-off-ed-ness." When someone would put explosives (cherry bombs or M-80's) down the toilet and the explosion would take out the plumbing in the whole building, instead of cheering on the perpetrator at a party later held in his honor, he'd get all upset about it and call the police and there would be a big investigation and such. I can hear him now, "I know it was you Spinks, you or one of your no-good friends, and I'm going to catch you one day, don't think you are getting away with anything because you're not."

At one time, Coach West was a real coach up the hill at the college. But by then he was the manager of the apartment complex and I guess he felt some responsibility to keep things like the whole place

1969 Yearbook - Jackson Courts on fire again

burning to the ground from happening. I remember the Fire Department being called in at least once a quarter. They should've just gotten rid of all those asphalt speed bumps all over the place and we wouldn't have had to keep burning them down to level all the time. I mean how are you going to have a decent drag race in the parking lot with a bunch of speed bumps everywhere? Just because we had a Budweiser Beer checkered flag in our apartment did not mean that we were behind any such activity as speed bump burning or drag race organizing. But try to tell Coach West that, especially when you've consumed about eight beers. All he cared about was filing another police report and then sending me up to see Dean Pershing at the college.

"You won't be laughing about this when you get kicked out of school!" He'd go on and on about that, and I was ending up about once a week with a regular appointment about some so called "believed misbehaviors" at my personal residence. Actually Dean Pershing thought it was as funny as I did. I mean, he knew Coach West, too.   Pershing's response was always evenly given with as much sympathy as seriousness: "All I can tell you is that one day you guys will push Coach West a little too far. Your partying will get out of hand, and I won't be able to save you."

On my way back from one of those weekly visits from the Dean's office, I ran into Walter Carmichael cutting across campus headed to the school newspaper to turn in an article he'd been working on. That spring, Walter was part of a crew of students staying in a house on Lovvorn Road they named "The Animal Farm." (Some of that group ended up forming the SAO fraternity that eventually became the Kappa Sigs.)

Walter had been living for a while at the Animal Farm but had just found other arrangements he felt better suited his needs. So he gave me the news that the Animal Farm was up for grabs and I had the right of first refusal.

It was an offer I couldn't refuse. This particular week I was finally being evicted from the Courts for causing yet another disastrous event— just a normal party really, but it was the final straw on Coach West's back.

And that's when my story of the Farm began. I enlisted five of my closest friends to live as one and hopefully be able to make the rent payments to Dr. Cruz, who owned the place. We were now a group of six with the same qualifying credentials—little money, no grade point average, and a communal "need to party" beyond the constraining boundaries of Jackson Courts as they pertained to all forms of debauchery, legal, and illegal.   We became the nucleus that would eventually grow into a real brotherhood of the likeminded.

That first summer, that whole summer, was one long party featuring quick trips to Uncle Roy's or Bobby Altman's Bay Station for kegs of beer, usually stopping by Skinner's Grocery to stock up on popcorn for the night, or a quick stop at the Jitney Jungle for some Slim Jims and Beanie Weenies. We may have been short on rent money but we were never short on that "foam of glory."

People came and hopefully went throughout those hot summer months. College students, high school students, town folks, teachers, faculty, coaches, and assorted misfits wandered through for a good time. Sooner or later all roads for refugees fleeing the realities of the late sixties led to the Farm. "Animal Farm" referred to the tenants, but we did have some chickens and there were two barns on the property. One of those barns mysteriously burned down one night. Even though Farm Brothers had advertised a big barn fire for that night, they all swore to Dr. Cruz that it was just a freak accident, a coincidence. It was the truth. There were freaks involved.

Now, you need to remember that back then, West Georgia was a suitcase college, causing party nights to be backwards from other institutions. With no one to party with on the weekends, the big parties ran Sunday through Thursday nights. We were mostly country boys, and Wednesdays were customarily the "big party nights" because we came from small towns that had a long tradition of closing up on Wednesdays. The "hump night" parties were usually rocking by dark-thirty and ran until you passed out. The music was on vinyl and blasted through big speakers powered by tube amps— the primo sound that our digital children have never been privileged to experience.

Walter was a genius at hooking electrical things up and, when he lived at Jackson Courts before the house on Lovvorn Road, he made a strobe light from scratch for that full disco effect, although discos had yet to be invented. That light show of his at Jackson Courts led to its becoming our former residence. All these strobe lights were red. The Carrollton cops showed up, this time saying that somebody had reported one of the apartments converted to a house of ill repute, a whore house. It seems that flashing red lights, or any red lights, really, displayed out in front of any residence were a universal statement that lewd sexual goings on were going on inside. (We wished!)

Farm Party Day

But at the Animal Farm we never worried at all about such things. It was great. We partied on till the dawn. I remember the last song played was always *AMEN* by the Impressions. The still-standing would circle up and we all drank from this big glass bowl we called The Holy Grail.

Mornings were always a treat. The stench of the beer on the floor and the record player kicking off again announced we had survived through another night. Ah, "*Sunshine of Your Love*"—one more time, baby.

The cast of roomies grew out of Rockmart, Cedartown, Griffin, Jackson and Dallas. They were KC, Bobo, Spinks, the Lindsey Brothers, Walter and Trooper Cooper. We were the nucleus, we who lived at the Farm. Plenty of folks just dropped in. On a Sunday night in September we all sat together and began the creation of an organized Farm Brotherhood. We came up with FARM standing for "For A Real Man". On the Farm we were independent of the school's control and loved it!

There came a time when we thought we wanted to be like the other fraternities on campus. A few of us showed up at the monthly inter-fraternal council meeting so as to approach the council with our intentions of becoming a real and recognized fraternity. I remember they all just laughed at us. They didn't even acknowledge our request as a request. All still laughing, they all got up at once and simply turned the lights out and left our little group there in the dark. I remember. We got the message—full throttle of Brotherhood forever!

We were still an organization, in the roughest sense of the word, so we were allowed to participate in intramural sports and did so most enthusiastically. We may have lost a few games but we never lost a party after a game, and a game was a perfect reason for a party.

I believe we had the best parties of all. We were a brotherhood, but not like the prevailing Greek organizations.

To be in the Farm Brotherhood, all you really had to do was **want** to be in the Farm Brotherhood. There were no such things as "black balls" or national organizations you had to kiss up too. Looking back, I guess the Farm actually was a kind of breeding ground for other off-shoots, like Foster's Store. When those off-shoots wanted to really party, they came to the back to the Farm. And the main thing those off-shoots were looking for at a party was the girls. The Farm had a sisterhood made up of sweethearts, dates and good old gals who loved to dance and party the night away with the guys. They helped cook, plan and make changes as well as show a little love and affection. They loved the "Grain Parties" where *Purple Jesus* was the featured drink and you know what kind of chaos that drink could lead to—Wow!

Ed Hass and others at Party

There's neither enough time nor space to go into much detail about some of the many characters or the images that to this day still resonate in my mind. I can see Jimmy Dennis bouncing like a rubber ball through a throng of partiers. And there goes some guy on his motorcycle down the hall in the Farm House. We will forgivingly forget the name of the person up there on the roof in his underwear signifying by his presence there that another party was about to begin. I have lots of images like those and more.

The Farm offered something special to those students who did not want to be a part of the "regulated community." It was the best of times; it is the best of memories. And there are a lot of memories.

Recipe for Purple Jesus

One large plastic trash can or one clean bath tub, 3 to 5 fifths of golden grain alcohol, 8 gallons of Welch's grape juice, chopped mixed fruit, one six pack of sprite, top with ice.

Mason and Moonshine jar

Chapter 33

My Last Days at Foster's Store

By Wayne Lankford

I remember when it was over, when I realized I wasn't going to be a college student anymore. When I got the piece of mail directing me to show up at the Registrar's Office one day, I thought I was finally going to be put out of my misery, that I'd be told that because my grade point average was so low, that I would never ever graduate, and the best thing for me would be to just walk away. I put off going to the office for a couple of weeks, the quarter was almost over when I screwed up my courage just enough to walk in there with that piece of paper in my hand. I remember I went in there and handed over that well-worn parchment quite expecting some sort of universal dismissal document all ready filled out with my name on it telling me in so many words that I should go ahead and hit the road, my college days were over. Yes, I had more than 40 hours more than I needed to graduate, but my GPA was so low that if it were a blood pressure, I would be pronounced you know what. I didn't know what was happening. Georgia Martin, the registrar, took my very wrinkled and sweat soaked piece of paper and simply asked me how tall I was and then took a tape measurer and put it around my head. Next, she asked for Ten dollars. Really, I had no idea what was going on. Then I said, "ten dollars? What's the ten dollars for?" Yes, you could have knocked me over with a feather when I heard her say that it was for the cap and gown, she was now handing me and adding. "You are graduating next Tuesday."

To say I was stunned would be an understatement of huge proportion. Really, all I could do was stand there like an idiot as she asked me for the ten bucks again; she was already filling out a receipt. For some reason, I remember, I actually had ten dollars to give her, which I did quickly, if not smoothly, handed it over to her in quick hopes that she would not recognize her mistake and that I'd maybe yet make it out of this crazy institution with a diploma. Something I knew would make my suffering parents quite happy.

Two minutes latter, I'm walking back towards the student center and my car. Every few steps I look into the bag she'd put the cap and gown in. It was still there. It was not a dream at all, no matter how much it felt like one.

Five years ago to next Tuesday, what just happened? I didn't believe it. I was on a list that said I was about to graduate from college. How did that happen? What about all those F's and D's I made my freshman and sophomore years, last year? I mean I spent half my college days on academic probation. Yeah, I always came back with at least a couple of C's to keep from getting kicked out of this place, but my point average was always a few points below what I knew I'd need to graduate. Then it hit me! I had slipped up the last couple of years and had started taking courses in stuff that interested me. I had even had made a few decent grades. But no, this was some grand joke being played on me. Any minute, somebody is going to surprise me and laugh like crazy that I would ever believe that I could actually graduate from this place. I decided not to tell anybody and just go about my business. I still had two term papers to write and there were a couple of pre graduating meetings, practice things,

I was supposed to attend. Certainly there, somebody with some sense would wake up and recognize that I really wasn't supposed to be in this thing and that in fact, I was to be ejected from this place summarily, not graduate. What kind of fool would believe I could do that? "Sorry about the typo snafu thing Wayne." Somebody would say that to me eventually. That would be the end of it. I'd be out of my misery.

I guess it was the next morning that my philosophy teacher announced that graduating seniors would need to have their term papers in by Friday, a full week before I had any real plan of even starting to write one. Then, being as nonchalant as I could, I asked my teacher if he had a list of the seniors in the class who were to graduate? He glanced down at what ever was on his lectern, turning a few pages quickly, it seemed like an eternity to me, and "Yes, looks like you're going to graduate next week. I mean, provided you get that paper in by Friday."

I was awake. I was on another list. It was Tuesday. I was going to have to write two term papers, in two graduate level courses, one in Philosophy, and the other one in Psychology in three days' time. I hadn't thought of a title or checked out a single book to use as a reference yet, but I could do all that. I could write fuckin term papers. That's all I'd done for the last year in a half.

What people maybe didn't realize about us guys at Foster's was that most of us eventually graduated. I admit that Foster's store was a poor environment to study in, but all that meant was that I, for one, could find another way to accomplish that objective off site or at times when no one else would ever guess, that I was engaged in any sort of academic pursuit. "Academic Pursuit!?", that would be stretching it, but you know what I mean, just doing enough to get by. As a liberal arts major, most of the classes I took the last couple of years had more to do with term papers and a few major tests than anything else. The tests were primarily discussion type and the term papers were about 15 to 20 typewritten pages. I don't have any real memories of what you might describe as actually studying for tests. All I did was read the material. I either got it or I didn't. I either read it or I didn't. I usually read it. In fact I almost always read it. I remember sitting for hours in the smoking room at the library. That was "my place" until I discovered that I could go to the desk and get a key to a "conference room upstairs" and have it all to myself, my own private on-campus office every afternoon or morning. I just told the Liberian on duty that my "study group" was meeting there; I'd need a room for 6 people. Yea, then I had the whole thing to myself. I think I even took a date there one night, but that's another story. We drank *Old Milwaukee* from Styrofoam coffee cups. Yeah, they had coffee up there too.

Studying was pretty much impossible for me back at the Store. Five minutes there and somebody would want to go get a couple of cases of PBR and there would be a lit joint passing by you ever couple of minutes. Not very conducive to study; I mean you could read John Paul Sartre when you were stoned. It was fun, but it was real slow reading, as I remember, and I would always get hung up on single sentences, or the book cover itself.

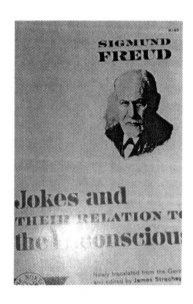

Funny Book Cover Example

Term papers, though, that was another story. I had this *JC Penny* electric typewriter that my parents had given me when I was a freshman. As a Junior and a Senior I had really worn the thing out writing term papers. I was a lousy typist (still am) and it took me more than all night long to type up a 20 page term paper. The problem was all the typos I had to go back and correct with one of those eraser pencils. That was when I discovered Coffee, *Folgers's' Crystals*, to be precise. No I didn't drink it, I just ate a big spoonful of the stuff and washed it down with cold water. The caffeine kicked in a little faster that way and besides, in those days I hated the taste of coffee. One major downside of that method of consumption was the coffee breath. The whole inside of your mouth turned brown, teeth and everything. You got to remember, I was putting myself thru all this because I really did want to graduate from college some day, but the real deal was Viet Nam. Flunk out and you're there. For me, though, I had run out of deferment and had already taken my Army physical. Thank God and Jehovah or whatever you pray to personally, I had failed the physical and had been reclassified as 4 −F. For me, at that time, when I graduated, it meant that I was going to have to get a real job. I think I was as afraid of that as I was of anybody's boot camp. I didn't have a clue about what I wanted to do work-wise, but I was sure that a degree in Sociology, would be at the end of a job searching day, about as valuable as the paper it was printed on. My future job prospects were anything but bright. But there I was, a virtual term writing tornado, whizzing out the last two I'd ever do. Just enough for a "B". A "B" was the same as a C in Graduate courses.

So what? What am I trying to say here? I guess it's that the way it played out, I never really had anytime at all to think about the graduation process. I was too busy just trying to get there all of a sudden and suddenly I had no time to even think about it. In less than a week I would have no place to go. And that was the way I felt standing in line with that black cap and gown on. I had no place to go. I felt emptier inside than I had ever felt in my life.

Thank goodness for all I had learned about drugs and alcohol while in college. It really helped me in my professional career. I was soon to find that all the people I would be working with for the next 30 years had pretty much the same extracurricular involvements as I, but just like me, had managed themselves to fool their way thru school, and were still at it today, just with shorter haircuts and coats and ties.

Eclectic Art 1970

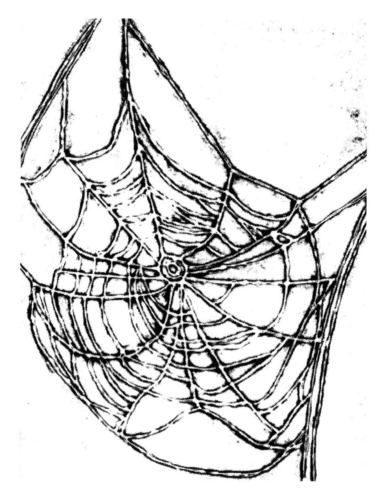

Triska Loftin

The Art of Fosters Store

White Longhair

THE WEST GEORGIAN

Walter Carmichael

MAY 21, 1971

What Can We Do?

Do you have some friends who got busted Monday night? I do. What can we do to help them?

I know, let's get mad. Let's go into Carrollton and burn the place down. Let's throw rocks and block traffic. If the facts in the case aren't gruesome enough, let's make up our own. We can tell them that a 10-year-old boy is in jail and even though that is a lie what difference does it make? If they don't believe you, then cuss them out with everything you can think of.

If you were a citizen of Carrollton and you saw a bunch of people that you really didn't understand and they came into your town blocking traffic,

WALTER CARMICHAEL

throwing rocks, and talking about burning the place down, what would you do?

You would keep an open mind, wouldn't you? You would walk in the courthouse and sit in the jury box with no opinion whatsoever. Maybe we can get the people in town so scared that they will be afraid to find our friends guilty. Isn't that what you think?

Yes, let's get mad and let's scare the hell out of everybody in town. That has got to be the way to help our friends. I guess we could go as individuals and talk to the people and try to make them understand what drugs are all about. No, that would never work.

And you people in town, what can you do? How can you stop the use of drugs? I know, let's put

those communist-backed weirdos in jail. That will straighten them out. I mean, just because they don't see themselves as doing anything wrong, jail will teach them how wrong they are, won't it?

And if we send these kids to jail, there won't be anybody else to take their place, will there? By sending these kids to jail it will keep other kids from starting on drugs. Hasn't that worked in the past?

REALITY

We've got to get these kids out of their doped up world and show them reality. We've got to get them in the churches so they can learn how to lead a life of peace and not go off protesting a war that is killing for peace. We've got to tell them about a world that can be over for everybody and everything just by pressing the right button. That's reality, isn't it?

I know, let's give them some heroes to look up to. How about Rusty Calley? I mean, there is a good American — he followed the system, he did his duty without question. It's a lot more of a crime to smoke grass than it is to kill women and children. Why else would our president let him off the hook? Isn't that who you want your son to be like?

Or maybe we could go to the kids as individuals with an open mind and try to understand their problem and maybe they could help us with some of ours. No, that would never work would it?

Chapter 34

BROTHERHOOD OF THE STORE

By Phil Spackman

Americal Patch

I recall being a senior in High School in Atlanta. Bill Harrell and I were about to graduate together from Avondale High School and I was trying to talk him into joining the army with me. We talked about how much fun it would be to drive jeeps through the woods and spend so much time in the outdoors. Bill said that it sounded great but doubted that the Army would be able to guarantee us that they'd keep us together. Bill went ahead to West Georgia and I, well, I joined the Army and delayed my education for a couple of years, my college education that is.

My return from Vietnam in late September, 1969 was marked by the Allman Brothers' free concerts in Piedmont Park and my acceptance to West Georgia College. All three events had a distinct impact on how things went for a twenty-one year old retired Army officer and aspiring college student.

My afternoon with Duane, et al reawakened my life-long love of blues and soul music and hearing it played by long-haired country lads with such ability was awe inspiring.

The last year of my Army time was spent in combat, and in retrospect I came away mostly whole, thrice wounded, often decorated, as was the wont of my employer at the time*.

As it turned out, the West Georgia connection that was about to unfold would have the most pleasant effect on my life. I had the good fortune to meet and befriend many native Carrolltonians as well as Doctors of History, Professors of Political Science, even a future Speaker of the United States House of Representatives. Most importantly, I added brothers to my heart. Dr. Melvin Steely had an impact on me measurably across decades for which I wish to thank him in print. He showed me the path to understanding through the study of history – i.e. all this has been done before, sometimes better than others and the value of courage as it occurs naturally in Americans – Thanks

Phil catching Frisbee

Richard Duncan, my room mate and coconspirator at Fosters Store, was an excellent young man, raised in a great family, a very recent graduate of West Georgia and a hell of lot of fun to run with. During our tenure in the "Honeymoon Suite"(previously know as The Worm Ranch or the Feed N Seed) behind the store, we traveled often, worked constantly, offered hospitality to all who sought it and, most of all, had more fun than most are ever allowed.

Up the hill the Storehouse was occupied at the time by Frank Brown, Chip Purdue, Mark Pitstick and a few others over the three years Duncan and I lived there. Of course Candy Carmichael occupied the little room under the store for a time, for which we were grateful since she provided artistic guidance, kindness and her stunning good looks. Steve Ensign and Ron Lightsey were always around although I don't really remember if those guys actually ever really had an address as such.

Candy Carmichael

Ron Lightzey

Steve Ensign

Phil Admiring Plants

After we finished our formal educations down the street at the college, Duncan and I, along with Lightsey and Ensign, began working for a company called General Corrosion Services out of Odessa, Texas. During our years of employment with the firm we worked in most all Southeastern states as far west as Texas and as far north as Virginia on projects for natural gas distribution companies. We maintained our residence at Foster's Store, although, absent there from for months at a time. Prior to one such absence we were able to pay our friend and landlord, Mr. L. R. Foster five months rent in advance and we always felt that act endeared us to him forever.

I remember the Student Activities Committee of West Georgia College in the early seventies. They were an odd group charged with booking weekend entertainment for a college whose students weren't on campus at the time. Many of their efforts were sad, some laughable but one effort stands out as exceptional.

Spackman in "Those Days".

Vince Vance and the Valients graced the West Georgia gym stage with a rock-a-billy flash worthy of Bill Haley and Carl Perkins. They played well, looked good and drank hard. The group was invited to the store following the show by the Texas lads there in residence for the purpose of a late night jam, a joint, a beer, etc. This is about the time that the natives in residence met Crissy LeBlanc----Vince's girl.

One of my store mates felt that this Louisiana hottie deserved better than she was getting in the Vance organization and offered her the moon----and delivered same as I recall. Once in the trap that was Foster's Store, our post concert music session degenerated rapidly when Vince realized Crissy had thrown in with one of the long haired Georgians and wasn't anywhere to be found, putting an end to our jam session.

As it were, Vince's dutiful road crew guys returned at least twice that evening to retrieve the now otherwise engaged Ms. LaBlance, but alas *and* alack, they were met only by outsized Texans loyal to the local talent. Eventually, Ms. LeBlanc was delivered to her bus in excellent spirits in an MG-B GT at six am for the balance of the tour and one might assume her life. I've never forgotten her odd but beautiful speech, but then again I didn't know her as well as my lucky store mate. He might remember more, but never tell.

Any Saturday afternoon at the Feed n Seed

Another time of note occurred while working over in Tuscaloosa, Alabama one week. Duncan and I had been on a pipeline job there for a while. We worked over there, for so much that we saw fit to rent a second residence, an apartment there for a time At the same time while we working so hard we were really hitting our stride with our foosball skills.   We even saw fit to buy our own table and took it with us every time we moved as our worked dictated.

We had kept records and it was something like 98 wins 2 losses over a certain period.

One night we went to a bar in downtown Tuscaloosa called the "Silver Dollar Saloon" and as customary, had some long neck Pabst Blue Ribbons and put our quarter on the foosball table while we stood at the bar politely waiting our turn.

The Silver Dollar was popular hang-out for University of Alabama students, especially, it seemed to us, with gents and ladies belonging to Greek organizations on campus and the play was fast and fun. The standard bet was the cost of the game and two beers to the winners. I should point out that my partner and I had not had hair cuts in four years and our challengers were rather clean cut. The U of Alabama campus is a pretty stylish and ritzy place, it turns out. That night, some of these pretty boys were really hogging the table it seemed to us, so finally, out of desperation; we said "what about our quarter? We've been waiting 45 minutes over here to play the winners".

After a couple more of our polite but pointed interruptions, one of

these straight laced and pretty frat guys finally said, "OK wise guys, then step up and take your punishment."

Richard Duncan in his prime

Of course, as if there could have ever been any doubt to the outcome of such a contest, it was simply and predictably, another great night for team Spackman and Duncan. We kept playing these over-privileged losers for about 1 1/2 hours without a single loss. It is a wonderful thing to get to play foosball all night in a strange bar and allow complete strangers to pick up the tab for it. At some point Richard and I had expected these guys to throw in the towel of defeat and let another, perhaps a more skilled pair of foosballers take us on, but it never happened. This whole activity, foosball, was just a great way for us to unwind after a long day spent working in the sun. We could play all night; even after a bathroom break. We came back and played and kept winning for another 2 hours. At some point after midnight our beer total stood at eighteen.

In those days, the gentlemanly and generous Mr. Duncan was always pleased to have longneck beers be distributed to whatever young ladies might linger some nights to observe the finer points of serious foosball competitions. They always seemed agreeable and often pleased, as easy and pleasant conversation abounded. However, sometimes, and this particular night, their escorts were not so enamored with our harmless gestures of friendship, and challenged us to a final game for one hundred dollars. A hundred dollars wagered by guys who had been taking a waxing for three hours seemed like pretty easy money and neither Richard nor I seemed at all concerned over the amount. I should've sensed something right then as the frat guys didn't seem to be concerned either over what was in those days, to most people, a pretty sizeable wager.

Richard Duncan never played better, there being money and women involved and all too quickly our young Alabama Frat friends were noticeably upset over their rapid defeat. Their offer to go double or nothing was respectfully declined in that we were actually making progress with a couple of the ladies by then.

The next part of this recollection is that it all happened very fast and much adrenaline was involved. While Richard headed up the narrow stairs to the men's room, the "Bama boys", thoroughly defeated by two handsome longhairs, and now quite fully alcohol-oiled and feeling the confidence in their numbers and numb to any good sense that they might have been raised with, plainly informed me that they intended to kick our hippie asses, regain their money and defend the honor of their dates.

I guess I was a bit surprised by these guys and their now stated intentions. "Dam", I thought to myself, "we going to have to fight over foosball?" Confronted like this all alone, all I could do was ask them if I might go retrieve my partner to bring the odds up to two one hundred fifty pound long hairs versus five or more healthy frat lads? They seemed agreeable to my request so I went up the long stairway to the second floor where Richard and the bathroom were.

I could hear a bunch mumbling and rumbling and turned around, as I was up the stairs, to see that there must have been 15 guys creepily following me, all the while hollering about whipping our asses. Quickly I arrived at the locked men's room door where I knocked loudly and sounded off to Richard to unlock the latch and let me in quick! Once inside the door, I closed and latched it behind us, then I blew by Duncan, and went to immediately kick the bathroom window out of its frame and by my actions and words apprised Richard of the quickly deteriorating situation just outside the plywood door and beseeched and assured my foosball playing partner, "that the drop to the shed roof was only eight feet down and an easy drop from there to the ground" and safety. (Being blind with his contact lenses he had to trust me and the pounding at the door audibly confirmed that this was the time for action and not deliberation). Hey, I only lied by about four feet regarding the distance to the ground. Trusting me fully and grasping the seriousness of the situation fully, Richard followed my order immediately as I passionately suggested to him that he jump first as I held to the door against the onslaught of a horde of drunken Greek attackers. He jumped right away and when I heard him laughing, that was my cue to sacrifice the door to the losers, just a thickness of plywood between us, and I followed Richard head first, employing a parachute landing fall, to a roll, to some success, and came up running, hopping to the dumpster, quick onto the ground, to the MG and headed homeward, bound for safety.

But alas, just about that same instant, the still unvanquished and ever so angry mob figured out what had happened came pouring out the front door en masse yelling, "There they are." "Let's go get 'em", quickly closing the distance between us across the grey gravel parking lot.

L to R, Spackman, Duncan & Carmichael cars

My old car was a good one...a real classic, but it did have one curious thing about it that I could have lived without. Sometimes the fuel pump wouldn't work and I would have to lean out the door and take a wrench to reach under the car and tap it good a few times to get it to pump fuel. Wouldn't you know it? It chose that exact moment to act up and wouldn't work just as the mad crowd of frat guys was closing in on us. Somehow, I managed the presence of mind to lean out the door, tapped it just in the right place with just the right amount of force to make the motor come to life, and we took off like a bullet in the Alabama night, grey gravel dust and rocks giving our former foosball mates a last and memorable farewell. I held my breath until I cornered it around the block back towards our part of town and safety. I still remember that neon sign in my rearview mirror, lighting up the whole group of what "coming up empty looks like". It was just their turn this night, and, no, we didn't go back there for a very long time.

When we got home we decided not to share this story with our outsized roommates, Jim Hill, Joe Don Hughes, Kurt Hughes, Bill Lupardis and Joe D. Brown from Midland, Texas, in that they would have considered such behavior less than courageous. I thought it was great fun and besides we didn't want to shoot those young men anyway. One hardly ever gets a date after shooting the escort, even in Alabama.

Phil was one of the most highly decorated combat veterans of the Vietnam War. Besides being awarded the Distinguished Service Cross (The DSC is the Nation's second highest award for valor) Phil, an Armored Calvary Platoon Leader, 11th Light Infantry Brigade, American Division, also received four bronze stars with V device, three silver stars, Combat Infantryman's badge, Airborne Wings Ranger Tab, and three Purple Hearts for his "heroism in battle".

Steve Ensign and Frank Brown
Horseshoes was another Foster's Favorite Activity

(Editor's note: This is Bill Harrell's last cartoon for the WEST GEORGIAN.)

The Art of Fosters

old fresh
winds blow
across falling
lands
  singing the
answer
  singing the unquestionable
word
  telling me
to regulate
my changing
nature
  so I may
purify this
senseless
system
  so blows
this valuable
wind
  blowing me
too

Bill Harrell

Winter Eclectic 1971

Do you remember back to Chapter 2 of this Book? It was called Snapshots. This chapter is called "More Snapshots".

The deal here, just like in Chapter 2, there are just more stories than a single book can cover. Chapter two dealt with things that occurred during the early years of Foster's. This chapter deals with the latter There is a whole nother book in this chapter.

The world had certainly changed. Just look at these snapshots

Chapter 35

More Snapshots

By various people

Snapshot 1

I dated a guy who was living at Foster's Store - the Feed and Seed - when I started at WGC in the Fall of 1974 until 1977 when he graduated. His name was Mike Robinson. He lived there for a time with another guy named Mike, whose last name I don't remember but was from Carrollton. A guy from Jasper GA, known to me only as Ravin' Dave, was Mike R's roommate for a time at the Feed & Seed and also lived for a while in the store proper up by the road. A woman named Mary but known to all as Sunshine lived below Foster's Store with her boyfriend, who's name I cannot recall. Mike R. and I lost touch after he graduated, but I heard he passed over sometime in the 80's.

Winston Spacy's "story" brought back some memories. He writes "...Beyond that there was the remains of what looked like an old couch and a large wire spool just in front of what must of been the ruins of the old Feed n Seed." I spent a lot of time at the Feed and Seed, sitting on a couch on the front porch; there was a wire spool there too. I remember one afternoon in particular when Mr. Foster was cutting the grass beside Foster's Store, to the west of the driveway. The grass had been waist to chest high for a long while, so Mike R. had been growing a pot plant in a container out there, where it was hidden by the grass but still got sun. Anyway, Mr. Foster cut the grass (not the pot), and exposed the plant, which was at least waist high, to the traffic whizzing by on the highway. Fortunately Mike R. was there and rescued the plant before anything of note occurred. I still remember Mike running up to Mr. Foster saying "Wait, Mr. Foster, wait!" as he grabbed the container and moved it behind the house. (I think it was harvested shortly thereafter.)

In case you haven't heard from anyone regarding the store in post 1974, I thought I'd fill you in on this little bit. Thanks for bringing back the memories.

Sincerely, Susan Carter

Snapshot 2

Hansard is not supposed to have any corresponding info on me or my family...there are approx 16 people who have restraining orders on "Hog Body". The only thing I remember about Fosters Store is that I became engaged twice to three different girls and one goat during the summer of 1969....enough.....you are welcome to stay in touch...

but not the "hog"....Vance

Snapshot 3

Hi,

My name is Kerry Godard. I moved into the basement of the Store when Candy moved out; summer 1973, I think. It was a trick living there with the ceiling height of about 6 feet and me being 6'2". Chip, Frankie, and I moved to Tyus at the end of the summer.

I have a couple of questions. Does the t-shirt with the picture of the store only come in black? And, when are you going to tell us who the folks are in the pictures at the reunion? It would be nice to put names with the faces.

Snapshot 4

So many memories. Phil Hart, class of '74, just sent me the info. I came to WGC in 1969 and graduated in 1974. I knew Candy, Shelley, Sam, Frankie, Bobo, Turkett, Walter, Spackman, Chip Perdue, etc. As you said, I came to school, at age 17, in the fall, wearing Villager skirts, little flats, and nylon stockings. By the next spring, I had only jeans, halter tops, and was usually barefoot. When I moved out of the dorm and into my house with Tish Baker, Carol Smith, and Linda (she later lived in Roopville with Roger Crysler), my life changed dramatically.

But as you described it, the world had changed dramatically, too. People I had gone to high school with in my little hometown of Cedartown, GA had been killed in Vietnam, and others I knew well were serving in Vietnam. When I think of the front pages of the newspapers at that time, all I can remember are the body counts that they listed every day. I also remember that Bobo and Spackman never would talk about being over there.

Yet, with everything else, I loved just about every moment at WGC and had a few very enjoyable times at Foster's Store, Headqarter's, the Farm, Resurrection City, Jackson Courts, and all the outdoor concerts. We were young and didn't need a lot of money. Bill Holden (Red) and I were married in March, 1974, and we moved to Marietta that summer. We were divorced approximately three years later., but remained close because of our son, Reid. Bill died two years ago and I saw Bobo, Nancy, Turkett, and a lot of folks. Thanks for putting all this together. I can't wait to see the book and the movie!

Myra Ray Holt

Snapshot 5

Hey Wayne

Great effort. Very impressive and evocative of...well...like **Tommy Carlisle** of *Eric Quincy Tate* said to me awhile back (we were at

Piedmont Park for the *Blues Musicians Photo Project* and discussing those **WGC** days, where they played the **STD** (!?) house regularly... [Tommy doesn't indulge at all now, BTW]

"Man...I don't know if I can drive home, just <u>talkin'</u> about this."

I'm a photographer now, as I was then, and have various photographs of **Headquarters** (where I ran the head shop when it moved out to the solarium) and I lived directly overhead with fellow art-student Josie Hays in the 3rd floor room that had the balcony/cupola. We threw firecrackers down on the small 2nd floor balcony below, where Son Baxley often entertained the Mann brothers and various shroomers. HQ was a wild and wooly place with characters worthy of film.

My favorite shots are of the two marches I covered, hanging out of my white '59 Triumph TR-3 (which was easy to do, as the doors are rudimentary).

A long line of hippies snaking down Maple Street to the town square...What sedition!

Remember when dissent was legal?

Democracy was nice... while it lasted. Funny how I'm battling the same fascists now as then...but the deck is now so stacked.

I was a Journalism minor (Art major) and did a research project on the Mandeville house, interviewing the last surviving granddaughter. I have <u>never</u> used the term *Civil War* <u>since</u>, as she gave me a 20-min. tongue-lashing on precisely WHY a good southern boy DID NOT use that *Yankee-forced* designation, when I had "slipped" and indeed evoked that heretical term in a question to her.

Understand, this was AFTER a 30 second silent gaze from her stone-cold blue eyes at my near-unforgivable faux paux.

I do go on...Anyhow, keep up the shocking nostalgia... *It makes all the parents nervous now.*

Later,
Paul Shoffner

Left Georgia College/ HQ
Summer of '69 to Fall of '74

Snapshot 6

Hey Wayne,

I've got the picture for ya!
Unfortunately, most of it is filled with these two girls that Perdue and I
were hanging with during one of our parties. Got to admit, the picture
does capture the unique atmosphere of that room. Just think about
how many people have partied in that room over the years! Check-out
all the stuff hanging on the walls and ceiling. Cool!

I've got a couple of other pictures during the party, but they really don't
have a perspective of the house. There's pictures of a bunch of us laying
on my water-bed in a bedroom. Come to think of it, some time ago I'd
send some of these pictures to Perdue in a Xmas card. Write a note to
his wife like "can you believe this guy looked like this"! We probably
should see if he hung on to any of them.

Don't know who would have been the last to live at the store. I know I
came back once after the typical group had all moved on. I was kind of
a professional student and was around longer than the others.

Enjoy!

Mark

Snapshot 7

I am a West Georgia alumnus (1990). In the six years that I was there I
heard from time to time stories about Foster's Store and the Farm. The
late 60's and early 70's were times that I was too young to remember
and really be apart of. The stories and pictures from that time fascinate
me to this day. I would greatly appreciate any of the material you have
to offer. I do plan on buying the book. May those times always be close
to your heart just as the times I had there are to mine. Sincerely, Ron
Martin (class of 1990)

Snapshot 8

Mr. Lankford,

After wondering how in the world I'll be able to keep in touch with all of my soon-to-be graduating friends, I just looked down and realized that it's at my fingertips. Yeah, everyone loves handwritten letters (if the handwriting is legible)--but what can be better than sending an email half way across the world and having it land right in front of their eyes within seconds. Yup--emails are wonderful...they serve the lazy and the busiest. However, www.fostersstore.com gives me the idea to create a similar website (oh how I wish I were computer literate! *calling all computer nerds*).

My father is John Penny, WGC student from '69-'72. He lived in Jackson Court Apartments and, at some point, in an old lady's vacant chicken coup--I can only imagine the feathers he and his friends ruffled! He can't really remember exactly where Jackson Court or the coup were--but then again, college was a *high*light of his life. Speaking of *my* father, I'm Annalee. I'll be graduating May 11th with a degree in Mass Communications and a minor in Marketing (my plans are to host and eventually produce a cultural travel show--but you know how that goes once someone graduates...I could become a dirty politician for all I know :] --I'm pretty set on my idea of traveling, though!). Here I go getting off on a bit of a tangent...but, once again, as a Mass Comm major, talking/writing is breathing (haha). My dad told me about the article in the Perspective on Foster's Store. I haven't had the chance to get my hands on the article, though I did something that gave me more insight. After scrolling down the opening page of fostersstore.com (before reading a single thing), I realized that I'll be in for some good reading and laughs. And was I wrong? Am I ever?!! Haha--just to let you know how much I enjoyed the articles and pictures, I check back with the site to read any new updates (or anything I might have missed before). And to REALLY show you the impact it's had on me--I want to include the site and quotes in my upcoming article for my Feature Writing course. My professor loves the idea so much that he asks me every class period about it...and the West Georgian's editor (also in my class) wants to run my story. My general topic is "alumni" (kind of a 'where are they now' & their 'WGC' life)...and I mostly want to focus on www.fostersstore.com and the likes of Jackson Courtsonians. I love your (and everyone who's helped out) website and I tell other students to check it out as well. I hope you grant me the 'o.k.' to go through with my article, using your website as a reference. The following is a short summary of what I turned into my professor:

From today's standpoint, living (as a college student) during the late 60's and early 70's could have been one of the best time periods in history—depending upon which aspects. Compared to my $395 rent, there were West Georgia College students (years '66-'74) who had to dish out a low—or to some, a mediocre—$40 a month. Foster's Store (an old retail grocery store that was located on the right side of HWY 166) was a "home" to a handful of students while they attended (or partied away) WGC. Now, as WGC alumni (many in their 50's), Foster's Store residents (or of the liking—Jackson Court Apartments) have the opportunity to reminisce about their high times in life (no pun intended). Mr. Wayne Lankford has recently taken something that was non-existent during the '60's and 70's—the Internet—and created www.fostersstore.com. This "far out" and humorous website allows the '66-'74 graduates to come together, share memories, and provide pictures of the presently successful grads (some of whom were probably wondering if they would even have time to squeeze graduation in amongst all the parties). www.fostersstore.com is bringing old buddies together and inviting new people (such as myself, a daughter of a WGC '72 grad) to have a laugh (or perhaps to shed a tear) at some of the best times of their lives—the college years!

I hope you don't mind me submitting what I did--I couldn't resist writing about something that I find clever and entertaining! Also, your style of writing grabbed my attention (none of this fluffy stuff--just straight to the point and lovin' it). I have several questions I want to ask...and would like your permission to quote you within my article. If you could scrounge a few minutes to give answers (I'm not asking that you reply to all--though, I'm definitely not going to argue if you do!!) I would be absolutely appreciative! Thank you for your website and the spark it created...congratulations on the website's success!

1. What is one thing you know now, that you wish you knew while you were in college?

2. Has www.fostersstore.com allowed you to talk to college buddies whom you never thought you would see again?

3. Would you mind naming a few of the bands that performed (we all know that Love Valley has turned into Love Vacancy--I have not seen one single band since I've been here!!!)

4. Are the rumors true that beer companies would sponsor concerts

and parties--kegs included?!   ohhh, happy days....

5. If you could go back, is there anything you would have done differently during your college career?

6. Have you 'visited' Foster's Store lately?

7. Do you and your colleagues get together and think back on the lives in the fast lane (outside of fostersstore.com)?

8. What was your area of study?

9. What was your first job straight out of college?

10. Does your present job relate to your field of study?

11. What is your personal quote? (mine is: 'the two greatest things you could ever do...live & love')

12. Did you ever have Newt Gingrich as a professor?

13. Which professor influenced you the most? Favorite class?

14. Do you have children? Did (do) they attend UWG?

15. What is one thing that you would tell the 2005 graduates to prepare them for the real world?

If there is anything you would like to add, you are more than welcome!! Thank you Mr. Lankford for your creativity and want to share!

Sincerely,
Annalee Penny

Snapshot 9

Annalee,

This is my answer.

15. What is one thing that you might tell the next group of graduates to prepare them for the real world?

Think about what you think you may want to be doing when you are fifty, not next year. Then start doing it tomorrow. If you want to sail around the world, don't go to work in an office for 30 years and dream the whole time of the sea. Go to sea tomorrow! Maybe start off as a deck hand. Try to get in touch with your soul; it's your connection to the universe. Listen to that voice in your head. It knows what your destiny is. Trust the voice. It's the real you.

Eric, Billy and the Gremlin

Snapshot 10

By

Wayne Eliot Lankford

FADE IN:

EXT. RAIN WET TWO LANE HIGHWAY - JUST OUTSIDE OF MILOVILLE

A 1973 yellow AMC Gremlin is seen moving through a heavy morning fog.

INT. THE YELLOW GREMLIN

The car has two occupants. Billy Genevas is behind the wheel, Eric
Rodriguez slouches back in the front passenger seat.   Rain has just
stopped, but the windshield wipers are still wiping, making a terrible
rubbing noise against the now dry windshield.

Eric

> Hey man, You think you could shut off the
> windshield wipers!   I'm trying to sleep
> here!

A possum darts out in front of the Gremlin. Its two occupants look in
amazement at the shining red eyes reflected back from their bright
headlight beams. It quickly moves back across the road in the direction
it came from.

Billy belatedly decides that the headlights on all this time aren't
really helping and turns them off along with the windshield wipers.

Billy

> Man! Was that cool, or what?

Eric

> Really cool man. I mean did you see those
> eyes? I bet that possum is as about as
> hungry as I am.

Billy

> Me too, man.   Do you have any cash left
> over?
> I used all my pay up at the bar.

Eric (Frustrated-Exhausted)

> Hell, I'm broke too, and if I don't get
> something to eat pretty soon I'm going
> pass the fuck out.

Billy: (Laughing-jokingly)

> What! Not again, that would be like the
> third time tonight. Or, you want me to
> load up the hash pipe for a little taste?

Eric (Serious now)

Listen, we got all of Nathan's tools in
the back here. How about we go up to the
square and bust open a couple of drink
machines and then we'll do the pancake
house in a big way. I could really dig on
a big old stack of pancakes and a bowl of
grits!

                    Billy

Is that what your degree's in, busting
open drink machines? You must be crazy
man.   I'm not going do a coke machine for
a stack of pancakes. We've got a few cans
of Beanie Wienies back at the store. And,
what if we get caught?

                    Eric

Look, it's so damn early, the only living
things out today are us and that ugly
possum. You can wait in the car. This'll
only take a second or two and then we'll
be swimming in the 30 weight with Aunt
Jemima.

                    Billy

You're nuts, E.

               Eric (Smiling Bright)

Hey man, you can trust me. I'm a college
graduate!

FADE OUT - EXTERIOR SHOT -GREMLIN ON HIGHWAY

FADE IN - MANSION IN UPPERCLASS NEIGHBORHOOD

DISSOLVE TO INTERIOR - RUTLEDGE DINNING ROOM - SAME MORNING

Richard "Budd" Rutledge perusing his Sunday newspaper is seated at the
head of a very formal dining room table. He looks up away from his
paper, hearing something. He is very still. The camera follows the
sound of music as it gets louder and louder following away.

PAN TO - MASTER BEDROOM TO MASTER BATHROOM

In master bath of the house Lisa Rutledge sits before a mirrored
dressing table smoking a cigarette, dancing around in her seat,
listening to the Rolling Stones blaring through the small speakers of an
AM-FM Clock radio. "Honkey Tonk Women". She applies the finish to her
now hot pink fingernails. Finishing, she rises and in the same motion,
flushes the toilet and sweeps her pink silk dressing gown closed. She
wraps the drawstring tight around her trim waist, turns radio off and
exits towards the Dining room. She pauses a moment, reflecting to
admire her ample cleavage in a hallway mirror, then quickly passes down

the hall to the dining room, where husband is still engrossed in his Sunday morning newspaper.

MASTER DINNING ROOM

>   Lisa (Entering dinning room)
>
>   So, today's the big one, hey big -'n'!
>
>   Budd (Irritated)
>
>   Lisa, I wish you'd quit saying that. You
>   are about to drive me crazy. You were way
>   overboard last night at the club.
>
>   Lisa (Unsympathetic, Sarcastic)
>
>   Oh sweetie, you're just no fun anymore,
>   with all this "send our Bud to Atlanta"
>   talk everyday.

Lisa moves to the formal sideboard. She lifts a large pitcher of orange juice and pours herself a glass, then moves slowly towards her husband.

>   I'd be just as happy if you'd just get a
>   real job with some of these highfalutin
>   friends of ours. Hell, we don't need any
>   of it. I'd be OK with me if you'd just
>   keep on playing the big time "poly-sigh-
>   prof", down at the college.

The young Lisa pauses again and moves closer towards her older husband.

>   This campaign trail will be fine for a
>   while but, I mean, you better ride me too,
>   Cowboy, before I jump the fence on you.

Lisa bends forward towards her seated husband, she leans her ample breasts just in front of his face, and then pushes her right hand, palm down, and fingers spread between the pages of the newspaper and his eyes.

>   Lisa (Seductively)
>
>   You like my new nail color? I think it
>   will go great with all those red, white,
>   and blue garlands they'll have up on the
>   stage this afternoon at the lake.

Standing up straight, Lisa pulls her dressing gown open and she pushes her pubic area to the corner of the table and points a finger down towards her panties.

>   Lisa
>
>   And look at this, these nails; they go
>   pretty good with my new panties! I tell
>   you, red white and blue underwear is hard

to come by, at least for some people, in a
small town like this-n.

Budd stares dreamingly for a deep breath or two as Lisa breathes a bit
more into her husbands face, then blows on her now dry fingernails.

> Budd (Reshaping his paper, he sits back a bit in
> his chair)

> You are something else, darling. Did your
> Daddy know what a nasty girl you were?

> Lisa (Rises up and back, she walks easily back
> to the other end of the table where she seats herself)

> We don't worry about that anymore, do we?
> Why you still worry so much is beyond me.
> The guy you're running against can't even
> quack these days, he's limping is so bad.

> Budd (with a little laugh)

> Worrying, yeah. I just hope that crazy
> little brother of yours and his band
> doesn't forget to show up - and on time.

> Those guys really live on the edge but
> they do help draw the crowd.

> Lisa (Seductively)

> I know something you can draw, for me.

Budd moves aside the pile of newspapers clearing the dining room table
in front of him.

FADE OUT - DISSOLVE TO AERIAL SHOT OF YELLOW GREMLIN

The gremlin pulls up along side a Coke machine on the Miloville Town
square.

DISOLVE TO:

FADE IN - OUTSIDE OF FOSTER'S STORE

DISOLVE TO:

INTERIOR - WOMB ROOM - MAIN LIVING AREA

The floor is raised three feet making it impossible to stand up
straight. It has thick blue shag carpet, wall to wall.

Store resident Jesse Carroll sits cross legged, Indian style, strumming
his acoustic guitar, at the same time admiring his reflection in the
mirror behind the bar. He pays special attention to his new gold
earring and keeps jerking his face repeatedly forward and back to
observe his pierced earring sparkle in the reflected early morning
light.

Jesse (singing)

Let's see, G, C, Deeee!

Jesse strums the cord combination on his guitar, looks at himself and then makes a note in the spiral notebook beside him, then looks in the mirror repeating the process.

Jesse: (Singing, slowly)

"Budd Rutledge is the one.

He's the one to go to the Capitol one day.

He's the man with the fans…no no no."

(Pausing to make a change in the notebook
and looks in the mirrow)

"He's the one with the plan

He's the one man with the plan

Let's all give him a plan , that anyone
can understand

He is the man with the plan
And the plan is a…"

Jesse hears the front screen door spring expand and the door open and slam itself shut as fellow storemate White Longhair steps inside. He is with his date from the previous evening, the head of the math department over at the high school. She is heard complaining to White just outside the door by Longhair's white Volkswagen Beetle.

Math Teacher

Would you please hurry! I have to be in
church in 45 minutes! You know I'm
playing the organ today!

Longhair looks into the womb room from the hallway to Jesse.

Jesse

Plays the organ pretty good, does she?

Longhair (smiling, nodding affirmatively)

I'll be back in about 20 minutes. You
guys doing that Lake concert thing for Bud
this afternoon?

Jesse

Yeah, me and Richard. Nathan, Billy and
Eric are all volunteered for it. You
ought to come and help us set up.

(Still looking in the mirror)

   They'll be plenty of fried chicken out
there today.

                    Longhair

Maybe so. Right now, I guess I have to see
that this angel gets her soul back to
heaven before her hour of power kicks in.

                    Jesse

Does this mean that you're in love again?

                    Longhair

Absolutely Brother! Darlene, here, is the
real thing. And she does keyboards. But
we gotta go. Later.

                    Jesse: (continuing his song writing)

If the people only knew
That Bud here is a Jew.,,,,,,,,,

DISSOLVE TO TOWN SQUARE

EXT. MILOVILLE POLICE CAR

Just off the town square, police car with two city cops, listening to
Reverend Ike on the AM radio, having coffee and fried eggs sandwiches as
they "guard" the town center.

Behind the wheel is Corporal Mark, still considered a rookie cop to his
senior partner, Sergeant Samuel Suskind. He was the policeman that
everyone referred to as, "Sergeant Sunshine", least ways behind his
back.

                    AM radio speaker in squad car
              (Static - cracking) Voice of Reverend Ike

          And I've seen the rain , and I've a seen
          the wind, and I have seen powerful glory
          be to God-a in the-midst of a situation un
          defensibility in and out of itself in the
          midst's of it self, and all the world was
          glory in the days when the final wind
          came,...

          Sergeant Sunshine (Notices a commotion in front of them
and turns the radio volume down)

          Is that what I think it is?

> Corporal Mark (speaks very slowly, pretending to
> squint)

I don't know, if you see a yellow Gremlin,
and a long haired hippie with a crow bar
beating the crap out of a coke machine, it
looks like, then, maybe, I think, you and
I are seeing the same thing?

They hear the banging noise even as far away as they are parked.

> Sergeant Sunshine (turning the radio volume
> down further, then off)

He's really knocking the heck out that
thing, ain't he?

> Corporal Mark

I wonder if he knows the vending machine
guys just cleaned all the quarters out a
couple of hours ago.

Sergeant Sunshine smiles. He reaches under his seat and produces a heavy
brown paper bag, pats it a couple of times on the bottom, so the change
inside jingles.

> Sergeant Sunshine

Probably not.   Let's not tell him just
yet. These hippies tire easy. They'll be
easier to collar when they're too tuckered
out to run from us.

> Corporal Mark

Yeah,   and he ain't never gonna bust
through that steel box with that little
ole crow bar.

> Sergeant Sunshine

I guess he don't have a key. Wonder if
they got any good weed on them. I could
use a toke about now.

> Corporal Mark

Almost a sure thing. It's that same ole
yellow Gremlin, ain't it?

> Sergeant Sunshine (frustrated)

Yeah, It's damn worthless, fuckin-Billy-
Genevas. Again!

Corporal Mark starts car and pulls slowly away from curb and up the
street toward the parked yellow Gremlin.

DISSOLVE BACK TO FOSTER'S STORE

INT. WOMB ROOM

> Jesse (Singing To Himself)
>
> Budd Rutledge is the one.
> He's the one to hit Atlanta on the run.
> He is the man with the plan.
> But he ain't as good looking as I am.
> And his ear's not pierced and he's,…

DISSOLVE TO RUTHLEDGE HOUSE DINNING ROOM

INT.

Budd and Lisa sit at opposite ends of the dining room table. Bud flips back and forth between his Bible and his copy of The Federalist Papers. He picks them up, comparing them, one in one hand, and one in the other hand, weighs them, raising and lowering his hands, looking from one to the other.

Lisa sits relaxed, smokes a cigarette as she rests one bare leg atop the highly polished table. Above and behind her is a very large impressionistic painting of Monticello. As she exhales, she blows a perfect smoke ring and it floats out towards Bud and dissipates right over an overturned silver fruit bowl in the middle of the extra long table, its wax fruit contents scattered around it.

> Lisa: (Slowly, dreamingly)
>
> Hey Budd, how soon after we get to Atlanta, will we get to meet the President?

> Budd (Bothered, mind focused elsewhere now)
>
> If we can get our big butts into the capitol, I guess we will pretty soon. But there's a whole bunch of work to do before that. I'm just announcing my plans to run today.

> Lisa
>
> Hell Bud, Everybody and their brother's known for a year you were going to do this.

> Budd
>
> I suppose, but intentions without cash are just intentions my young bride.

> Lisa

Well, I'm your secret weapon, baby. You
know you can depend on me. And if you can
depend on me, then you know the rest. And
that's all you will ever need to know.

Budd stares and smiles at his young wife Lisa.

DISSOLVE TO TOWN SQUARE

The white Miloville squad car moves slowly to the Coke machine where
worn out, would-be bandit Eric, short of breath bends over and vomits
behind the machine. Billy is sprawled out in the drivers seat, fast
asleep.

Sergeant Sunshine surveys the scene, turns to Corporal Mark.

                    Sergeant Sunshine

        Have   that   read,   "Car   occupant
        unconscious."

                Sergeant Sunshine (Seated in the passenger side of
the squad car, leans out toward Eric)

        Hey, boy, you look like you might be in
        the market for some Dynamite?

                Eric (Startled, finishes puking, speaking slowly,
breathless)

        Holy shit! Sergeant Sunshine! What you
        doing up so early? This isn't what it
        looks like!

                Sergeant Sunshine (Shaking his head, his right
elbow jutting out the open squad car window and lifting slightly the
brim of his hat)

        Well, that's good to know, because to this
        trained eye, it appears that you two boys
        are   having   trouble   robbing   an
        uncooperative Coke Machine.

                    Eric

        No Sir, we just found all this. I was
        looking for some identification marks on
        the crowbar, maybe to return it to its
        owner.

                Corporal Mark: (Leans forward into the steering
wheel with intimate tone)

        Hey Eric, I thought you finished school
        and got drafted? What you still doing
        hanging around Miloville?

                    Eric

Yeah, I'm drafted. I have to report to
Fort Benning for my basic training two
weeks. I'm just killing time I guess.
Hey man, you guys aren't thinking about
arresting us, are you? I mean with me
fixing to head to Nam and protect you from
the commies and all.

                    Sergeant Sunshine

Eric, you get in the back seat here. Your
dazed partner in crime over there, if we
can wake him up, can follow us down the
street to the station and we'll let the
Chief figure it out. He'll be heading out
to church in a little bit. But I don't
know. You idiots really did a number on
that Coke Machine.

            Billy (waking up fully now)

I may still be too drunk to drive.

                    Sergeant Sunshine

You can drive a half a block can't you? Or
will we have to add some more charges to
being just plain stupid?

                        Billy

Stupid is OK, I guess, but we have a lot
of work to do. We got another gig this
afternoon, and we are so hungry!

Can we stop by the Pancake House and you
guys get us something to go maybe? There
any food at the jail this morning?

Billy gets out the Gremlin and than gets in again.

                Billy (Picks up something)

Almost forgot the crowbar.

                    Sergeant Sunshine

We wouldn't want you to forget any of the
tools of your trade.

                        Billy

Wouldn't want to do that.

DISSOLVE BACK TO FOSTER'S STORE

INT. WOMB ROOM

Jesse, by run through, finishes campaign song quick and does a quick singing of it. Richard Hurt plays along with him on his own acoustic guitar.

>   Together:

> Budd Rutledge is the one.

> He's the one to go to Atlanta in a run.

> He's the man with the plan

> He's the one man with the plan

Phone rings in the center hallway and Richard, closest to it, slides his legs down, through the crawl space opening, rises and walks to the end of the center hallway and picks up the phone.

FOSTER'S STORE - MAIN HALLWAY AND BACK AND FOURTH CUTS BETWEEN THE STORE AND THE JAIL

INTERCUT: Richard: (into phone)

>   Hell-o

>   Eric (Through receiver)

> Hey Man, what's going on?

>   Richard

> Eric, hey, fantastic! Jesse and I just finished Bud's campaign song. Where are you? Been trying to find you all morning?

>   Eric

> That's what I'm calling about. Looks like me and Billy are in a little trouble. They've got us locked up down here at the police station and the Sheriff says he's not going to cut us loose unless we can get somebody to go our bail?

>   Richard: (laughing)

> You fuck-head! What did you guys do this time?

>   Eric

> Well, they say that we were destroying private property or something; I think they are talking about a Coke machine up here on the town square or someplace.

Richard

I told you guys to ease off on the beers
last night! Did you spend you all the
money you made at the gig on beer?

Eric

Yeah, the gig, yeah that too. They say
we'll have to play there three more times
before we can get even with them for all
the beer we drank during the breaks and
afterwards. But I figure they'll let that
slide when I leave for the Army. Anyway,
we're innocent here, I keep telling them.
We weren't actually caught in the act.

Richard

Yeah, sure!

Eric

No, really. That Coke machine was
committing suicide when we got there. We
were wrestling the crowbar away from it
when Officer Sunshine and good-old Private
Mark pulled up.

Richard

You idiot! Ok, I'll call Bud. I'm sure
he and Lisa will do the bail thing for
you? Did they say how much it was?

Eric

Usually it's five hundred dollars. Each.

Richard

Hang in there. I'll get back with you.

INT. THE JAIL

Eric hangs up the phone on the counter, and a female deputy pulls it
off. A buzz releases the lock and Eric turns and walks through the
steel door back to Billy sitting alone on a long dark wooden bench that
faces a couple of steel case desks and three other doors that lead out
to other areas of the jail. No one else is around.

Billy (To Eric)

Is everything OK?

Eric

I guess. Richard is going to call Bud.
Maybe he'll come and bail us out? If
not, we'll have to do a week or so here in
the jail when we're not picking up trash
all week out on the highway. Who the fuck
knows?

                    Billy

Hell, this is my entire fault! We didn't
have to be here if I had gotten around to
harvesting my pot plants instead of
putting it off until today.

                    Eric

Are you still claiming to have a bunch of
weed growing out there somewhere?

                    Billy

Hell yeah! Those plants were about six
feet tall ten days ago. And with the rain
we had the other day, I bet you it's grown
another foot. Six of ten of them are
doing great! I should be able to sell it
for all the money we'll need for a while.

                 Eric (Shaking his head)

To be from such a rich family, you seem to
have even less money than any of us.

                    Billy

Oh I'm absolutely fucked financially until
I'm 25, like my big sis was until she
graduated last year. What I have to live
on now a year hardly keeps me in beer and
guitar stings.

You know about it, everybody does. When I
dropped out of school the cash flow
practically disappeared. That was my dead
parents deal in their will.

Billy shifts his body to a ready-for-more-sleep-again-position

                    Eric (sighing as he moves
into a similar position)

I wish I could disappear about now. But,
I hear they have great pot in Viet Nam.

Eric and Billy descend into silence on the long wooden church pew type
bench. Eric drifts off first, dreaming of a peaceful jungle far away.
Billy, exhausted from the long night, finishes the egg sandwich and cup
of water from a church lady representing Alcoholics Anonymous. Billy
eyes the card she left him about meeting times, as he drifts into deep

sleep. The card drops to the floor, and as it does, a multi colored Fu dog casually walks through the scene slowly, pausing to breathe deeply, the audience can hear it breathing into its nostrils the odors of Billy and Eric. The Fu dog turns, and passes towards the wall and disappears.

DISSOLVE the fu dog, then the whole scene

INT. FOSTER'S STORE

Richard leans into the womb room, speaking in a business like manner to Jesse.

                    Richard

          I guess it's left up to us again. I'm
          giving Budd a call to ask if he can go
          down there this morning before church and
          bail out our drummer and bass player.

                    Jesse (Seemingly, unconcerned)

          I guess so, brother. . .

          But, you haven't said anything about my
          new earring.

          What do you think?

                    Richard   (shaking   his   head   all
around)

          All the earring stuff for guys; it's still
          too confusing for me, Jess.   It's OK I
          guess, but for me, I can't ever remember
          if it's the right ear or the left ear that
          means you're gay or straight.   And you
          know when you're facing somebody left is
          right and right is left and when you're a
          little stoned it's just too much to have
          to fucking think about. I mean, for me.

                    Jesse (Smiling big)

          Then you never met Marva did you?

Richard moves back form the womb room door opening a few steps down the hall to the wall phone and begins to dial one of fifty phone numbers scratched into the cheap wall board paneling.

DISSOLVE BETWEEN STORE HALLWAY AND RUTHLEDGE MANSION MASTER BEDROOM AND BACK AND FORTH

Bud is in the final motions of tying his tie in front of the bathroom mirror. Lisa, sitting on the bed, takes off her right ear ring and answers the phone ringing from the bedside table.

                    Lisa (In her normal Voice)

Rutledge residence, this is Lisa.

On the other end of the phone is Richard back at the store.

                    Richard

          Morning Lisa, it's Richard.   It sure was
          good to see you last night.   You were
          dancing up a storm out there!

                    Lisa

          Hey Cutie!   Yeah baby, I had a great time!
          It was like old times till old "Stick in
          the Mud Budd" here makes us leave-just
          when I'm getting fired up!

                    Richard

          That husband of yours is a Lucky man!
          Is he there?   Seems like our drummer and
          our bass player could use a little of his
          legal expertise this morning.

                    Lisa

          That fuck-head brother of mine again!
          What did he do this time?

                    Richard

          The idiots got busted this morning for
          trying to beat up on a Coke machine on the
          Town Square.

Lisa laughs out loud, then attempts to control it. Bud, his tie tied
walking towards her to take the phone.

                    Lisa (to her husband)

          Looks like you are going to miss Bible
          class this morning, baby. A couple of your
          personal worshipers are in the calaboose
          and need you and your white horse again.

Bud shakes his head and glances at this watch, it's 9:35 AM.

                    Bud

          What's it this time!

                    Richard

          It's a long story, but the short is it is
          that the High Sheriff is holding a couple
          of your musical supporters down at the
          Jail House.   And, because you are the only
          guy we know in town who wouldn't laugh at
          us, we have selected you from this very

short list, to give you the chance at the
honor of bailing these two idiots out of
jail on this fine Sunday morning in
Georgia.

                    Bud (hurried)

OK. I'll take care of it. You guys just
make sure that you're at the lake set up
and playing by 4:o'clock. The mayor and
everybody is going to be there. Hell, the
whole fuckin Party of Georgia is going to
be there. I just got it confirmed this
morning that the Attorney General is
planning to make a surprise appearance!
Can I depend on you guys? You have to be
on time this time!

                    Richard

You want to hear the song we wrote for
you?

                    Bud

Love to, but I have to go down to the jail
right quick. See you guys later, and we'll
all get together in about a week and maybe
have a real party over here.

                    Richard

Sounds good to me. Thanks a bunch, Bud.
See you this afternoon.

DISSOLVE TO EXT. MUNICIPAL COURT HOUSE - CITY JAIL

INT. SHERRIF'S OFFICE

Sheriff Jenkins sits behind his desk facing Bud Rutledge. Jenkins,
silver haired, is dressed this morning in a dark blue business suit like
Buds, ready to head out the door to the same church down the street
attended by the Rutledges and half the elite of Miloville. Laid out on
his desk top are two open manila file folders. In bold letters they
read Eric H. Rodriguez and William J. Genevas.

                Sheriff Jenkins   (gazing out the window that's
behind him facing the town square)

You never can really tell, but to me, it
sure looks like a great day for a
barbeque!

                    Bud

Yeah, it sure does at that! Barbeque and
political campaigns, George Washington
swore by them.

                    Sheriff Jenkins (Looking now back directly at
Bud with a growing smile)

          Yeah, and   nothing like a little music to
          spark those doings.

                         Bud

          You and Dorothy still planning to come
          today. You know we have a seat for ya'll
          at the main table!

                         Jenkins

          We hope to make it. But you never know
          what'll happen in this job, and my main
          responsibility is to protect the citizens
          form danger and disorder. You just never
          know what the next minute will bring, like
          that little incident this morning.

                         Bud

          You do a great job Sam, specially with the
          puny resources you have to work with these
          days.

                         Jenkins

          I guess a dollar won't ever buy what it
          used to.

                         Bud

          That's a tradition we could do without.
          But, speaking of dollars, what do we need
          to do about those two fast asleep fools
          down there in your basement hall? I wanted
          to, but I hate to wake them.   They need
          their rest if they are going to do this
          thing this afternoon.

                         Jenkins

          Bud, you have way too much going for you
          without the trouble of that Billy and
          Eric.   Ever think about sending them to
          Europe or someplace for a while?   I mean
          Hell! What a couple of idiots!

          I know Billy's had a hard time of it, but,
          Hell, he's gone wild as a goat!

                    Bud (Now Serious)

          Lisa and I are trying Sam, but I think
          with Billy it's about being so young
          still, that's most of it.   His Dad was a

blade, and his father before him. You
know the legend "he" was in this county.

We were all young once. Well, maybe not
you or I. But it takes all types. These
guys are set to help me out a lot on the
campaign trail. It's a long road. They're
really pretty good musicians, if not
upstanding citizens. I'm not even sure
you can have one with the other at the
same time. I don't think they are even
made that way anymore.

I promise to keep Billy reigned in better.
Hell, I have a lot to lose if I don't.

      Jenkins (Shaking his head and glancing towards
the window again)

He and Lisa have both been knocked pretty
hard.

      Bud

They're not really as stupid as they act
all the time. Eric was in Graduate school
and he just got drafted. He'll most
likely be in Viet Nam in six months.
Billy, well, he is a bit touched in the
head still, but he's harmless. He's a
good musician, he'll find himself one day.
They almost all do, you know.

Chief Jenkins glances down at the two manila folders. He touches the
edge of one, pauses, and then slowly pulling it towards and over its
partner, folds the two together, closing them both, and with his left
hand, then creases, flattens them together.

      Jenkins

OK, Bud, I guess I can make these go away
for you <u>this morning.</u> But what about the
Coke machine?

      Bud

What Coke Machine?

      Jenkins (laughing as he lets the two folders
drop from his hand into a waste basket)

Yeah right, what Coke machine? I heard it
committed suicide anyway. I don't think
we have a form for that kind of demise.
You want to go give them the news?

      Bud

Don't have time this morning. I'm late
for Sunday school, you coming?

Jenkins

I'll see you over there later. I need to
get it right with the deputies.

Bud

Thanks Sam. I owe you.

DISSOLVE SCENE TO EXTERIOR OF COURT HOUSE

Budd emerges from the court house through a side door and walks toward
the white Lincoln Town Car where Lisa is parked. We see Bud get in the
car on the passenger side.

Lisa

I tried to get you a cold drink but the
machine over there is broken. Looks like
somebody tried to break into it.

Budd (laughing)

Not funny baby, not funny at all!

The car slowly pulls away and around the block to the main street, it
makes a right turn down an Oak tree lined street, one block and into the
Church parking lot.

DISSOLVE - BACK TO FOSTER'S STORE

EXT. PARKING AREA IN FRONT OF STORE

Eric and Billy make it back to Foster's store in the Gremlin. Jesse and
Richard have already left for the gig, with plenty of planned setup time
for the sound check scheduled at 2 PM.

Eric exits the Gremlin's passenger side

Eric (walking away towards the Feed N Seed)

Well man, I'm beat! I'm going to crash for
a couple of hours.   What time are we
supposed to be at the lake for Bud's deal?

Billy

The sound check is supposed to be about
2:30, if I remember right. If you wake up
and I'm not here,. I'll see you over
there.

Eric

Cool, what are you going to do?

                    Billy

The book says about two more weeks, but
I'm going to go over to my secret place
and do a quick plant check.

                    Eric

Oh yeah, the pot deal, yeah, see you
later.

White Longhair (Eric's roommate) comes up from the the Feed n Seed where
he greets the two almost out of it store mates.

               Longhair (Smiling big)

Hey guys, great job with the Coke machine!
What you going to do for an encore? Kidnap
a potato chip machine?

                Billy (laughing)

I hadn't thought of that. But all I had
this morning was an egg sandwich at the
jail. You got any money you could lend
me? All we have to eat around here is a
few cans of beanie weenies and soda
crackers.

                    Longhair

Sure, man, let's hit the T-Burger. I'll
take care of us. I just got paid
yesterday, so I'll be rolling in the dough
for about two whole days.

DISSOLVE

INT. THE T-BURGER RESTURANT

Billy turns to Longhair.

                    Billy

White, you want to go with me after we
leave here to look at my plants?

                    Longhair

You mean your secret farm?

                    Billy

It won't have to be a secret anymore if I pull the plants today. I think they're past ready any way and I really need the money.

Longhair

Sure. How far?

Billy

They're out towards Lovorn road a ways, off this dirt road, and down a path. They're hidden really good! You couldn't spot them from a helicopter the way I spread them out. Jim Kent use to grow his plants out there a few years ago. Back before he moved to Colorado.

Longhair

Oh yeah! I smoked some that stuff. Pretty fine weed!

Billy

Remember that Jesus weed we had last year. That Panama Red?

Longhair (enthusiastic)

Do I ever. Who could forget that stuff? It was like tripping.

Billy

I saved a bunch of the seeds. A few of them grew into these 8 or 10 plants we're going to get today.

The two finish up their lunch.

DISSOLVES ALL

EXTERIOR GOD VIEW

Longhair and Billy drive out towards Lovourn Road in Billy's Gremlin.

ADDITIONAL VIEW

Jesse, Richard, and the other band members set up for the concert.

PRERECORDED MUSIC PLAYING

Many people are already starting to arrive at the Lake rally point. From the shore we see a few have brought their lunch coolers and set up picnic tables all the way out to the surrounding woods. A young hippie couple tosses a frisbee back and forth. Other hippie types paint signs with bright flowers and peace signs.

There are people down at the lake's shoreline. The sun has climbed past its midway point and beyond. Besides the band's own pickup truck and the equipment trailer, other set up vans unload electrical cables, which we see being laid from the main meeting house up the hill and back down to the staging area. A large white tent has been erected just behind the bandstand.

Two TV station vans from Atlanta have come over to cover the story. A radio news helicopter takes off and lands at the ball fields adjacent to the meeting area. A circus atmosphere pervades. A professional catering service cooks hot dogs and hamburgers. Clowns entertain children; making animals and hats out of balloons as they pass form the parking lot over to and in front of the band stand. Bright colors are everywhere.

A local DJ plays music from the AM-FM radio station Van. It's shaping up to be a pretty big crowd.

JUST WEST OF THE CITY LIMITS

The camera discovers Longhair and Billy completing their mile long trek through some heavy woods to a cleared circle, barely twelve feet across surrounded by privet hedges. They admire one six foot tall extremely bushy plant and dance around it five times. Billy pulls it out of the ground.

LATER

INT. FEED N SEED

Cameral tells condensed chronology of Longhair and Billy drying an ounce of pot leaves in the oven. They roll it into one huge oversize joint and start smoking it. Longhair and Billy sit in a marijuana cloud filled room when Billy, becomes distracted in a beer sign glowing from the darkness of the black walled party room to inside the den where he is muttering to himself.

                    Billy

          Miller Time, it's Miller time right now.

          Oh man, the gig, I'm late,! It's now, and
          I have to show everybody this beautiful
          pot plant.

Billy wobbles off the couch and darts out the door and into his car, weaving through town to the lake.

LAKE CARROLL - STAGE 4:35 PM

Up on stage, Richard straps into his guitar, and Eric and his drums are beginning to make some noise, as the pre-show sounds emerge from the various speaker arrays. Jesse is sound checking the microphones.

Jesse (into microphone-softly)

Budd Rutledge is the one, two three four.

There is a small rumble of cheering form the gathering crowd.

All this is going on until it is almost ready for Bud to be brought in
from behind the stage where he and Lisa are sequestered, waiting till
the time when the Attorney General will introduce them. That entire
crowd is now, inside the big white tent and the band is getting nervous.
Billy, their bass guitar player, is not there yet, and it's 4:45 PM.

From behind the stage, Lisa walks up and gets Richard's attention.

Lisa

Lisa (irritated)

What's the deal? Why aren't you guys
playing yet?

Richard (irritated himself)

Sorry Lisa, Our Bass Player is late. You
know "our" bass player! Waldo is setting
up another guitar in case he doesn't show.

Lisa

Well, get it together guys! You know the,
(she mouths the word "fuckin" under her
breath) Attorney General is back here!

Jesse focuses out beyond the crowd of about 1000 people on Billy's
yellow Gremlin stopped from parking by Sergeant Sunshine as he attempts
to enter the small area behind the stage where all the other band
members and dignitaries are parked.

Officer Sunshine confronts Billy.

Officer Sunshine

Little late, ain't you, boy?

Billy

Yea, no kidding! Really!

Officer Sunshine

I think your partners in crime up there
have been waiting on you for a while.

Maybe you need to steal a watch next time.

Billy

> Aw, come on, Sergeant Sunshine. I got to get to the gig here.
>
> Officer Sunshine
>
> Well, I hear what your mouth is saying. But I see what the rest of you is saying too.
>
> You'd be pretty messed up on that marijuana right now ain't you?
>
> Billy (whining in agreement)
>
> I was pretty fucked up this morning. I'm way past pretty fucked up right now, maybe all the way to totally messed up! Which is where you will probably be if you don't let me in there.
>
> Officer Sunshine
>
> All right, I guess you're pretty normal, given what normal looks like for guys like you.
>
> Try not to crash before you get it in the gate.
>
> Billy
>
> Thanks Dude. I'll dig you latter.

Billy mashes the accelerator just a bit too hard. The back wheels spin in place in what was almost pasture a few hours before, but now rain-soaked, Georgia red clay. A jet of that mixture is spun up and spit out and on to Officer Sunshine's crisply laundered dark blue uniform pants.

Now the good Sergeant notices a small patch of green plant from a spread-out army blanket in the back of the Gremlin. As the hatchback trunk lightly bounces, loosely held down by red speaker wire much too long for the job at hand, leaving a trail in the fine mud surfacing the road.

The sergeant makes a note in his mind, decides to do nothing about it right then and just casually closes the gate behind Billy.

THE MAIN STAGE

Jesse and the other band mates notice Billy's entrance from the top the main stage.

> Jesse
>
> Thank Goodness! Let's go help him with his gear!

Jesse and Richard put down their guitars and hurry down the wooden steps to a broadly smiling Billy getting out of the Gremlin, they notice Billy's red eyes staring up at them.

> Billy (as wild eyed and crazy as any pot head in recorded pot head history could be, smelling like marijuana smoke to high heaven)

Hey man, you're not going to believe this!

> Richard (Realizing Billy's condition)

I believe we're about to get fired if you don't get up there on that stage and strapped in to that bass of yours as quick as you know how too! Man are you too, hey, you are a, you're too fucked up to play! You are a mess!

> Billy

Far Out man, you got to see what I got back here!

Billy moves to the rear of the Gremlin and opens the hatch-back to reveal a blanket that now only partially conceals a very bushy pot plant, dirt still on the roots pot plant. Almost six feet long, Billy pulls the entire plant out from the trunk, flings dried dirt from its roots as he jerks it completely out of the Gremlin for their admiration.

> Billy (spinning himself around)

Zonk you! And zonk you! I zonk all of you!

Look at this thing! Have you ever seen a more beautiful pot plant? Longhair and I have already sampled it. We dried it out in the oven for about ten minutes on low, and,

> Jesse (Interrupting)

Are you nuts!

Just then Richard reaches in to the middle of them and quickly grabs the plant away from Billy's hand and re-covers the giant pot plant with the army blanket. But the blanket is not big enough and the plant is still sticking out of the back of the car, root end out now. They are right out in the open! Richard quickly reaches down the plant stem a couple of feet, breaks it, folds enough allowing the trunk to be closed, after he stuffs the speaker wire aside, and inside the back area.

> Billy: (surprised, sorrowful)

Hey man, you broke my plant!

> Richard (Serious, Slowly)

Billy, can you hear me? You're going to
get us all thrown in jail! But we don't
even have time for that; your sister has
been all over my ass about not starting
yet! We're late! Get you bass and,

(just then looking around the Gremlin and notices) (a breath taking
pause),

Where the fuck is your guitar?!!

Billy (Looking inside the Gremlin himself now)

Oh Man! I must have left it back at the
store!

Jesse (businesslike)

I have the other guitar already set up.
We're ready now!

(And leaves)

Richard

Billy! You! Get in the car and don't do
anything. Don't go anywhere! OK? You are
too fucked up right now to play and you
don't even have a guitar.   Do you
understand?

Billy

I can play man.   How about some air
guitar?

Billy goes into motion of someone playing a guitar without a guitar.

Richard

Yea, stay here and play the air guitar.
OK, but inside the car! I don't have time
for this!

Richard turns and heads back up to the stage as the band has already
started playing an introduction with *I wish I was in Dixie*, leading up
to a big introduction of the candidate and a bunch of banners beginning
to unfold and saying "Vote for Bud, Rutledge is the One"!

Bud comes out on the stage with the Attorney General and the crowd
cheers as Jesse sings into the microphone.

Jesse (singing)

Budd Rutledge is the one.
He's the one to go.
He is the man, with the plan.

Behind the stage, Billy is back in his car talking to himself and deciding he'll just head on back to the store and get his real guitar and return for the long set after the announcements and all the dignitaries say all they have to. He backs his car up and then heads forward towards the closed gate and Officer Sunshine who is standing there, still, arms folded, in front of the closed iron gate.

>   Billy (leaning his head out the window)
>
>   Hey man, could you let me out-a-here?
>   Seems I forgot my guitar and I need to go
>   back home and get it. Would you mind
>   saving my parking place for me while I'm
>   gone?

Officer Sunshine walks forward; he pushes his cap back on to the back of his head and bends forward then squats beside Billy and his open car door window, brushing a few flakes of dried mud from his pant leg, glancing to the back of the Gremlin and the very lumpy army blanket.

>   Officer Sunshine
>
>   Well, I don't know Billy. How long do you
>   think you'll be gone this time?

>   Billy
>
>   Probably, no more than 30 minutes, I don't
>   guess.

>   Officer Sunshine (relaxed)
>
>   Thirty minutes! Sure Billy. (He smiles
>   bigger now) I'll save a place for you.

OVERHEAD VIEW

From above, we see Officer Sunshine walk slowly over to the gate and unlatch it, swing it open and gesture Billy and his car forward as if he were a real dignitary.

As Billy drives forward he again presses a bit hard on the accelerator and unknowingly troughs a new spray of mud on to officer Sunshine's uniform pants. But the officer seems not to care as Billy pulls further away and up the hill to where another Miloville police car pulls in behind Billy and just out of sight, light flashing, pulls the yellow Gremlin over for the second time today.

Officer Sunshine turns his attention back to the stage where Bud is taking in all the sound of cheering for him and a standing ovation.

>   Officer Sunshine (To Himself)
>
>   A bit more than 30 minutes this time boy;
>   more indeed.

END ACT I

The Art of Foster's Store – Eclectic 1971

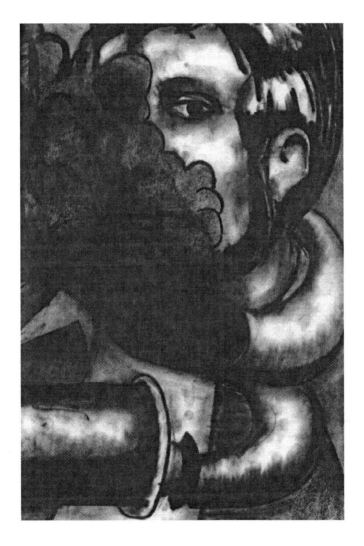

Michael Kuczmarski

MAY 1, 1970

Chapter 35

Dean McCarthy - Last Man at Foster's

By Dean McCarthy

Picture of Dean 1975 while at West Georgia

Foster's store basement was really just a place to keep my mattress while I shacked up with a girl for free at Tyus dorm. The school said I had to have an address and at the time, Foster's was the cheapest place I could find. The one room cement block basement that I rented was either 60 or 40 dollars a month. The ceiling was only about five feet high, so I had to do the limbo or squat or crawl to get in there.

I can really only remember sleeping in there once. While I was there in 1975 I don't think anybody had lived upstairs in a while as far as I could tell. It just looked to me like it was full of cobwebs.

The Feed & Seed was still back there and while I was there a guy by the name of Mike Robinson lived down there by himself. His place seemed like a Mexican hacienda, and he had an old fabric couch on his front porch, where he was usually sprawled with a beer and a smoke. He went to WGC but died soon after graduation I heard. He was a hemophiliac.

WGC was a wonderful adventure.

I'd like to share with everyone that GOD sent me to WGC and keeps sending me places. My room mate from Tyus Hall and I got married after I moved to Louisiana, 27 years ago. Have you heard a song that has the lyrics, "I am a friend of God. He sent me here." I'd like to add, and he sent me here to you.

Foster's Store Today

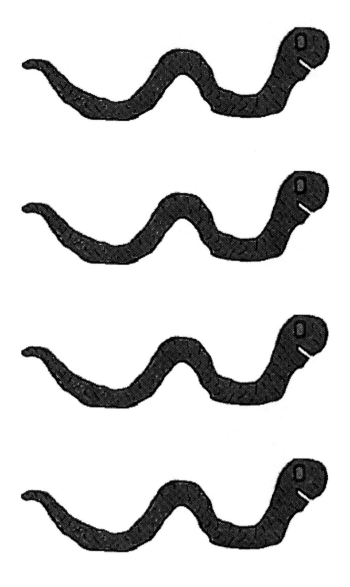

Chapter 36

The Fosterian Society

Foster's Store Alumni to Seek Research Grant from University of WG

By New Foster's Store Staff Reporter Haywood Jablowme

October 19, 2005 - Atlanta Georgia

Today, Butch Gungii, lead counsel for The New Foster's Store Development team and his long time law partner, Kenton Clapsaddle, announced that group's intention to develop a research park adjacent to the already-planned mega complex, The New Foster's Store. Gungii stated that because of current research into long-term use of marijuana, the former residents of Foster's Store and some of their good friends have a unique opportunity to "give back something to the community and advance scientific research at the same time." He then handed out a white paper entitled *Effects in the Brain caused by long term use of marijuana.*

Assisted by several scientific illustrations, Gungii summarized the findings contained therein:

MRI Brain Image (think what that looks like)

"Using the latest Magnetic Resonance Imaging (MRI) technology, new research presents evidence indicating that the active ingredient of marijuana, tetrahydrocannabinol (THC) remains in the brain forever. That means that the amount of THC a marijuana smoker took into his body smoking pot 30+ years ago is still inside his brain today. Further, all the THC ingested during an entire lifetime remains in that marijuana smoker today, within the living brain. You can not remove it, and as you can see from the MRI exhibit, it is easily detectable."

THC Molecule (think what that looks like)

"Think about it," said Gungii, "every molecule of THC you ever took in is still with you today, in your brain. A former or current marijuana smoker doesn't remain high forever, the research explains, because the THC does not settle in the region of the brain used for conscious thought. But it's all still there, every bit of it, and we are here to announce today that there is a way to get it back, even recycle it."

Gungii continued, "At this point I want to introduce my good friend and law partner, Kenton Clapsaddle. Ken heads up our Commodities Trading Division and his area of the firm will set up the architecture for what we believe will be a another area of revenue to be plowed into community philanthropy by the newly formed *Fosterian Society*, planned to be headquartered in Carrollton, Georgia."

Clapsaddle thanked Gungii for the introduction and described himself as a lawyer with over 30 years' experience in the Commodities and Futures markets both in Chicago and in Atlanta. He and his wife were already looking for residence in the Carrollton area: "My attachment to this endeavor is to assure confidence and security for those individuals who may wish to participate in this important research project, scheduled to begin after the first quarter of 2006. My first responsibility to this project is to provide an atmosphere of trust and to guarantee absolute anonymity for all current and future participants in the Foster's Store Residents' and Friends' THC Reclamation Project, or, *The Fosterian Society*.

The Plan (stop thinking now)

"The first thing you will need to understand is the newly formed **Fosterian Society** itself. In order for this research to go forward, we need actual human brains. We need specific brains of specific individuals known to be heavy marijuana users over a long time frame. It was a former resident of Foster's Store who brought this idea forward, provided the current scientific research and a detailed plan to actualize what we are presenting today.

Secondly, this plan calls for former Foster's Store mates to donate their brains to this research. **Fosterian Society** staff will take possession of the Former Foster's Store mate's disembodied brain soon after death, dissect and dehydrate it.

Then a meeting of the Society will be called at some secret location, where society members will roll the dried brain tissue into joints and smoke it, and thereby ritually, pay homage to the departed store mate.

It is theorized that very little smoke will be needed to produce a high for the participants. In fact, most of the dried brain matter will be stored, like fine wines. Then, after much research, the remaining brains not directly smoked by Fosterians themselves will be sold on the open market to be created via the New Foster's Store Mega Site.

Clapsaddle continued, "All store mates contacted thus far have agreed, at the end of their lives, to bequeath to this project their no longer needed grey matter."

Clapsaddle said that it was too early to estimate the value of any one brain of any particular former Foster's Store resident or friend. But certain former residents were still today unaccounted for, and he now feared for their lives. "We believe some notorious former store mates of the 1970's are especially today in the greatest danger of having their brains harvested before their time by unscrupulous THC brain pickers, a strange cult already rumored to exist on the West Coast.

Walking THC Banks

"My responsibility to the Society is to see that its investors receive a decent profit down the line," said Clapsaddle. "I'm a Commodities and Futures guy, but if I were some of these guys who are still missing today, I'd make a beeline for the safety of the Fosterians."

At that point, Butch Gungii returned to the podium and said that future news releases will be available soon and regularly. He expressed his optimism about receiving a large investment from the investment portfolio managers at the University of West Georgia. Then he added, "No doubt, because of this new technology, a new Masters Program will be added to the already extensive curriculum at the University."

In an effort to determine the long term viability of the project described above, this reporter contacted a former Foster's Store resident now residing North Georgia, who for purpose of this article, wishes to remain anonymous. When I asked if he had been previously alerted to the existence of the *Fosterian Society* and its intentions, the former resident said that he had and would gladly donate his own brain to the project: "Sure man, I mean, like, this is far out! If I live longer than some of the other guys, I mean, think about it, man, a brain literally cured in THC for almost forty years. Smoke that shit and I bet you'd, maybe . . . Well, who knows, man? Who cares? And then the ceremony of it all, having your best friends smoke your brains! Far out man, really far out."

At that point the former Foster Store mate offered me a chocolate brownie from a batch just taken out of the oven by his live-in girlfriend "Shirley." He also offered me an opportunity to review the legal document he had just endorsed, signing over his brain to the society upon his death. He suggested I include it in whatever article I might write about this project. I contacted Butch Gungii, of Gungii, Clapsaddle and Obberwolfer, Attorneys at Law, and gained permission to reprint the complete document here. According to Gungii, it may be completed by any former resident or friend of Foster's Store who believes that he or she may today have large amounts of THC lodged in their brains and would like to donate it to the society as per the guidelines described above.

Permission to remove my Brain when I die

I, _____, a friend or resident of Foster's Store between the years of 1969 and 1974, do hereby donate my brain to the Fosterian Society upon my death.

I understand that the dried remains of my brain will be used in whatever research projects that the **Fosterian Society** may conceive of and that certain portions of my brain may be smoked by Society members as per their collective will.

Signature_____   Witness_____

Date_____   Date_____

Mail signed document to: Brain Donation, Keaton Clapsaddle, Attorney at Law, P. O. Box 36168, Hoover, AL 35233

As I sat there on the front porch steps enjoying a very delicious brownie, I couldn't help ponder the possibilities of this bold research initiative. I thought about the universe, how large it is. I thought about "Shirley" and me together. I wondered if she would share her brownie recipe with me. I pondered changing careers. Maybe I could qualify as a "New Fosterian" someday, start my own cult and have worshipers, like Pastor Legg himself. I could teach people a thing or two about what kind of nuts growers should plant and harvest for chocolate brownie makers, what subsidies they might legislate for and create maybe an entirely new class of constituents. We could all apply for grants and I could be right there next to the statue carved in ice pissing champagne into everybody's crystal glasses, a big name band playing softly while the sun goes down. Maybe write a book to promote my vision. Then a sequel. I can see it all.

Wait a minute! That's all been done before. Pass me a brownie and we'll start over.

Acknowledgements

Who would have believed that somebody would ever write a book about Foster's Store? I can tell you, absolutely no one.   I'm about to thank a lot of people in this section of the book but I think you might want to know just how all this came about as well. You can think of this section of the book as a template to do this kind of thing yourself one day if you'd like.

When all this started happening, I was actually working on another book, *Crane Hill,* when I realized one day while reading the West Georgia Alumni Paper, *Perspective*, that they did reviews of books written by alumni so, not being one to shy away from a chance to shamelessly self promote myself, I decided to send them a copy of *The Bike Path*, a book I had just written and released about mountain biking and metaphysics.   In the process of getting all that set up I had the occasion to correspond a bit with Sally Roberts, the copy editor for the <u>WGC Perspective</u>.

After the book review ran, Sally asked me if I'd like to contribute any writing to the paper. I really had no intention of doing anything like that, but mentioned to her in an email message, that maybe I could do a piece about Foster's Store. I got back a one word reply, "Humm". Talk about non-verbal communication! That one utterance told me that she had heard of Foster's Store, even knew its reputation and more. So then, I was intrigued, and the next day I got another message from her saying to go ahead and write something if I wanted to and we'd just see what happens; if they felt like they could use it or not, she didn't really try to encourage me much further than that.

I went ahead and wrote the piece and soon after it appeared in the alumni paper, I began hearing from people who I hadn't heard from or seen in over thirty years. I got emails from former WGC students everywhere. It was just amazing! Totally unsolicited, I got emails from former store mates and other people who had partied there over the years. I got accounts of things that were just hilarious to downright crude. But mostly, I received an overwhelming avalanche of good feeling from people I could barely remember or never met in my life. I got to hear from people whom were my best friends in the world back then, but by now, I hadn't even laid eyes on them forever.

At the same time all this was happening, I set up a webpage, **www.fostersstore.com,** and it started experiencing a lot of hits, way more than I ever imagined. It still is today. It became a place where all of us could get together and share all these outrageous photographs taken back then, as well as a place to retell and recall all those crazy times.

Things just really began to snowball after that. What was so neat was that I had a reason to get in touch with all these people I hadn't seen in so long, to introduce them to the website and to ask them if they'd like to contribute to it in some way, either in words or with old pictures they might still have. I started the site with two pictures, two, that's all I had left of a place which holds some of the nicest memories of my life, two out of focus black and white Polaroids.

One of the first things I did was to get out my copy of the 1999 edition of the Alumni Directory and find Richard Haliburton, who was living now in Bremen Georgia. I seemed to remember somewhere in the recesses of my mind that he had a picture or two of "Proud Mary". Talk about "Kismet". I called him up, he answered the phone, and we began talking like we were still store mates today and it was only yesterday since we last spoke. I would recognize his voice anywhere anytime. It was the same for him. I asked him, eventually, if he still had any of those old photographs from the store days.

Without a pause, he answers, "Yea, I think I have some here in my desk drawer, yea, here they are, here's one with you and O'Conner, Teter and Mr. Foster, I got a bunch of them".

That was the way it went, over and over again. Right now there are almost 600 graphic images on the website. (I started with only two.)

You may know that photographs like these can degenerate over time. They may not be of the best quality today, but now, thanks to this project, they have been archived and saved for all of us and for anyone else in the future who may want to learn a little more about who we were back then. What a wonderful time to be alive.

The next person to weigh in with some photographs was Candee Carmichael. She had a bunch. After that it just got nuts. Terry Farner, Steve Craft, Chris Berry, and yes, even Ethel Foster herself, came thru with a bunch of great pictures. Then, it was Dean Nations who sent me two whole albums of nothing but pictures from both Foster's Store and Jackson Courts. And it didn't stop there. Right quick like I set up a Friends of Foster's page and I received a whole lot of pictures from Becky Herrin, Charles Balance, Sid Shortt, and Steve Aderhold. Without these folks there might not have ever been a book today.

Those pictures drove people to the webpage and the stories about those days began to flow. I was there to tell my own, but I was joined by a few more tellers of tales, and before long, I knew there was a book here. *Crane Hill* could wait till next year. Along with the stories came the memories of a time in our history when we were divided as a country, as Bob O'Kelley pointed out in so many words, "Mayberry was no more".

Store mate Walter Carmichael has been the biggest help to me in producing this book. I got with him about all this coincidentally, practically the same day he stepped down as the Editor of the *Butts County Progress Argus* in Jackson Georgia. I hope Walter will let me publish a book of his editorials from the past five years. They are a hoot!

Bob O'Kelley, Terry Farner, Chris Berry, Mike Sorrell, Richard Hurt, Richard Duncan, Phil Spackman, Phillip DeLoach, Larry Bouie, Mickey Spinks, and Allen McMillan contributed chapters. This was a group effort, yes, but, to me it was about as effortless as anything I'd ever done in my life.

A bunch of other people also contributed but asked not to be named. That would be people like all of the above (at one time or another) and Frank Brown, David Jack, Jim Kent, Steve Zoromsky, Jay Heard,

Rodney Abernathy, and a bunch of people whose name I really can't mention because I'm afraid they might try and sue me.

I need to mention that while researching some of these stories that there were a number of females who wished not to have their names printed here or on the webpage. Less timid about that were of course, Candee Carmichael, Becky Herrin, Eileen Howell, Jolaine Battey, Mic Chambers, and Mary Huff. Thank you all.

Besides all the photographs in the book I managed to pry a few pieces of Art from a few people. All this art and graphics work really helps to add to the experience. Some of the people we need to thank are Candee Carmichael (again), Allen McMillan, Bill Harrell, Michael Kuczmarski, and the still missing, Dan O'Conner.

Then finally, everybody who has ever written anything, knows, that without a good editor, anybody's writing, no matter how creative or enthusiastic they are, can easily turn out be nothing but shit. Last but not least, so as this all not be shit, I thank former store mate and West Georgia English teacher Peter Bryg, for volunteering for this duty. Running into Peter again was just another example of why I think this book will work somehow. Along with Peter, , my Ante Charlotte and my cousin Allison helped us proof this thing to the end of it. Sally Roberts and Roger McCook really did a great job with the galley copies. There are still some mistakes in this book, but what may look like errors, maybe aren't really. Maybe they are something else, from somewhere else?

I think it's noteworthy to point out that a lot of the Foster's crowd turned out to be very successful. Despite all the things we did to ourselves that would tend to make people believe the opposite, most everybody I spoke with turned out very well. But success doesn't seem to have spoiled the magic spell, which is, that all the true friendships that were born back then are alive and well today. That's a lot to be thankful for in itself, this thing called friendship. Friendship is just another word for love.

All of us seem to have learned that friendship is a special thing. Maybe more special than we had ever thought. I think it's timeless.

All the people in these pages are of an age today where we've lost people whom we've loved. We've gone through that fire apart from each other, individually, but share the pain of loss. I think because of things like that, we know now what's important and what isn't. Remembering Foster's Store has been a balm to me personally. I hope all who spend some time with this book will feel at the end of it as rejuvenated as I do now.

Now, let's party!

Wayne Lankford

Glossary

$5.17 - The price of a case of Pabst Blue Ribbon beer in returnable bottles in 1968 sold down at Skinner's Grocery.

20th Century – The century where all the action in this book took place except for the hallucinations and short periods of time skipping phenomena.

250 mg-psilocybin kicker – Something you really don't want to know about, but just plain old LSD laced with something to make it even more mind expanding.

401 Maple Street – Address for Headquarters and The Mansion.

4-F – Selective Service classification meaning not physically fit enough to learn how to kill people.

62 – My number in the names-in-the-hat deal.

Abernathy, Rodney – Famous race car driver of the Hwy 166 west track. Also does a pretty good Elvis Presley impersonation. Well, not just pretty good, really great actually!

About 1300 miles – Distance from Carrollton to Canadian border.

a loaded 45 caliber automatic pistol – What some people used to put under their pillow in order to get a good night's sleep. Very popular with returning home Viet Nam Veterans.

a lot of screwing going on – Primary reason for a potential college student to pick one institution of higher learning over an other. It never was about Football.

Academic Pursuit – A game, the same thing as *Trivial Pursuits* except that if you lost at this it could mean your life.

Accident scene – What all crime scenes are before they become that.

Acid Head – This term might describe a person who took a lot of LSD.

Age of Aquarius – Supposed to be characterized by an amount of time where Peace, Understanding and Harmony are existent and prevail throughout the universe.

Ajax – The preferred disinfectant and cleaner for Terry Farner and other residents of The Worm Ranch.

Altman's Bay Station – AKA: Bobby's Bay Station, 310 Maple Street. A lot of people bought beer and gas and rubbers there.

Americal Division – US Army Division formed for the Vietnam War. General Westmoreland was the boss.

American Civil Liberties Union – In the days of Foster's Store they were the only legal defense who perhaps believed that the laws pertaining to the use and possession of marijuana were too severe.

Andre Cold Duck – The first bottle of this stuff ever brought into Carroll County was purchased by Store mate Chris Berry. AKA: Cold Quacker.

Anonymous – This could be Jimmy Tingle, Steve Zoromsky, Frank Brown or any of about fifty other people.

Army – Not where most people wanted to be during the era of the Viet Nam war.

Arons, Mike – Famous Humanistic Psychologist.

Athens – Where the University of Georgia is located.

Atlanta- A place to go to buy hard liquor and other goodies not available in Carrollton.

Atlanta Constitution – Atlanta Morning newspaper – Lewis Grizzard's articles were the best thing in the paper.

Atlanta Journal – Atlanta Newspaper – The newspaper nobody ever read in those days because Lewis Grizzard's articles were in the Constitution.

AUSTRAILOPITHICUS AFRICANAS – A kind of basketball game played at Foster's Store sometimes, an expanded version of HORSE.

Avondale High School – Atlanta, Georgia High School attended by Bill Harrell and Phil Spackman.

Aycock – Men's Dormitory where Lankford lived while he flunked English Composition three times. Moved out of there and eventually passed.

Babe magnet – A magnet that attracts babes

Baby Boomer generation – Generally speaking, people born right after the end of World War II

Ballew's Music Store – Music store located in Downtown Carrollton for a while owned by Neil Ballew. Nathan Barfield worked there for a while.

Bama Boys – Hapless Frat boys

Banning Mill – A great place to party over on the Snake River

Baptists – The predominant religion in Georgia. They could be very strange people sometimes. Like, in stead of going into a liquor store and buying a bottle of whiskey themselves, often they would call a taxi and have the taxi driver buy them their liquor and then deliver it to them at their home address. It seems that they all drank a lot but were in a big denial scene. The worst thing that could happen was to be seen by somebody you went to church with in a liquor store.

Bateman, Bill – A guy who it is believed died a long time ago. Once lived at Foster's Store.

Barfield, Nathan – A great guitar player and a person who died fighting a horrible disease.

Bay Station- See Altman's Bay Station

Beatles – Musical group from England

Beer can baseball – A variety of regular baseball except that instead of a ball an empty beer can is used.

Being brain dead – A condition where your brain isn't working anymore. For me, it was how I felt after an hour of taking notes in Biology class.

Bell bottoms – The style of pants we all wore back then for a while. They are popular again today.

Bike Path, The – Book about Nature and Metaphysics, written by store mate Wayne Eliot Lankford. You should buy a copy of it. The ISBN # is 0-9745125-0-8. Go to Amazon.com.

Black Beard – Famous pirate and model for Store mates in 1970 Halloween party.

Black Student Alliance – Had a great football team. They could have run the score up on the Green Jay Rushers, but didn't.

Blissville – If you got it just right, that's where you were.   Not to be mistaken for Blairsville.

Blue Diamond Match Box – Very early on what small portions of marijuana were sold in by undercover agents.

Blotter Acid – A kind of LSD that was packaged on a small piece of paper. A drop of the liquid containing the acid was dropped on the paper and allowed to dry. It could be swallowed later.

Body Count – Every week for about 8 years, somebody would walk around and count up all the dead bodies lying around in a certain southeast Asian country. The total of that number was said to be the body count. You just want to make sure that "their" number was higher than "yours".

Bomb scare – It's what you have when somebody calls the school and leaves a message that there is a bomb about to explode somewhere on campus in the next few minutes. For a while there we were getting them about once a week.

Booby traps – What the Viet Cong would set up out in the jungle to and try to kill you with. Where's a Hallmark card when you really need one?

Book Experience – That sort of over all glow you get when you finish reading a good book. But more likely, as a college student, it could be a bad thing when you find out that some piece of shit history book that you had to purchase one quarter will cost over fifty dollars. Then it only gets worse because at the end of the quarter you find out that it won't ever be used again and the bookstore where you bought it three months ago will only give you fifteen cents a pound for the thing.

Boone's Farm – Yes, it was a cheap wine, but it was a good wine. There was Apple, and later they came out with a Strawberry flavor. It was very good when your throat became parched by smoking inferior weed.

Boots, a pair of – All that's left of you sometimes after a rocket hits you.

Boundaries – A modern-day term used to describe certain limits one should recognize and abide by under certain socio-psychological situations. A totally alien train of thought for any residents of Foster's Store.

Bowdon – Where Store mate Jim Kent was from. Ten miles west of Foster's Store.

Brown Owsley – A popular type of LSD manufactured in California by little dwarfs who hung around and dressed alike.

Buffy – Buffy Wuffy's first name.

Buff-Wuff Hotel, The – Luxury hotel planned for west side of Carrollton.

Buffy Wuffy – Mr. Foster's dog.

Burning bras – What women of the sixties did to demonstrate their irritation with a governmental and social system that treated them as second class citizens. It was a form of Protest.

Candymen – Band Larry Bowie played in.

Capricorn Records – Phil Walden's record label name. Think Alman Brothers and Eric Quincy Tate et al.

Carpet bombing – A benign term describing the principal activity of a B-52 bomber in a time of war.

Carroll County – The name of the county where West Georgia College was.

Carrollton – Where West Georgia College was. Today, the University of West Georgia is in the same place where the college used to be.

Cascade School- Atlanta Georgia Grammar school attended by store mates Wayne Lankford and Bob O'Kelley.

Catch 22 – Only a crazy person would put their life on the line like they do sometimes in war. But this type of being crazy was not an excuse to be excused from war, even though war is a completely crazy way to decide differences. In there somewhere is the description of catch 22.

Cavalier – An attitude adopted by some of the student body characterized by an unhealthy desire to wear a large headdress with horns on the top, or, to at least be photographed within a group of intoxicated guys on a staircase where one of the guys is wearing the horned headdress.

Chromosome Damage - What the Government wanted you to believe that ingesting LSD would cause.

Chitterlings - The intestines of hogs. To this day, they are still the favorite food of Rodney Abernathy.

Chu Lie – A beautiful beach in Vietnam.

Church of the Cleansing Fire, The – Made up name of a made of church, but famous for their great collection of outer wear and things that glow when the batteries are charged.

Clapsaddle, Slomo T. - Name of guy who owned pawn shop in Carrollton

Cold Slaw – River in Alabama near Tuscaloosa.

Cold war – To some, better than no war at all.

College – A good place to go during a war.

College deferment – The reason you ended up in college in the first place. The alternative was unthinkable. Get one of these and you're safe from the draft for 4 years.

Committee on Un-American Activities – Good excuse for guys who like to hunt together without getting dirty or spending all day in the cold winter weather.

Communism – A system where all the marijuana and beer are divided by the number of people you have and distributed out.

Communists – All you need to know is that you need to kill all of them.

Conscientious Objector Status – If you could pull this off you wouldn't have to be drafted. For many, it was their last attempt to avoid being drafted.

Confession – Something law enforcement people advise you to make and tell you at the same time that it is the best thing for you but may not be, really.

County Land Fill – Place where Proud Mary ended up.

Crack Back Block – The block where you go to take your bad crack back to. Is this a test?

Criminal Justice Majors – Lost souls end up following this course of study.

DSC - The Distinguished Service Cross – One of many medals awarded to store mate Phil Spackman.

Daisy Cutter Bomb– Benign term describing the effect of a 5,000 pound bomb. I wonder what we would call it if anybody ever dropped one of them on us.

Divinity School – A Place during the Viet Nam war to go to so you wouldn't have to go to where you really didn't want to go.

Dog Meditation – Something you will see your dog doing a lot of when he converts to Buddhism.

Dope – Generic term for all illegal drugs, also what that guy in the hat with the horns thinks he looks like 30 years later.

Draft Dodger – Depending on which side of the fence you stood philosophically, it could be a term of disdain or honor.

Drunk – A state of being, a judgmental term sometimes. To some, an undesirable condition, while to others a worthy goal for ones life work.

Drunkenness – The condition described above, but with zest.

Durkee's Mayonnaise – Lankford's favorite brand of mayonnaise when making cold slaw or potato salad, great with bologna and bread as well.

Dylan, Bob – Wrote the song, "The Times They Are A Changing'" and a guy who knew what he was singing about.

Ed Tant – Former Editor of the West Georgian. As opinionated as ever, today he writes a column for an Athens Georgia newspaper.

Electric Kool-Aide – Regular Kool-Aide with LSD added; great for bobbing for apples in at Halloween parties.

Elvis – See Rodney Abernathy. Really, go to Cartersville Georgia and see Rodney Abernathy.

Ethel's Five Minutes – Every Fall quarter during the first big party at Foster's Store, Ethel would knock on the door real hard. We would all think it was the police (a sign of our paranoia) but it would be Ethel come to lay down her own laws about noise and limitations to our partying.

Existence Justification – A solution to a dilemma in which certain individuals become uncertain of their being and have to talk themselves back into a state of being and accept that condition as real. A process that could often take all night under some conditions.

Fall Quarter Party – A celebratory ritual characterized by group participation, consumption of large amounts of beer or other extracurricular substances designed to produce a heightened sense of exuberance and social interaction, with both stated and unstated goals.

Far Out – Common expression of the late 1960's and early 70's. Mostly used as a retort expressing agreement and enthusiasm at the same time.

Farm Party – A place to go to for unrestrained fun.

Fat Fox – Band Richard Hurt used to play in.

Feed & Seed or Feed N' Seed – The building behind the store.

Filler – What some people will say this glossary is. In literary terms, useless and redundant information included only to take up space to increase page count.

Flask – Usually small tin or glass containers designed to conceal alcoholic beverages on one's person.

Flower Power Revolution – A sociopolitical movement associated with the late 1960's. Participants tended to group together, dress alike and smoke marijuana. As revolutions go, not a bad way to spend in service to your country.

Flunked Out – What would naturally happen if you were a student and never went to class.

Foosball – A game played on a table.

Folger's Coffee – What I used to use to stay awake during finals week.

Forfeit – What the Green Jay Rushers did on days that they were just too fucked up to go play football.

FOSTER 500 – A loosely structured automobile race in front of Foster's Store characterized by complete lack of planning and rules. Set the garbage cans on fire on Hwy 166 and let 'em race!

Frank Brown – Named after its inventor, a term used to describe any mixed drink prepared on a Sunday afternoon. Usually that meant what ever liquors or mixing ingredients were left over from the previous night's partying. For some reason, most often a combination of Bourbon and Orange juice.

Free love – A good deal at the right price if you were ever lucky enough to find it.

Frisked – What you were during the drug bust.

Fu dog – Chinese in origin, refers to a dog seen one night by Store mate White Longhair after ingesting an unknown amount of LSD.

GBI – Georgia Bureau of Investigation

Georgia –Southeastern state where Foster's Store was located.

GI Bill - An educational funding source for veterans. This legislation made it possible for millions of veterans to attend college after WW II and beyond. I mean the ones that lived thru it.

Girlfriend – A less than super serious relationship with a woman; a romantic if not sexual friendship, as in girlfriend – boyfriend. Most desirable situation sometimes, if you lived in Carrollton and they lived in Atlanta or anywhere not too close to where you lived, as having more than one girlfriend at a time could be hazardous to your health. Just ask Richard Duncan. .

God – Supreme Being

Gore, Al - Son of a Senator from Tennessee. Met and came close to befriending Bob O'Kelley in Vietnam. Quit the army and went to Divinity School.

Grace Slick – Lead singer for the Jefferson Airplane.

Grades – College would have been a lot more fun if we didn't have to worry about these things.

Grant's Lounge – A Macon Georgia night club, infamous as a place frequented regularly by members of the Alman Brothers Band and the Eric Quincy Tate Band. Ronnie Thompson, mayor of Macon, used to have a armored half track with a cannon mounted on it. The barrel of the cannon was usually aimed directly at the front door of Grant's Lounge from the middle of the town square where the vehicle was usually parked when not in use.

Grass Huts - What we would all still be living in if they had invented Viagra before they invented the wheel. What most of the population of the world lives in today even without Viagra. See Yin Yang. No, don't really.

Great Depression, The – From about 1929 to he end of World War II, a place in our history where economically, things weren't really too great at all.

Green, Mike – A great Artist.

Grinding Paranoia – What you get after a few years of watching a war you might have to go fight in on TV. Most severe on Thursday evenings when they reported the weekly dead and wounded totals.

Gungi – A variety of marijuana that was supposed to be pretty powerful.

Gungii, Butch – The greatest lawyer in the world.

Gungii, Clapsaddle, & Obberwolfer – Name of a fictitious law firm. But don't tell them that.

Halloween – Great excuse for a party!

Hallucinogens – Family of drugs that became popular in the late 1960's and early 70's. Ingesting a drug of this type might make you see things that aren't really there. (Or, are they really there all the time, but you can only see them when you take this kind of a drug?) You might choose to take a drug like this at a time in your life when you really aren't sure about the things that were there and you could already see.

Haines City Florida – The city on Florida where Steve Zoromsky was from.

Hard Rock – A style of music still popular today.

Hari Krishna – As a movement, people who believed in peace but hated body hair. Eyebrows were on their hit list along with any kind of meat. Liked to dress in bed sheets and play the tambourines.

Harman, Mama Kate – Owned and operated snack bar at WGC from 1962 to 1967 when new Student Center opened. Mama Kate was well loved and a great cook. She believed she was forced to retire against her will. She also owned the Fishing Shack where Larry Bowie lived for a while.

Harrell, Bill – Creator of Cartoon strip *Ink Lines*.

Hay Bales – Mr. Foster theorized they might be inter-galactic vehicles.

Head Shop – A retail store where you could buy drug paraphernalia like cigarette rolling papers, pipes, bongs, psychedelic posters, incense, music, clothing and literature like: books, newspapers and magazines.

Headquarters – Carrollton's own home grown Head Shop owned and operated by Sid Short

Heflin, Bob – Senior Class President 1970 or 71 maybe.

Hippie Culture – The integrated system of beliefs and the manifestations which defined and control the appearance, lifestyles and choices of its practitioners.

Holy Shit – Shit blessed by the Pope.

Hooka – A big water pipe used to smoke marijuana and hashish.

Horeshoes – A game played for hours and hours out in front of the Feed N Seed.

Horne, Al – Famous A.C.L.U lawyer from Atlanta. His business card was stapled to the wall in the store house right beside the telephone.

Humanism – A Branch of Psychology.

Ink Lines – Bill Harrell's infamous cartoon strip.

Insincere losers – What the Foster's Store intramural Football team became after losing a game.

Institutions of Higher Learning – Places to hide out for a while and legally avoid being drafted.

Jackson Courts – An apartment complex located right next to the West Georgia campus, the scene of some pretty outrageous behavior.

Jane Fonda – AKA Hanoi Jane. But my favorite was Barberella, a movie where she wore a see through shirt made out of plastic and floated around a lot.

Jason - The name of Candee Carmichael's coker spaniel.

John Paul Sartre – Existentialist who many thought of or not.

Karma – The law of cause and effect; the apparent spread of energy through thoughts, words and deeds.

Keg – An aluminum barrel containing much beer, or not.

Keith and Larry – The names of the ducks that lived at Foster's, pets of Dean Nations and all Foster's children.

Kennedy – Chris Kennedy had six toes on one foot so he got a medical deferment. I remember one day asking him if having six toes on one foot ever caused him any trouble. He said that sometime if he would get to running real fast he would tend to get more traction with the leg that had the six toed foot. That would tend to cause him to run in circles.

Kent State – A college in Ohio where students tried to trade bullets for flowers with the National Guard. Unsuccessfully.

KIA's – Government abbreviation for "Killed In Action". Actually saying the words "Killed In Action" took too long and brought everybody down big time. They were talking about people, how many people got killed in a specific time period, most often, one week's time.

Kubrick, Stanley – Director Movie, *2001, A Space Odyssey.*

Laing, R. D. – Prominent British Psychologist

Large animal tranquilizers – What you might want to get your hands on some weeks if the KIA numbers were especially high.

LeBlacce, Crissy – Girl who rode around in a big bus and played hide and seek games with the road crew when it made stops.

Legg, Jacob – Leader of the Church of the Cleansing Fire. He fervently opposes construction of The New Foster's Store.

Left Coast Look – Obtained by mimicking styles of speech, dress and behavior thought to be popular in California during the years of 1966 to 1974. Fit perfectly with the cultural habits being portrayed in the media and the arts of "those times".

Left Georgia – Another name for the Western section of Georgia. Carrollton is in the left portion of the state of Georgia.

Liberal Arts Major – Isn't it funny, they don't even offer a "Conservative Arts Major! But if they did, this would be the complete opposite of that.

Like a Rolling Stone – What everybody felt like during their college days**.**

Longham, Wade – AKA: Lank Wayneford

Lottery system – You'd think a country a big as the USA could come up with a better way to send fifty thousand young men to their deaths. It was the same thing as a "names in the hat deal".

LSD – A perfectly sane thing to do would be to experiment with a mind expanding drug like LSD in a world that was insane.

M-16 –A piece of shit rifle nowhere as good as a Chinese made AK – 47, but it made a pretty good bong when you weren't in the bush.

Maddox, Lester – Former Governor of Georgia. Died of AIDS.

MGB- GT – Kind of car owned by Richard Duncan.

Make-It-Take-It – The style of basketball played at Foster's Store. As long as you kept on scoring you got to keep bringing in the ball offensively. That meant that when you were playing against O'Conner, you never got to shoot the ball at all.

Mandeville, L. C. – Used to own and reside in what is today known as the Maple Street Mansion.

Maple Street – The main drag in Carrollton aka Hwy 166.

Maple Street Mansion – Figure some of this shit out for yourself, would you!

Marijuana – Illegal substance that was a lot of fun to smoke until you got all paranoid and couldn't stop thinking about bad shit that never happened. Mostly it made you giggle a lot.

Marine Corps – A place you would go to lose weight. Some people lost it all.

Georgia, Martin – West Georgia College Registrar. Very nice lady, let Wayne graduate despite his dazed- like behavior.

Mayberry - A mythological all-American town.

Meaningless Drivel – This glossary would qualify as meaningless drivel. But I just love glossaries, so I thought I'd just throw this one in.

I figured it might be fun for some of the stranger people I know. I got the idea from a book by Al Franken.

Memory – Something that you can lose all at once or a little bit of every day. It can be the other way around too.

Mescaline – I don't know what it is, but one day when I took some with Sleepy Jack, my whole idea of reality came under attack. I saw some things that were real neat and didn't bite.

Mother Ship – Mr. Foster and I believed that it was the space ship that leaves all the baby space ships around in everybody's back yard.

Multi-dimensional beings – Beings that travel from one dimension to another at will. Usually multi colored.

My Lai Massacre – A point in History where it began to look like we were the bad guys.

Nads, The – Name of Foster's Store's first flag football team. "Go nads go!

Name That Puke! – Name of a game popularized by the members of the Okeefeenokee Yacht Club.

Nathan Barfield – One real nice guy who died too young from a disease he couldn't beat.

National Guard – During the time of this book, a place of refuge.

Newt Gingrigh – Former History teacher at WGC.

Nixon - AKA Tricky Dick . Liked the names in the hat deals so long as his name wasn't in there somewhere.

Nuns – What there weren't any of at Foster's store.

O'Connor, Daniel J. – Of the unknown artists of the 1960's, Dan was the least known. This is why his Art is so very valuable today. There isn't any. Nothing is so expensive!

Okeefeenokee Yacht Club – Group of guys from Carrollton who, well I can't say, I promised. You know what I mean and you know who you are.

Old Milwaukee – Better than no beer at all but not much. Very inexpensive. Along with PBR, a staple at Foster's.

Orgy – Three or more people engage in lascivious sex acts together. Or, that's the rumor around here.

Other dimensions – Dimensions other than the ones we are in now. Well, I can only speak for myself here.

Pabst Blue Ribbon – The beer brand of choice for many West Georgia undergraduates.

Panama City - Coastal city in Florida, Sorrell's neo fish put to se there.

Panty Raid – Ancient clandestine operations involving male college students where the object is to gain entrance into a girl's dormitory and pilfer as much of their underwear, preferably panties, as possible and not be caught by the campus cops.

Paranoia – What a little bit of is a good thing.

Paris Island - Before the Atkinson Diet and The Betty Ford Center there was an island off the Coast of North Carolina where you could check in for about 6 to 8 weeks and really get into great shape. Not only would you exit in the best health condition of your entire life, but you'd then know at least 50 ways to kill somebody.

Peace with Honor - Nobody knows what that means or ever did, but it is assumed a President or Statesman will start to use that phrase at times when he doesn't know what the fuck is going on himself anymore.

Peanut Butter Jar – What kind of jar Rodney Abernathy packed Dean Pershing's keys in.

Peep Hole – In the main store house, a hole drilled in the kitchen wall and into the bathroom. It was covered by an iron frying pan most of the time. Yes we saw what you were doing in there. Please forgive us.

Pillow – Sometimes surreal during these times.

Phenomenology – A course of philosophy where you begin to look back in bewilderment at stuff that just a day ago made perfect sense but doesn't come anywhere close to that today.

Philosophical Dilemma – A place in your thought process where you don't know the right thing to do anymore because you began to actually think about what you were doing for the first time in your life.

Player number 42 - Jimmy Tingle

Political Careers – Things that go on for politicians, sometimes even past their deaths.

Ponce de Leon Ave. – Street in Atlanta where you had to go to take your Draft Physical.

Possession – A good thing or a bad thing.

Propane Gas Tanks – Camouflage for extraterrestrials.

Puken – The gerund or gerundive forms of the verb "Puke". Dialect for "Puking."

Purple Jesus – Recipe used to get everybody drunk in a hurry down at the Animal Farm. *As Follows:* One large plastic trash can or one clean bath tub, 3 to 5 fifths of golden grain alcohol, 8 gallons of Welch's grape juice, chopped mixed fruit, one six pack of sprite, top with ice.

Pershing, Dean John J. – The Dean of West Georgia College during the years of Foster's Store. He was much respected and well liked by all who knew him

Pertussin – A decongestant sometimes used to heighten or deaden one's awareness. Some people would actually use it as a decongestant.

Quaalude – A drug that relaxes you too much.

Ray, William Cotter – A West Georgia student who got killed in Viet Nam

Red Wigglers – The kind of worms Mr. Foster raised and sold right there next to the store. He'd put a big sign out by the road on the weekends when he had some to sell. I remember helping him feed them. He kept them underneath large pieces of plywood. We'd lift up the plywood and put a stack of newspapers on top of the worm bed. The worms ate the old newspaper.

Ritz Carlton – A place to spend the night that you'd never confuse with Foster's Store.

Rock Garden – A band Larry Bowie played in.

Rocket – A Rock Band comprised of members Nathan Barfield, Ricky Fowler, Don McWhorter, Russell Daniel and Doug somebody.

Rockmart – Home town of Bob Abbott and other store mates.

Sandose – The Drug company that developed the first batch of LSD.

Sanity - As a metal condition, it's much over rated. There was not much of it going around between the years of 1965 and 1974. As I recall, there were a lot of prescriptions you could take for it. None of them worked.

Scene(s) of chaos - The only places they ever did "Live Broadcasts" during the time this book talks about.

Sexual revolution – That's where one sex decides that it doesn't want to be on the bottom anymore.

Shallowmar – A Rock Band of the era of this book.

Shit – Can be very deep at times.

Shit Eating Grin – Something that went perfectly with that "Left Coast Look".

Shot Gunning – A style of marijuana smoking where one person fills their lungs with marijuana smoke and then, after holding it in their own lungs for a few moments, puts the lit end of a joint in their own mouth, fire side first, and plows the smoke back they previously inhaled and had been holding in their lungs into their fellow pot smoking friend's mouth where he or she in turn inhales the then, double dose of smoke, into their own lungs supposedly receiving a double dose of smoke.

Sid in custody – Where Sid Shortt would have rather not been.

Sid Short – Famous, or infamous, (you pick it) Store owner and Restaurateur. Owned and operated Headquarters in the Maple Street Mansion. Later moved to Helen, Georgia where today he owns, and operates the Wurst Haus. Go by and see him.

The Silver Dollar Saloon – A dive bar in Tuscaloosa Alabama where fraternity guys learned to drink beer and play foosball poorly.

Skinner's Grocery - Probably sold more than just beer there but you couldn't prove it by me. Unknowingly (I'm sure), Mr. Skinner catered to the underage college crowd.

Smoking dope- Dope that has been set on fire tends to behave in this way.

Sociology – Who knows what this means?

South Park- Carrollton Apartment complex where a lot of students lived.

South Vietnam – The Viet Nam we supported. South Viet Nam good. North Viet Nam bad. Neither exist today.

Southwestern Company – A company that used college students to sell bibles.

Spreading like rats – Hey, I don't know why this term is here.

Stay-awake-pills – Before the term "speed" was popular, this is what students called amphetamines. Most people took them during Final Exam week in order to stay up all night and study.

Steely, Dr. Melvin – A great History Teacher.

Stoned – The desired effect from smoking marijuana.

Straight head – A person who would never get stoned.

Student Center – Building in center of campus that resembled a flying saucer. Or, the absolute center of a student.

Study Group – A group of people who were forced to work with each other for a time in order to complete some kind of stupid group project that a professor might assign. Most often consisted of about five people who wouldn't even speak to each other in public if they weren't forced to be in a group like this. The object was to help each other better understand some sort of subject matter. Usually the group could determine who its weakest link was pretty quick and devour the runt.

Swami Gone Bananas – Name of a great band from Atlanta.

Sweetwater – The name of Terry Bonner's leather shop.

Sword of Damocles – Thing that hung dangerously over all our draft eligible heads.

Tuscaloosa – A Great town for foosball.

Tazer Guns – Great things for our kids to play with.

Thompson, Hunter – The founder of Gonzo Journalism and in no way an influence for writing this book or any other that I might choose to be a part of.

Tight Butt Cheeks – A condition which might describe someone who was extremely worried about their future.

Insane mindset – Opposite of a sane mindset, but some days much more fun.

The whole fuckin' universe – Yeah!

Thunder – The name of Bill Bateman's malamute dog.

Trailer hitch – A device used by females to measure their sexual appetites and prowess. The amount of chrome removed orally was a way of measuring this talent.

Trips – (As in LSD trips) The term used to describe the overall experience one had while ingesting an amount of LSD or other hallucinogenic drug.

Tuna Fish Surprise – Name of a food dish which was cheap and easy to prepare, consisting of one can of tuna fish, an onion, two stalks of celery, one can of cream of mushroom soup, a can of water, all poured eventually over a heaping mound of egg noodles. Also known as tuna douche.

Tyus Road – Pass the store on the left.

Varsity, The – Past the store on the right, going the other way from Tyus road. On the corner of I-75/85 and North Ave.

Vego – Pronounced "Vee-go". Dan Withrow's German shepherd. Great dog. Seemed always to be in the "aroused" condition, especially when co-eds were near. Just like the guys who lived at Foster's store and the Worm Ranch.

Viet Cong – Guys who wore black pajamas all the time and carried AK-47's. During the Viet Nam war, it was their job to kill us. Over in North Viet Nam they were thought of as Freedom Fighters.

Vince Vance and the Valliants – A band.

Viet Nam War – A conflict where you could get killed very easily, especially if you were a young American male and had some bad luck and got drafted.

Virgin pins – The name for a small piece of jewelry worn during the late 1960's by women who had never been to a party at Jackson Courts.

Vomit – Consisted mostly of beer.

Vomit bag – Where organized individuals kept their vomit. Usually came with matching gloves.

Wacki Tabaki – My favorite name for marijuana.

Water buffalo hairdos – With their hair parted in the middle, women applied copious amounts of hair spray in order to achieve this look. Store mate Allen McMillon was always very attracted to women who wore their hair this way. Sadly, he was more attracted to real water buffalo.

West Coast – Area of great unrest and revolution.

West Georgia Perspective- The thing you get after living in the western part of Georgia for a few years.

Westgeorgenous Pabstblueribbineous – Genius Species name of ape like creature believed now residing somewhere in and around the former grounds of Foster's Store. Some characteristics resemble former residents, Richard Duncan and Phil Spackman.

Whiskey – Hard to come by in Carroll County during the time frame covered in this book, yet, much was consumed.

White Longhair – Most famous store resident. Ended up writing books about metaphysics and spirituality, and most used alias for Wayne Lankford.

Wild Dogs – The dogs that ate the Chitterlings.

Willingham, Wylly – The best pool player ever to attend West Georgia College

Womb Room – Room in the main storehouse characterized by its raised floor and thick shag carpeting.

Woodstock – A town in New York State where a lot of people had a good time. After I saw the movie I was a different person, but I looked the same.

Worm Farm House, or Ranch – Also know as the "Feed in Seed". One legend persists about its origin: L.R had it built for Ethel and some guy she was engaged to for a while. At some point that marriage fell through and eventually so did the roof. The legend about Ethel was never true. The deal about the roof is true.

Wurst Haus, The – Restaurant owned ad operated by Sid Short up in Helen, Georgia.

Yin Yang – There is this mythological place of balance in the universe and in you. A place where all secrets are revealed and peace and harmony abound. In order to get there you have to understand the balance of things like good and evil, lightness and darkness, up and down, tax laws and how to avoid contagious disease. Thinking about Yin and Yang won't get you there, but it won't get you in any deeper than you already are. So, go breathe will you!

Zachariah Foundation – Founded to honor the memory of Steven Z. Smith. Raised money for various charities. Zachariah was the name of a band Steve once played in.

Zen Buddhism – It's a kind of religion that was catching on fast back in the late 60's. I remember store mate David Jack seemed to spend a lot of time sitting in the lotus position. I came to believe that the practice of this religion hurt your back and made your pupils get bigger.

Ziggurat – Another band Nathan Barfield once played in, along with Nightwing.

Art/Illustrations/Photographs – Contributors

Page #	Description	Contributor
5	Milo, our mascot	Bill Harrell
6	1955 photograph of L. R. Foster	Ethel Foster
16	Group Photo –West Side of Store	Wayne Lankford
17	Side of Store – Poloroid	Wayne Lankford
18	Student Center from Super 8	Walter Carmichael
19	WGC ID Picture 1970-71	Walter Carmichael
21	Bob Greer running	Yearbook
22	Mini Master of Ceremonies *InkLines*	Bill Harrell
25	"Oh My God, I'm in a Book" *InkLines*	Bill Harrell
27	Bill Craver Cooking in Store	Dean Nations
31	Mr. Foster & Buffy Wuffy 1968	Ethel Foster
32	L.R from 1930's (Mandeville Oil days)	Ethel Foster
38	Student Center 1968	Charles Balance
39	Spanada Bottle Pencil & Ink	Allen McMillan
40	Dean Nations Driving	Dean Nations
40	Dean Nations rent receipt	Ethel Foster
41	Chris Berry	Chris Berry
42	Dean Nations Store front	Dean Nations
43	Chris Berry's rent receipt	Ethel Foster
43	Ducks, Keith & Larry	Dean Nations
44	Two Unidentified girls in Womb Room	Mark Pitstick
46	Eclectic Art 1970	Phillip DeLoach
48	Terry Farner Store in Background	Terry Farner
49	Chris Berry and Terry Farner	Chris Berry
50	Storemates in Dune Buggy	Terry Farner
51	Party Patrol-Dean Nations-Bonnie Bubb	Dean Nations
51	Steve Craft and Cathy Kent	Dean Nations
52	Terry Farner sideways at store	Terry Farner
53	Carlos Penedo and date	Dean Nations
53	Skipper Glover and date	Dean Nations
54	Vee-Go and friend, good friend!	Dean Nations
58	Mr. Foster, Buffy-Wuffy & Ponies	Ethel Foster

149	Basketball Fans Haliburton et al	Chris Berry
150	*InkLines* Come to end war	Bill Harrell
151	Reclining Nude pencil 1970	Allen McMillan
152	Storefront Impression	Wayne Lankford
154	Group in the sun	Chris Berry
159	*InkLines* Tic-Toc	Bill Harrell
161	Rear Admiral Duncan	Wayne Lankford
161	Girl Pouring Drink	Jolaine Hall Battey
162	Passed out Partier	Unknown
163	Candee Carmichael pre-headstand	Wayne Lankford
166	Girls Dorm Party	Georgia Aderhold
167	Puked on car	Wayne Lankford
168	Coed sharing beer with goat	Jolaine Hall Battey
169	Big Thing in Sky Eclectic 1970	Bill Harrell
171	*InkLines* A Billion Flies	Bill Harrell
172	Eclectic Art 1970	Sylvia Hanson
174	Keith and Larry	Dean Nations
176	Hallucinogenic Art	Dan O'Conner
176	Candee with Art Project Lips	Wayne Lankford
179	Mr. Foster and friends	Ethel Foster
180	*InkLines* Out of Crosses	Bill Harrell
182	Mr. Foster and Store mates	Wayne Lankford
185	Barry Edwards with beard	Walter Carmichael
186	David Jack making movies	Walter Carmichael
191	Exactly What It Looks Like	Dan O'Conner
192	Mac and Date	Allen McMillan
194	Z's basketball yearbook picture	Yearbook
194	Z escorting unidentified beauty queen	Yearbook
196	Acid Man	Dan O'Conner
201	Fu Dog	Wayne Lankford
202	Lankford Tripping at Feed N Seed	Wayne Lankford
208	Z's Army Photograph	Z
212	*InkLines* Lost Arrow	Bill Harrell
215	Bob O'Kelley	Dean Nations
218	Zig Zag Man	Allen McMillan
219	*InkLines* Smoke Disappearing Trick	Bill Harrell
220	Eclectic 1970	Michael Kuczmarski
221	Walter Carmichael	Walter Carmichael
225	Possom Trot Band	Charles Balance
229	Unknown Student USA flag	Walter Carmichael
230	Historical Store 1950's	Ethel Foster
235	Candee Carmichaels Meal ticket	Candee Carmichael

236 Eclectic Art Fall 1970   Michael Kuczmarski

298 Bob Abbott in front of SC	Walter Carmichael
301 Green Jay Rushing practice	Wayne Lankford
303 Nude Beauty pencil drawing	Allen McMillan
304 *InkLines* Spring	Bill Harrell
305 UFO or Propane Tank	Wayne Lankford
306 Hay Bales or UFO's	Wayne Lankford
308 InkLines Kite or UFO	Bill Harrell
319 Skipper Glover's Shirt	Wayne Lankford
323 Group Farm Picture 1969	Yearbook
325 Jackson Court Fire 1969	Yearbook
326 Animal Farm Officers	Yearbook
328 Farm Party	Yearbook
329 Farm Party Interior Steve Smith et al	Yearbook
330 Ed Has and others at Farm Party	Yearbook
331 Linda Mason with moonshine	Wayne Lankford
335 Freud book cover	Steve Aderhold
337 Eclectic Art	Trista Loftin
338 PBR Pool Player	White Longhair
340 Phil Catching Frisbee	Candee Carmichael
341 Candee talking to Jason	Candee Carmichael
341 Ron Lightsey	Candee Carmichael
341 Steve Ensign Brushing teeth	Becky Herrin
342 Spackman in the garden	Walter Carmichael
342 Spackman in Those Days	Becky Herrin
343 Saturday afternoon Feed N Seed	Candee Carmichael
344 Richard Duncan in his prime	Candee Carmichael
347 Sports Car days at the store	Candee Carmichael
348 Steve Ensign & Frank Brown	Candee Carmichael
349 *InkLines* Saying good-by	Bill Harrell
350 Ink Thingy Eclectic	Bill Harrell
389 Eclectic 1970	Michael Kuczmarski
380 *InkLines* Characters Meeting	Bill Harrell
391 Dean McCarthy	Dean McCarthy
392 Foster's Store Recent	Walter Carmichael
393 Foster Store 1971	Walter Carmichael
394 Worms	White Longhair
400 *Inklines*	Bill Harrell

Foster's Store Index

Not like a real index, more like horseshoes, but pretty close.

Pavlovian, 262
PBR, 55, 179
   another empty case of, 259
   case of, standing on, 258
   standing on own, 259
PCP, 72
Peace sign, 107, 152, 406
Peace with Honor, 127
Peace, 71
peanut butter jar, 94
peanut butter, 99, 167
Peepers, Sergeant, 193
Peephole, 52 - 53
Penedo, Carlos, 48 (See Carlos)
Penny, Annalee, 356
Penny, J. C., typewriter, 335
Penny, John, 356
Pentecostal Tent Revival, 29
Perdue, Chip, 265
Perkins, Carl, 342
Perkins, Kathy, 32
Permission Form, 399
Pershing, Dean John J., 93, 99, 108, 325
Pertussin, 179
Petrouski, Terry, 80
Petty, Richard, 61
Phenomenology, 293
Philanthropy, 396
Philosophy final ditching, 197
Philospphy, 200
phone sex, 109
physical flunking, 112
physical world, 202
Physicists, 141
Pi Kappa Alpha, 21
Piano Reds, 286
pickers, brain, 397
pickles, 243
pickles, sweet relish, 245
Piedmont Park, 339
Piedmont Park, 354
Pier One, 41
PIG, 143
Pike County, 20
Pike party, 321
Pikes, 21

pills, stay awake, 204
pimp, 281
pin drop, 146
pipe, sewer, ducking, 166
pipe, water, 174
pipes, 253
Pirate Number 3, 190
pirate, 188
Pirates of the Caribbean, 181
pirates, 118
pistol, 127
Pitstick, Mark, 44, 265, 282, 340, 355
Place on Paces, 282
platoon, the, 135
Pleaka Central Highlands, Viet Nam, 311
Plymouth, 1953, 116
Plymouth, or something, 102
poker game, 197
poker player, 194
Police Lieutenant, 260
police, 138, 225
Police, Campus, 105
Police, City of Atlanta, 280
Police, dropping by, Carrollton, 324
Police, Fulton County, 280
policeman, 82
political power, 112
political statement, pot smoking as, 254
political, agenda, hidden, 322
polyester, 156
Ponce de Leon Ave, 315
Pontiac Lemans, 60
pool tables, 296
porch, front, 200
Porno movies, 22
Porsche, 286
possession, 186, 187
Possum Trot band, 225
Pot, 68, 195,
   against the law, 297
   bag of, 183
   bust, 101
   cleaning, 98

Other books by Wayne Lankford

ISBN: 0974512508

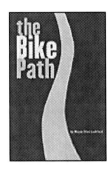

Book Description

Experiences, both physical and metaphysical can be profound out on The Bike Path. This trail ride will take you from the top of a very small hill to the outer reaches of the universe then back down into the vastness of the human soul. As you explore the activity of mountain biking through Lankford's eyes you will perhaps begin to see deeper into an understanding of Nature and the evolving spirit of humankind.

From the Publisher

The Bike Path is the first of a series of books about mountain biking and universal connectivity. Already a coffee table edition of this work is being planed which will incorporate the Author's digital ink renderings into the storyline. The blending of metaphysics, spirituality, mountain biking and nature come across genuinely through the heart-felt stages of a discovery process, which occurred for the author himself, out along the winding path of a single-track mountain bike trail. We believe that there is artfulness in this work that will not only allow the reader to marvel at the images contained herein, but also find enjoyable a stream of consciousness style of writing that's both inspiring and captivating. This is a one of a kind book, or we hope, the first of a one of a kind series of books that simply reflects from the adventure of life itself.

Sample Reviews:

Librarians will have a tough time trying to categorize The BikePath because it could easily fit on several different shelves, though not for long. Yeah, it's about self-discovery, but it's not a self-help book. It's about mountain biking, but not how-to. It's about spirituality, but not religious. It's funny, but not .... well, you get the picture. The BikePath deserves its own kiosk, because it is, simply, like nothing you've read before. The BikePath is about the metamorphosis of a man, a soul, a writer. The author begins as a two pack smoker, 6 pack drinker - out of shape, out of control. In fact, the author's writing style very closely parallels his mountain biking skills. Awkward and slow at first, but by mid-book, the biker is becoming a master of the trail, while the writer is becoming gifted artist. It's really fun to watch the evolution of both. Whether or not you are motivated to try mountain biking isn't the point. Doing SOMETHING is.

Is The Bike Path about mountain biking? Yeah, and Moby Dick is about sailing.
Imagine if you would: In a last ditch effort to save their sanity, Jack Kerouac and Deepak Chopra take up mountain biking, then inexplicably decide to collaborate on a book about the experience. It may be redundant to call something absolutely unique, but The Bike Path by Wayne Eliot Lankford falls squarely in that category. We are along for the ride as Lankford jumps from the corporate treadmill onto a mountain bike and begins to see life not as a continuing series of problems, but as a continuing adventure. Soul searching on a 17-mile loop around Oak Mountain, Lankford explores where he is in his life and how he got there. This book combines the lyrical rhythm of a songwriter with insights and wisdom that come only after serious reflection. Highly recommended

Rose's Cantina

Oak Valley Press

Coming 2007

Printed in the United States
50872LVS00004B/4-63